Seasons of Thoreau
Reflections on Life and Nature

Selected by
Peter Saint-Andre

No rights reserved.

This book is licensed under the Creative Commons
Public Domain Dedication:
http://creativecommons.org/publicdomain/zero/1.0/

Published by the Monadnock Valley Press,
Parker, Colorado
http://www.monadnock.net/

Cover image by Amy Meredith
https://www.flickr.com/people/jjandames/

ISBN: 0-9991863-0-2
ISBN-13: 978-0-9991863-0-5

Seasons of
Thoreau

SPRING

SEASONS OF THOREAU

March

In whatever moment we awake to life, as now I this evening, after walking along the bank and hearing the same evening sounds that were heard of yore, it seems to have slumbered just below the surface, as in the spring the new verdure which covers the fields has never retreated far from the winter. —Journal, 1837-47 (undated)

March fans it, April christens it, and May puts on its jacket and trousers. It never grows up, but Alexandrian-like "drags its slow length along," ever springing, bud following close upon leaf, and when winter comes it is not annihilated, but creeps on mole-like under the snow, showing its face nevertheless occasionally by fuming springs and watercourses.

So let it be with man — let his manhood be a more advanced and still advancing youth, bud following hard upon leaf. —Journal, March 1, 1838

The phenomena of the year take place every day in a pond on a small scale. Every morning, generally speaking, the shallow water is being warmed more rapidly than the deep, though it may not be made so warm after all, and every evening it is being cooled more rapidly until the morning. The day is an epitome of the year. The night is the winter, the morning and evening are the spring and fall, and the noon is the summer. —Walden, "Spring"

I feel as if I had got my foot down on to the solid and sunny earth, the basis of all philosophy, and poetry, and religion even. I have faith that the man who redeemed some acres of land this past summer redeemed also some parts of his character. I shall not expect to find him ever in

the almshouse or the prison. He is, in fact, so far on his way to heaven. When he took the farm there was not a grafted tree on it, and now he realizes something handsome from the sale of fruit. These, in the absence of other facts, are evidence of a certain moral worth.
—Journal, March 1, 1852

The greatest impression of character is made by that person who consents to have no character. He who sympathizes with and runs through the whole circle of attributes cannot afford to be an individual. Most men stand pledged to themselves, so that their narrow and confined virtue has no suppleness. They are like children who cannot walk in bad company and learn the lesson which even it teaches, without their guardians, for fear of contamination. He is a fortunate man who gets through the world without being burdened by a name and reputation, for they are at any rate but his past history and no prophecy, and as such concern him no more than another. Character is Genius settled. It can maintain itself against the world, and if it relapses it repents. It is as a dog set to watch the property of Genius. Genius, strictly speaking, is not responsible, for it is not moral. —Journal, March 2, 1852

Soon after John's death I listened to a music-box, and if, at any time, that event had seemed inconsistent with the beauty and harmony of the universe, it was then gently constrained into the placid course of nature by those steady notes, in mild and unoffended tone echoing far and wide under the heavens. But I find these things more strange than sad to me. What right have I to grieve, who have not ceased to wonder? We feel at first as if some opportunities of kindness and sympathy were lost, but learn afterward that any *pure grief* is ample recompense for all. That is, if we are faithful; for a great grief is but sympathy with the soul that disposes events, and is as natural as the resin on Arabian trees. Only Nature has a right to grieve perpetually, for she only is innocent. Soon the ice will melt, and the blackbirds sing along the river which he frequented, as pleasantly as ever. The same everlasting serenity will appear in this face of God, and we will not be sorrowful if he is not. —Letter to Lucy Brown, March 2, 1842

Evidently some buds are further advanced than others even when the winter comes, and then these are further expanded and matured in advance of the others in the very warm days in the winter. —Journal, March 2, 1860

Happy I who can bask in this warm spring sun which illumines all creatures, as well when they rest as when they toil, not without a feeling of gratitude! whose life is as blameless — how blameworthy soever it be — on the Lord's Mona-day as on his Suna-day!

Thus much as least a man may do: he may not impose on his fellows — perhaps not on himself. Thus much let a man do: confidently and heartily live up to his thought: for its error, if there be any, will soon appear in practice, and if there be none, so much he may reckon as actual progress in the way of living. —Journal, March 4, 1838

In society you will not find health, but in nature. Unless our feet at least stood in the midst of nature, all our faces would be pale and livid. Society is always diseased, and the best is the most so. There is no scent in it so wholesome as that of the pines, nor any fragrance so penetrating and restorative as the life-everlasting in high pastures. I would keep some book of natural history always by me as a sort of elixir, the reading of which should restore the tone of the system. To the sick, indeed, nature is sick, but to the well, a fountain of health. To him who contemplates a trait of natural beauty no harm nor disappointment can come.

The doctrines of despair, of spiritual or political tyranny or servitude, were never taught by such as shared the serenity of nature. Surely good courage will not flag here on the Atlantic border, as long as we are flanked by the Fur Countries. There is enough in that sound to cheer one under any circumstances. The spruce, the hemlock, and the pine will not countenance despair. Methinks some creeds in vestries and churches do forget the hunter wrapped in furs by the Great Slave Lake, and that the Esquimaux sledges are drawn by dogs, and in the twilight of the northern night, the hunter does not give over to follow the seal and walrus on the ice. They are of sick and diseased imaginations who would toll the world's knell so soon. Cannot these sedentary sects do better than prepare the shrouds and write the epitaphs of those other busy living men? The practical faith of all men belies the preacher's consolation. What is any man's discourse to me, if I am not sensible of something in it as steady and cheery as the creak of crickets? In it the woods must be relieved against the sky. Men tire me when I am not constantly greeted and refreshed as by the flux of sparkling streams. Surely joy is the condition of life. Think of the young fry that leap in ponds, the myriads of insects ushered into being on a summer evening, the incessant note of the hyla with which the woods ring in the spring, the nonchalance of the butterfly carrying accident and change painted in a thousand hues upon its wings, or the brook minnow stoutly stemming the current, the lustre of whose scales worn bright by the attrition is reflected upon the bank.

We fancy that this din of religion, literature, and philosophy, which is heard in pulpits, lyceums, and parlors, vibrates through the universe, and is as catholic a sound as the creaking of the earth's axle; but if a man sleep soundly, he will forget it all between sunset and dawn.
—Natural History of Massachusetts, Spring 1842

Let us not underrate the value of a fact; it will one day flower in a truth. It is astonishing how few facts of importance are added in a century to the natural history of any animal. The natural history of man himself is still being gradually written. Men are knowing enough after their fashion. Every countryman and dairymaid knows that the coats of the fourth stomach of the calf will curdle milk, and what particular mushroom is a safe and nutritious diet. You cannot go into any field or wood, but it will seem as if every stone had been turned, and the bark on every tree ripped up. But, after all, it is much easier to discover than to see when the cover is off! It has been well said that "the attitude of inspection is prone." Wisdom does not inspect, but behold. We must look a long time before we can see. Slow are the beginnings of philosophy. He has something demoniacal in him, who can discern a law or couple two facts. We can imagine a time when — "Water runs down hill" — may have been taught in the schools. The true man of science will know nature better by his finer organization; he will smell, taste, see, hear, feel, better than other men. His will be a deeper and finer experience. We do not learn by inference and deduction, and the application of mathematics to philosophy, but by direct intercourse and sympathy. It is with science as with ethics — we cannot know truth by contrivance and method; the Baconian is as false as any other, and with all the helps of machinery and the arts, the most scientific will still be the healthiest and friendliest man, and possess a more perfect Indian wisdom. —Natural History of Massachusetts, Spring 1842

This has indeed been a grand winter for me, and for all of us. I am not considering how much I have enjoyed it. What matters it how happy or unhappy we have been, if we have minded our business and advanced our affairs? —Letter to Daniel Ricketson, March 5, 1856

I read an account the other day of a snipe, I think it was, which, though neither plucked nor drawn, underwent no change but that of drying up, becoming a natural mummy for some unknown reason, as has happened to other, larger bodies. Methinks that many, if not most, men are a sort of natural mummies. The life having departed out of them, decay and putrefaction, disorganization, has not taken place, but they still keep up a dry and withered semblance of life. What the salt is that saves them and robs the worms I do not know. Some bodies there are that, being dead and buried, do not decay, but after the lapse of years are found as fresh as if they had died but yesterday. So some men, though all true life was long ago extinct in them, wear this deceitful semblance of life. They seem to live on, without salt or season, from mere toughness or dryness or some antiseptic quality in their fibre. They do not mellowly dissolve and fatten the earth with their decay.
—Journal, March 7, 1853

The mystery of the life of plants is kindred with that of our own lives, and the physiologist must not presume to explain their growth according to mechanical laws, or as he might explain some machinery of his own making. We must not expect to probe with our fingers the sanctuary of any life, whether animal or vegetable. If we do, we shall discover nothing but surface still. The ultimate expression or fruit of any created thing is a fine effluence which only the most ingenuous worshipper perceives at a reverent distance from its surface even. The cause and the effect are equally evanescent and intangible, and the former must be investigated in the same spirit and with the same reverence with which the latter is perceived. Science is often like the grub which, though it may have nestled in the germ of a fruit, has merely blighted or consumed it and never truly tasted it. Only that intellect makes any progress toward conceiving of the essence which at the same time perceives the effluence. —Journal, March 7, 1859

There is no ripeness which is not, so to speak, something ultimate in itself, and not merely a perfected means to a higher end. In order to be ripe it must serve a transcendent use. The ripeness of a leaf, being perfected, leaves the tree at that point and never returns to it. It has nothing to do with any other fruit which the tree may bear, and only the genius of the poet can pluck it.

The fruit of a tree is neither in the seed nor the timber — the full-grown tree — but it is simply the highest use to which it can be put. —Journal, March 7, 1859

We can only live healthily the life the gods assign us. I must receive my life as passively as the willow leaf that flutters over the brook. I must not be for myself, but God's work, and that is always good. I will wait the breezes patiently, and grow as Nature shall determine. My fate cannot but be grand so. We may live the life of a plant or an animal, without living an animal life. This constant and universal content of the animal comes of resting quietly in God's palm. I feel as if I could at any time resign my life and the responsibility of living into God's hands, and become as innocent, free from care, as a plant or a stone.

My life, my life! why will you linger? Are the years short and the months of no account? How often has long delay quenched my aspirations! Can God afford that I should forget him? Is he so indifferent to my career? Can heaven be postponed with no more ado? Why were my ears given to hear those everlasting strains which haunt my life, and yet to be prophaned much more by these perpetual dull sounds?

Our doubts are so musical that they persuade themselves.

Why, God, did you include me in your great scheme? Will you not make me a partner at last? Did it need there should be a conscious material? —Journal, March 8, 1842

When the frost comes out of the ground, there is a corresponding thawing of the man. The earth is now half bare. These March winds which make the woods roar and fill the world with life and bustle, appear to wake up the trees out of their winter sleep and excite the sap to flow. —Journal, March 9, 1852

I was reminded, this morning before I rose, of those undescribed ambrosial mornings of summer which I can remember, when a thousand birds were heard gently twittering and ushering in the light, like the argument to a new canto of an epic and heroic poem. The serenity, the infinite promise, of such a morning! The song or twitter of birds drips from the leaves like dew. Then there was something divine and immortal in our life. —Journal, March 10, 1852

Shall the earth be regarded as a graveyard, a necropolis, merely, and not also as a granary filled with the seeds of life? Is not its fertility increased by this decay? A fertile compost, not exhausted sand. —Journal, March 11, 1854

When it was proposed to me to go abroad, rub off some rust, and *better my condition* in a worldly sense, I fear lest my life will lose some of its homeliness. If these fields and streams and woods, the phenomena of nature here, and the simple occupations of the inhabitants should cease to interest and inspire me, no culture or wealth would atone for the loss. I fear the dissipation that travelling, going into society, even the best, the enjoyment of intellectual luxuries, imply. If Paris is much in your mind, if it is more and more to you, Concord is less and less, and yet it would be a wretched bargain to accept the proudest Paris in exchange for my native village. At best, Paris could only be a school in which to learn to live here, a stepping-stone to Concord, a school in which to fit for this university. I wish so to live ever as to derive my satisfactions and inspirations from the commonest events, every-day phenomena, so that what my senses hourly perceive, my daily walk, the conversation of my neighbors, may inspire me, and I may dream of no heaven but that which lies about me. A man may acquire a taste for wine or brandy, and so lose his love for water, but should we not pity him?

The sight of a marsh hawk in Concord meadows is worth more to me than the entry of the allies into Paris. In this sense I am not ambitious. I do not wish my native soil to become exhausted and run out through neglect. Only that travelling is good which reveals to me the value of home and enables me to enjoy it better. That man is the richest whose pleasures are the cheapest. —Journal, March 11, 1856

It is strange that men are in such haste to get fame as teachers rather than knowledge as learners.
—Journal, March 11, 1856

There is always some accident in the best things, whether thoughts or expressions or deeds. The memorable thought, the happy expression, the admirable deed are only partly ours. The thought came to us because we were in a fit mood; also we were unconscious and did not know that we had said or done a good thing. We must walk consciously only part way toward our goal, and then leap in the dark to our success. What we do best or most perfectly is what we have most thoroughly learned by the longest practice, and at length it falls from us without our notice, as a leaf from a tree. It is the *last* time we shall do it — our unconscious leavings. —Journal, March 11, 1859

It is essential that a man confine himself to pursuits — a scholar, for instance, to studies — which lie next to and conduce to his life, which do not go against the grain, either of his will or his imagination. The scholar finds in his experience some studies to be most fertile and radiant with light, others dry, barren, and dark. If he is wise, he will not persevere in the last, as a plant in a cellar will strive toward the light. He will confine the observations of his mind as closely as possible to the experience or life of his senses. His thought must live with and be inspired with the life of the body. The death-bed scenes and observations even of the best and wisest afford but a sorry picture of our humanity. Some men endeavor to live a constrained life, to subject their whole lives to their wills, as he who said he would give a sign if he were conscious after his head was cut off — but he gave no sign. Dwell as near as possible to the channel in which your life flows. A man may associate with such companions, he may pursue such employments, as will darken the day for him. Men choose darkness rather than light. —Journal, March 12, 1853

All enterprises must be self-supporting, must pay for themselves. The great art of life is how to turn the surplus life of the soul into life for the body — that so the life not be a failure. For instance, a poet must sustain his body with his poetry. As is said of the merchants, in ninety-nine cases out of a hundred the life of men is a failure, and bankruptcy may be surely prophesied. You must get your living by loving. —Journal, March 13, 1853

I see by the newspapers that the season for making sugar is at hand. Now is the time, whether you be rock, or white maple, or hickory. I trust that you have prepared a store of sap-tubs and sumach spouts, and invested largely in kettles. Early the first frosty morning, tap your maples — the sap will not run in summer, you know. It matters not how little juice you get, if you get all you can, and boil it down. I made just one crystal of sugar once, one twentieth of an inch cube, out of a pumpkin, and it sufficed. Though the yield be no greater than that, this is not less the season for it, and it will be not the less sweet, nay, it will be infinitely the sweeter.

Shall, then, the maple yield sugar, and not man? Shall the farmer be thus active, and surely have so much sugar to show for it, before this very March is gone — while I read the newspaper? While he works in his sugar-camp let me work in mine — for sweetness is in me, and to sugar it shall come — it shall not all go to leaves and wood. Am I not a *sugar maple* man, then? Boil down the sweet sap which the spring causes to flow within you. Stop not at syrup — go on to sugar, though you present the world with but a single crystal — a crystal not made from trees in your yard, but from the new life that stirs in your pores. Cheerfully skim your kettle, and watch it set and crystallize, making a holiday of it if you will. Heaven will be propitious to you as to him. —Letter to Harrison Blake, March 13, 1856

This afternoon I throw off my outside coat. A mild spring day. I must hie to the Great Meadows. The air is full of bluebirds. The ground almost entirely bare. The villagers are out in the sun, and every man is happy whose work takes him outdoors. I go by Sleepy Hollow toward the Great Fields. I lean over a rail to hear what is in the air, liquid with the bluebirds' warble. My life partakes of infinity. The air is as deep as our natures. Is the drawing in of this vital air attended with no more glorious results than I witness? The air is a velvet cushion against which I press my ear. I go forth to make demands on life. I wish to begin this summer well; to do something in it worthy of it and of me; to transcend my daily routine and that of my townsmen; to have my immortality now, that it be in the *quality* of my daily life; to pay the greatest price, the greatest tax, of any man in Concord, and enjoy it the most!! I will give all I am for *my* nobility. I will pay all my days for *my* success! I pray that the life of this spring and summer may ever lie fair in my memory. May I dare as I have never done! May I persevere as I have never done! May I purify myself anew as with fire and water, soul and body! May my melody not be wanting to the season! May I gird myself to be a hunter of the beautiful, that naught escape me! May I attain to a youth never attained! I am eager to report the glory of the universe; may I be worthy to do it; to have got through with regarding human values, so as not to be distracted from regarding divine values. It is reasonable that a man should be something worthier at the end of the year than he was at the beginning. —Journal, March 15, 1852

When I am opposite the end of the willow-row, seeing the osiers of perhaps two years old all in a mass, they are seen to be very distinctly yellowish beneath and scarlet above. They are fifty rods off. Here is the same chemistry that colors the leaf or fruit, coloring the bark. It is generally, probably always, the upper part of the twig, the more recent growth, that is the higher-colored and more flower or fruit like. So leaves are more ethereal the higher up and further from the root. In the bark of the twigs, indeed, is the more permanent flower or fruit. The flower falls in spring or summer, the fruit and leaves fall or wither in autumn, but the blushing twigs retain their color throughout the winter and appear more brilliant than ever the succeeding spring. They are winter fruit. It adds greatly to the pleasure of late November, or winter, or of early spring walks to look into these mazes of twigs of different colors. —Journal, March 17, 1859

Now, then, spring is beginning again in earnest after this short check. Is it not always thus? Is there not always an early promise of spring, something answering to the Indian summer, which succeeds the summer, so an Indian or false spring preceding the true spring — first false promise which merely excites our expectations to disappoint them, followed by a short return of winter? Yet all things appear to have made progress, even during these wintry days, for I cannot believe that they have thus instantaneously taken a start....

The sun is now declining, with a warm and bright light on all things, a light which answers to the late afternoon glow of the year, when, in the fall, wrapping his cloak closer about him, the traveller goes home at night to prepare for winter. This the foreglow of the year, when the walker goes home at even to dream of summer. —Journal, March 18, 1853

Each new year is a surprise to us. We find that we had virtually forgotten the note of each bird, and when we hear it again it is remembered like a dream, reminding us of a previous state of existence. How happens it that the associations it awakens are always pleasing, never saddening; reminiscences of our sanest hours? The voice of nature is always encouraging. —Journal, March 18, 1858

The first sparrow of spring! The year beginning with younger hope than ever! The faint silvery warblings heard over the partially bare and moist fields from the bluebird, the song sparrow, and the red-wing, as if the last flakes of winter tinkled as they fell! What at such a time are histories, chronologies, traditions, and all written revelations? The brooks sing carols and glees to the spring. The marsh hawk, sailing low over the meadow, is already seeking the first slimy life that awakes. The sinking sound of melting snow is heard in all dells, and the ice dissolves apace in the ponds. The grass flames up on the hillsides like a spring fire — "*et primitus oritur herba imbribus primoribus evocata*" — as if the earth sent forth an inward heat to greet the returning sun; not yellow but green is the color of its flame — the symbol of perpetual youth, the grass-blade, like a long green ribbon, streams from the sod into the summer, checked indeed by the frost, but anon pushing on again, lifting its spear of last year's hay with the fresh life below. It grows as steadily as the rill oozes out of the ground. It is almost identical with that, for in the growing days of June, when the rills are dry, the grass-blades are their channels, and from year to year the herds drink at this perennial green stream, and the mower draws from it betimes their winter supply. So our human life but dies down to its root, and still puts forth its green blade to eternity. —Walden, "Spring"

Walden is melting apace. It has a canal two rods wide along the northerly side and the west end, wider at the east end, yet, after running round from west to east, it does not keep the south shore, but crosses in front of the deep cove in a broad crack to where it started, by the ice ground. It is glorious to behold the life and joy of this ribbon of water sparkling in the sun. The wind blows eastward over the opaque ice, unusually hard, owing to the recent severe though transient cold, all watered or waved like a tessellated floor, a figured carpet; yet dead, yet in vain, till it slides on to the living water surface, where it raises a myriad brilliant sparkles on the bare face of the pond, an expression of glee, of youth, of spring, as if it spoke the joy of the fishes within it and of the sands on its shore, a silvery sheen like the scales of *leuciscu*, as if it were all one active fish in the spring. It is the contrast between life and death. There is the difference between winter and spring. The bared face of the pond sparkles with joy. —Journal, March 20, 1853

The peculiarity of today is that now first you perceive that dry, warm, summer-presaging scent from dry oak and other leaves, on the sides of hills and ledges. You smell the summer from afar. The warm makes a man young again. There is also some dryness, almost dustiness, in the roads. The mountains are white with snow, and sure as the wind is northwest it is wintry; but now it is more westerly. The edges of the mountains now melt into the sky. It is affecting to be put into communication with such distant objects by the power of vision — actually to look into rich lands of promise. —Journal, March 20, 1853

It is a genial and reassuring day; the mere warmth of the west winds amounts almost to balminess. The softness of the air mollifies our own dry and congealed substance. I sit down by a wall to see if I can muse again. We become, as it were, pliant and ductile again to strange but memorable influences; we are led a little way by our genius. We are affected like the earth, and yield to the elemental tenderness; winter breaks up within us; the frost is coming out of me, and I am heaved like the road; accumulated masses of ice and snow dissolve, and thoughts like a freshet pour down unwonted channels. A strain of music comes to solace the traveller over earth's downs and dignify his chagrins, the petty men whom he meets are the shadows of grander to come. Roads lead elsewhither than to Carlisle and Sudbury. The earth is uninhabited but fair to inhabit, like the old Carlisle road. Is the road so rough that it should be neglected? Not only narrow but rough is the way that leadeth to life everlasting. Our experience does not wear upon us. It is seen to be fabulous or symbolical, and the future is worth expecting. Encouraged, I set out once more to climb the mountain of the earth, for my steps are symbolical steps, and in all my walking I have not reached the top of the earth yet. —Journal, March 21, 1853

Whatever your sex or position, life is a battle in which you are to show your pluck, and woe be to the coward. Whether passed on a bed of sickness or a tented field, it is ever the same fair play and admits of no foolish distinction. Despair and postponement are cowardice and defeat. Men were born to succeed, not to fail. —Journal, March 21, 1853

I *suppose* that I have not many months to live; but, of course, I know nothing about it. I may add that I am enjoying existence as much as ever, and regret nothing. —Letter to Myron B. Benton, March 21, 1862

As soon as those spring mornings arrive in which the birds sing, I am sure to be an early riser. I am waked by my genius. I wake to inaudible melodies and am surprised to find myself expecting the dawn in so serene and joyful and expectant a mood. I have an appointment with spring. She comes to the window to wake me, and I go forth an hour or two earlier than usual. It is by especial favor that I am waked — not rudely but gently, as infants should be waked. Though as yet the trill of the chip-bird is not heard — added — like the sparkling bead which bursts on bottled cider or ale. When we wake indeed, with a double awakening — not only from our ordinary nocturnal slumbers, but from our diurnal — we burst through the thallus of our ordinary life with a proper exciple, we awake with emphasis. —Journal, March 22, 1853

A seed, which is a plant or tree in embryo, which has the principle of growth, of life, in it, is more important in my eyes, and in the economy of Nature, than the diamond of Kohinoor. —Journal, March 22, 1861

I spend a considerable portion of my time observing the habits of the wild animals, my brute neighbors. By their various movements and migrations they fetch the year about to me. Very significant are the flight of geese and the migration of suckers, etc. But when I consider that the nobler animals have been exterminated here, the cougar,

panther, lynx, wolverene, wolf, bear, moose, deer, beaver, turkey, etc., etc., I cannot but feel as if I lived in a tamed and, as it were, emasculated country. Would not the motions of those larger and wilder animals have been more significant still? Is it not a maimed and imperfect nature that I am conversant with? As if I were to study a tribe of Indians that had lost all its warriors. Do not the forest and the meadow now lack expression? now that I never see nor think of the moose with a lesser forest on his head in the one, nor of the beaver in the other? When I think what were the various sounds and notes, the migrations and works, and changes of fur and plumage which ushered in the spring, and marked the other seasons of the year, I am reminded that this my life in nature, this particular round of natural phenomena which I call a year, is lamentably incomplete. I listen to a concert in which so many parts are wanting. The whole civilized country is, to some extent, turned into a city, and I am that citizen whom I pity. Many of those animal migrations and other phenomena by which the Indians marked the season are no longer to be observed. I seek acquaintance with nature to know her moods and manners. Primitive nature is the most interesting to me. I take infinite pains to know all the phenomena of the spring, for instance, thinking that I have here the entire poem, and then, to my chagrin, I learn that it is but an imperfect copy that I possess and have read, that my ancestors have torn out many of the first leaves and grandest passages, and mutilated it in many places. I should not like to think that some demigod had come before me and picked out some of the best of the stars. I wish to know an entire heaven and an entire earth.
—Journal, March 23, 1856

I am reassured and reminded that I am the heir of eternal inheritances which are inalienable, when I feel the warmth reflected from this sunny bank, and see the yellow sand and the reddish subsoil, and hear some dried leaves rustle and the trickling of melting snow in some sluiceway. The eternity which I detect in Nature I predicate of myself also. How many springs I have had this same experience! I am encouraged, for I recognize this steady persistency and recovery of Nature as a quality of myself. —Journal, March 23, 1856

The change from foul weather to fair, from dark, sluggish hours to serene, elastic ones, is a memorable crisis which all things proclaim. —Journal, March 26, 1846

Magnanimity, though it look expensive for a short course, is always economy in the long run. Be generous in your poverty, if you would be rich. To make up a great action there are no subordinate mean ones. We can never afford to postpone a true life today to any future and anticipated nobleness. We think if by a tight economy we can manage to arrive at independence, then indeed we will begin to be generous without stay. We sacrifice all nobleness to a little present meanness. If a man charges you eight hundred pay him eight hundred and fifty, and it will leave a clean edge to the sum. It will be like nature, overflowing and rounded like the bank of a river, not close and precise like a drain or ditch. —Journal, March 27, 1841

I do believe in simplicity. It is astonishing as well as sad, how many trivial affairs even the wisest man thinks he must attend to in a day; how singular an affair he thinks he must omit. When the mathematician would solve a difficult problem, he first frees the equation of all incumbrances, and reduces it to its simplest terms. So simplify the problem of life, distinguish the necessary and the real. Probe the earth to see where your main roots run. I would stand upon facts. Why not see — use our eyes? Do men know nothing? I know many men who, in common things, are not to be deceived; who trust no moonshine; who count their money correctly, and know how to invest it; who are said to be prudent and knowing, who yet will stand at a desk the greater part of their lives, as cashiers in banks, and glimmer and rust and finally go out there. If they *know* anything, what under the sun do they do that for? Do they know what *bread* is? or what it is for? Do they know what life is? If they *knew* something, the places which know them now would know them no more forever. —Letter to Harrison Blake, March 27, 1848

When I witness the first plowing and planting, I acquire a long-lost confidence in the earth — that it will nourish the seed that is committed to its bosom. I am surprised to be reminded that there is warmth in it. We have not only warmer skies, then, but a warmer earth. The frost is out of it, and we may safely commit these seeds to it in some places. Yesterday I walked with Farmer beside his team and saw one furrow turned quite round his field. What noble work is plowing, with the broad and solid earth for material, the ox for fellow-laborer, and the simple but efficient plow for tool! Work that is not done in any shop, in a cramped position, work that tells, that concerns all men, which the sun shines and the rain falls on, and the birds sing over! You turn over the whole vegetable mould, expose how many grubs, and put a new aspect on the face of the earth. It comes pretty near to making a world.
—Journal, March 28, 1857

As I sit two thirds the way up the sunny side of the pine hill, looking over the meadows, which are now almost completely bare, the crows, by their swift flight and scolding, reveal to me some large bird of prey hovering over the river. I perceive by its markings and size that it cannot be a hen-hawk, and now it settles on the topmost branch of a white maple, bending it down. Its great armed and feathered legs dangle helplessly in the air for a moment, as if feeling for the perch, while its body is tipping this way and that. It sits there facing me some forty or fifty rods off, pluming itself but keeping a good lookout. At this distance and in this light, it appears to have a rusty-brown head and breast and is white beneath, with rusty leg-feathers and a tail black beneath. When it flies again it is principally black varied with white, regular light spots on its tail and wings beneath, but chiefly a conspicuous white space on the forward part of the back; also some of the upper side of the tail or tail-coverts is white. It has broad, ragged, buzzard-like wings, and from the white of its back, as well as the shape and shortness of its wings and its not having a gull-like body, I think it must be an eagle. It lets itself down with its legs somewhat helplessly dangling, as if feeling for something on the bare meadow, and then gradually flies away, soaring and circling higher and higher until lost in the downy clouds. This lofty soaring is at least a grand recreation, as if it were nourishing sublime ideas. I should like to know why it soars higher and higher so, whether its thoughts are really turned to earth, for it seems to be more nobly as well as highly employed than the laborers ditching in the meadow beneath or any others of my fellow townsmen. —Journal, March 29, 1857

Near the end of March, 1845, I borrowed an axe and went down to the woods by Walden Pond, nearest to where I intended to build my house, and began to cut down some tall, arrowy white pines, still in their youth, for timber. It is difficult to begin without borrowing, but perhaps it is the most generous course thus to permit your fellow-men to have an interest in your enterprise. The owner of the axe, as he released his hold on it, said that it was the apple of his eye; but I returned it sharper than I received it. It was a pleasant hillside where I worked, covered with pine woods, through which I looked out on the pond, and a small open field in the woods where pines and hickories were springing up. The ice in the pond was not yet dissolved, though there were some open spaces, and it was all dark-colored and saturated with water. There were some slight flurries of snow during the days that I worked there; but for the most part when I came out on to the railroad, on my way home, its yellow sand heap stretched away gleaming in the hazy atmosphere, and the rails shone in the spring sun, and I heard the lark and pewee and other birds already come to commence another year with us. They were pleasant spring days, in which the winter of man's discontent was thawing as well as the earth, and the life that had lain torpid began to stretch itself. One day, when my axe had come off and I had cut a green hickory for a wedge, driving it with a stone, and had placed the whole to soak in a pond-hole in order to swell the wood, I saw a striped snake run into the water, and he lay on the bottom, apparently without inconvenience, as long as I stayed there, or more than a quarter of an hour; perhaps because he had not yet fairly come out of the torpid state. It appeared to me that for a like reason men remain in their present low and primitive condition; but if they should feel the influence of the spring of springs arousing them, they would of necessity rise to a higher and more ethereal life. —Walden, "Economy"

My purpose in going to Walden Pond was not to live cheaply nor to live dearly there, but to transact some private business with the fewest obstacles; to be hindered from accomplishing which for want of a little common sense, a little enterprise and business talent, appeared not so sad as foolish. —Walden, "Economy"

Though the frost is nearly out of the ground, the winter has not broken up in me. It is a backward season with me. Perhaps we grow older and older till we no longer sympathize with the revolution of the seasons, and our winters never break up. —Journal, March 30, 1852

Perchance as we grow old we cease to spring with the spring, and we are indifferent to the succession of years, and they go by without epoch as months. Woe be to us when we cease to form new resolutions on the opening of a new year! —Journal, March 31, 1852

It would be worth the while to tell why a swamp pleases us, what kinds please us, also what weather, etc., etc. — analyze our impressions. Why the moaning of the storm gives me pleasure. Methinks it is because it puts to rout the trivialness of our fair-weather life and gives it at least a tragic interest. The sound has the effect of a pleasing challenge, to call forth our energy to resist the invaders of our life's territory. It is musical and thrilling, as the sound of an enemy's bugle. Our spirits revive like lichens in the storm. There is something worth living for when we are resisted, threatened. As at the last day we might be thrilled with the prospect of the grandeur of our destiny, so in these *first* days our destiny appears grander. What would the days, what would our life, be worth, if some nights were not dark as pitch — of darkness tangible or that you can cut with a knife? How else could the light in the mind shine? How should we be conscious of the light of reason? If it were not for physical cold, how should we have discovered the warmth of the affections? I sometimes feel that I need to sit in a far-away cave through a three weeks' storm, cold and wet, to give a tone to my system. The spring has its windy March to usher it in, with many soaking rains reaching into April. Methinks I would share every creature's suffering for the sake of its experience and joy. The song sparrow and transient fox-colored sparrow — have they brought me no message this year? Do they go to lead heroic lives in Rupert's Land? They are so small, I think their destinies must be large. Have I heard what this tiny passenger has to say, while it flits thus from tree to tree? Is not the coming of the fox-colored sparrow something more earnest and significant than I have dreamed of? Can I forgive myself if I let it go to Rupert's Land before I have appreciated it? God did not make this world in jest; no, nor in indifference. These migrating sparrows all bear messages that concern my life. I do not pluck the fruits in their season. I love the birds and beasts because they are mythologically in earnest. I see that the sparrow cheeps and flits and sings adequately to the great design of the universe; that man does not communicate with it, understand its language, because he is not at one with nature. I reproach myself because I have regarded with indifference the passage of the birds; I have thought them no better than I. —Journal, March 31, 1852

It is suddenly warm, and this amelioration of the weather is incomparably the most important fact in this vicinity. It is incredible what a revolution in our feelings and in the aspect of nature this warmer air alone has produced. Yesterday the earth was simple to barrenness, and dead — *bound out*. Out-of-doors there was nothing but the wind and the withered grass and the cold though sparkling blue water, and you were driven in upon yourself. Now you would think that there was a sudden awakening in the very crust of the earth, as if flowers were expanding and leaves putting forth; but not so; I listen in vain to hear a frog or a new bird as yet; only the frozen ground is melting a little deeper, and the water is trickling down the hills in some places. No, the change is mainly in us. We feel as if we had obtained a new lease of life. —Journal, March 31, 1855

SEASONS OF THOREAU

April

What I was learning in college was chiefly, I think, to express myself, and I see now, that as the old orator prescribed, 1st, action; 2d, action; 3d, action; my teachers should have prescribed to me, 1st, sincerity; 2d, sincerity; 3d, sincerity. The old mythology is incomplete without a god or goddess of sincerity, on whose altars we might offer up all the products of our farms, our workshops, and our studies. It should be our Lar when we sit on the hearth, and our Tutelar Genius when we walk abroad. This is the only panacea. I mean sincerity in our dealings with ourselves mainly; any other is comparatively easy. But I must stop before I get to 17thly. I believe I have but one text and one sermon. —Letter to Richard F. Fuller, April 2, 1843

The mode of founding a college is, commonly, to get up a subscription of dollars and cents, and then, following blindly the principles of a division of labor to its extreme — a principle which should never be followed but with circumspection — to call in a contractor who makes this a subject of speculation, and he employs Irishmen or other operatives actually to lay the foundations, while the students that are to be are said to be fitting themselves for it; and for these oversights successive generations have to pay. I think that it would be better than this, for the students, or those who desire to be benefited by it, even to lay the foundation themselves. The student who secures his coveted leisure and retirement by systematically shirking any labor necessary to man obtains but an ignoble and unprofitable leisure, defrauding himself of the experience which alone can make leisure fruitful. "But," says one, "you do not mean that the students should go to work with their hands instead of their heads?" I do not mean that exactly, but I mean something which he might think a good deal like that; I mean that they should not play life, or study it merely, while the community supports them at this expensive game, but earnestly live it from beginning to end. How could youths better learn to live than by at once trying the experiment of living? Methinks this would exercise their minds as much as mathematics. If I wished a boy to know something about the arts and sciences, for instance, I would not pursue the common course, which is merely to send him into the neighborhood of some professor, where anything is professed and practised but the art of life — to survey the world through a telescope or a microscope, and never with his natural eye; to study chemistry, and not learn how his bread is made, or mechanics, and not learn how it is earned; to discover new satellites to Neptune, and not detect the motes in his eyes, or to what vagabond he is a satellite himself; or to be devoured by the monsters that swarm all around him, while contemplating the monsters in a drop of vinegar. Which would have advanced the most at the end of a month — the boy who had made his own jackknife from the ore which he had dug and smelted, reading as much as would be necessary for this — or the boy who had attended the lectures on metallurgy at the Institute in the meanwhile, and had received a Rodgers' penknife from his father? Which would be most likely to cut his fingers?... To my astonishment I was informed on leaving college that I had studied navigation! — why, if I had taken one turn down the harbor I should have known more about it. Even the poor student studies and is taught only political economy, while that economy of living which is synonymous with philosophy is not even sincerely professed in our colleges. The consequence is, that while he is reading Adam Smith, Ricardo, and Say, he runs his father in debt irretrievably. —Walden, "Economy"

A single gentle rain makes the grass many shades greener. So our prospects brighten on the influx of better thoughts.

We should be blessed if we lived in the present always, and took advantage of every accident that befell us, like the grass which confesses the influence of the slightest dew that falls on it; and did not spend our time in atoning for the neglect of past opportunities, which we call doing our duty. We loiter in winter while it is already spring. In a pleasant spring morning all men's sins are forgiven. Such a day is a truce to vice. While such a sun holds out to burn, the vilest sinner may return. Through our own recovered innocence we discern the innocence of our neighbors. You may have known your neighbor yesterday for a thief, a drunkard, or a sensualist, and merely pitied or despised him, and despaired of the world; but the sun shines bright and warm this first spring morning, recreating the world, and you meet him at some serene work, and see how his exhausted and debauched veins expand with still joy and bless the new day, feel the spring influence with the innocence of infancy, and all his faults are forgotten. There is not only an atmosphere of good will about him, but even a savor of holiness groping for expression, blindly and ineffectually perhaps, like a new-born instinct, and for a short hour the south hill-side echoes to no vulgar jest. You see some innocent fair shoots preparing to burst from his gnarled rind and try another year's life, tender and fresh as the youngest plant. Even he has entered into the joy of his Lord. —Walden, "Spring"

Too late now for the morning influence and inspiration. The birds sing not so earnestly and joyously; there is a blurring ripple on the surface of the lake. How few valuable observations can we make in youth! What if there were united the susceptibility of youth with the discrimination of age? —Journal, April 2, 1852

It appears to me that, to one standing on the heights of philosophy, mankind and the works of man will have sunk out of sight altogether; that man is altogether too much insisted on. The poet says the proper study of mankind is man. I say, study to forget all that; take wider views of the universe. That is the egotism of the race. What is this our childish, gossiping, social literature, mainly in the hands of the publishers? When another poet says the world is too much with us, he means, of course, that man is too much with us. In the promulgated views of man, in institutions, in the common sense, there is narrowness and delusion. It is our weakness that so exaggerates the virtues of philanthropy and charity and makes it the highest human attribute. The world will sooner or later tire of philanthropy and all religions based on it mainly. They cannot long sustain my spirit. In order to avoid delusions, I would fain let man go by and behold a universe in which man is but as a grain of sand. I am sure that those of my thoughts which consist, or are contemporaneous, with social personal connections, however humane, are not the wisest and widest, most universal. What is the village, city, State, nation, aye the civilized world, that it should concern a man so much? the thought of them affects me in my wisest hours as when I pass a woodchuck's hole. It is a comfortable place to nestle, no doubt, and we have friends, some sympathizing ones, it may be, and a hearth, there; but I have only to get up at midnight, aye to soar or wander a little in my thought by day, to find them all slumbering. Look at our literature. What a poor, puny, social thing, seeking sympathy! The author troubles himself about his readers — would fain have one before he dies. He stands too near his printer; he corrects the proofs. Not satisfied with defiling one another in this world, we would all go to heaven together. To be a good man, that is, a good neighbor in the widest sense, is but little more than to be a good citizen. Mankind is a gigantic institution; it is a community to which most men belong. It is a test I would apply to my companion — can he forget man? can he see this world slumbering?

I do not value any view of the universe into which man and the institutions of man enter very largely and absorb much of the attention. Man is but the place where I stand, and the prospect hence is infinite. It is not a chamber of mirrors which reflect me. When I reflect, I find that there is other than me. Man is a past phenomenon to philosophy. The universe is larger than enough for man's abode. Some rarely go outdoors, most are always at home at night, very few indeed have stayed out all night once in their lives, fewer still have gone behind the world of humanity, seen its institutions like toadstools by the wayside. —Journal, April 2, 1852

It is evident that it depends on the character of the season whether this flower or that is the most forward; whether there is more or less snow or cold or rain, etc. I am tempted to stretch myself on the bare ground above the Cliff, to feel its warmth in my back, and smell the earth and the dry leaves. I see and hear flies and bees about. A large buff-edged butterfly flutters by along the edge of the Cliff — *Vanessa antiopa*. Though so little of the earth is bared, this frail creature has been warmed to life again. Here is the broken shell of one of those large white snails (*Helix albolabris*) on the top of the Cliff. It is like a horn with ample mouth wound on itself. I am rejoiced to find anything so pretty. I cannot but think it nobler, as it is rarer, to appreciate some beauty than to feel much sympathy with misfortune. The Powers are kinder to me when they permit me to enjoy this beauty than if they were to express any amount of compassion for me. I could never excuse them that. —Journal, April 2, 1856

Will you live? or will you be embalmed? Will you live, though it be astride of a sunbeam; or will you repose safely in the catacombs for a thousand years? In the former case, the worst accident that can happen is that you may break your neck. Will you break your heart, your soul, to save your neck? Necks and pipe-stems are fated to be broken. Men make a great ado about the folly of demanding too much of life (or of eternity?), and of endeavoring to live according to that demand. It is much ado about nothing. No harm ever came from that quarter. I am not afraid that I shall exaggerate the value and significance of life, but that I shall not be up to the occasion which it is. I shall be sorry to remember that I was there, but noticed nothing remarkable — not so much as a prince in disguise; lived in the golden age a hired man; visited Olympus even, but fell asleep after dinner, and did not hear the conversation of the gods. —Letter to Harrison Blake, April 3, 1850

It is surprising how the earth on bare south banks begins to show some greenness in its russet cheeks in this rain and fog — a precious emerald-green tinge, almost like a green mildew, the growth of the night — a *green* blush suffusing her cheek, heralded by twittering birds. This sight is no less interesting than the corresponding bloom and ripe blush of the fall. How encouraging to perceive again that faint tinge of green, spreading amid the russet on earth's cheeks! I revive with Nature; her victory is mine. —Journal, April 3, 1856

Hosmer is overhauling a vast heap of manure in the rear of his barn, turning the ice within it up to the light; yet he asks despairingly what life is for, and says he does not expect to stay here long. But I have just come from reading Columella, who describes the same kind of spring work, in that to him new spring of the world, with hope, and I suggest to be brave and hopeful with nature. Human life may be transitory and full of trouble, but the perennial mind, whose survey extends from that spring to this, from Columella to Hosmer, is superior to change. I will identify myself with that which did not die with Columella and will not die with Hosmer. —Journal, April 3, 1856

If you aspire to anything better than politics, expect no cooperation from men. They will not further anything good. You must prevail of your own force, as a plant springs and grows by its own vitality. —Journal, April 3, 1858

Most have sufficient contempt for what is mean to resolve that they will abstain from it, and a few virtue enough to abide by their resolution, but not often does one attain to such lofty contempt as to require no resolution to be made. —Journal, April 7, 1839

Some poets mature early and die young. Their fruits have a delicious flavor like strawberries, but do not keep till fall or winter. Others are slower in coming to their growth. Their fruits may be less delicious, but are a more lasting food and are so hardened by the sun of summer and the coolness of autumn that they keep sound over winter. The first are June-eatings, early but soon withering; the last are russets, which last till June again. —Journal, April 8, 1854

The communications from the gods to us are still deep and sweet, indeed, but scanty and transient — enough only to keep alive the memory of the past. I remarked how many old people died off on the approach of the present spring. It is said that when the sap begins to flow in the trees our diseases become more violent. It is now advancing toward summer apace, and we seem to be reserved to taste its sweetness, but to perform what great deeds? Do we detect the reason why we also did not die on the approach of spring? —Journal, April 9, 1856

I bought me a spy-glass some weeks since. I buy but few things, and those not till long after I begin to want them, so that when I do get them I am prepared to make a perfect use of them and extract their whole sweet.
—Journal, April 10, 1854

I do not so much regret the present condition of things in this country (provided I regret it at all), as I do that I ever heard of it. I know one or two, who have this year, for the first time, read a President's Message; but they do not see that this implies a *fall* in themselves, rather than a *rise* in the President. Blessed were the days before you read a President's Message. Blessed are the young, for they do not read the President's Message. Blessed are they who never read a newspaper, for they shall see Nature, and, through her, God. —Letter to Parker Pillsbury, April 10, 1861

I hear the sound of the piano below as I write this, and feel as if the winter in me were at length beginning to thaw, for my spring has been even more backward than nature's. For a month past life has been a thing incredible to me. None but the kind gods can make me sane. If only they will let their south winds blow on me! I ask to be melted. You can only ask of the metals that they be tender to the fire that melts them. To naught else can they be tender. —Journal, April 11, 1852

I observe that it is when I have been intently, and it may be laboriously, at work, and am somewhat listless or abandoned after it, reposing, that the muse visits me, and I see or hear beauty. It is from out the shadow of my toil that I look into the light. —Journal, April 12, 1854

The naturalist accomplishes a great deal by patience, more perhaps than by activity. —Journal, April 15, 1858

The evenings are considerably shortened. We begin to be more out of doors, the less housed, think less, stir about more, are fuller of affairs and chores, come in chiefly to eat and to sleep. —Journal, April 17, 1860

For the first time I perceive this spring that the year is a circle. I see distinctly the spring arc thus far. It is drawn with a firm line. Every incident is a parable of the Great Teacher....

Why should just these sights and sounds accompany our life? Why should I hear the chattering of blackbirds, why smell the skunk each year? I would fain explore the mysterious relation between myself and these things. I would at least know what these things unavoidably are, make a chart of our life, know how its shores trend, that butterflies reappear and when, know why just this circle of creatures completes the world. Can I not by expectation affect the revolutions of nature, make a day to bring forth something new? —Journal, April 18, 1852

Was awakened in the night to a strain of music dying away — passing travellers singing. My being was so expanded and infinitely and divinely related for a brief season that I saw how unexhausted, how almost wholly unimproved, was man's capacity for a divine life. When I remembered what a narrow and finite life I should anon awake to!
—Journal, April 19, 1856

An early morning walk is a blessing for the whole day. To my neighbors who have risen in mist and rain I tell of a clear sunrise and the singing of birds as some traditionary mythus. I look back to those fresh but now remote hours as to the old dawn of time, when a solid and blooming health reigned and every deed was simple and heroic.
—Journal, April 20, 1840

Most of the luxuries, and many of the so-called comforts of life, are not only not indispensable, but positive hindrances to the elevation of mankind. With respect to luxuries and comforts, the wisest have ever lived a more simple and meagre life than the poor. The ancient philosophers, Chinese, Hindoo, Persian, and Greek, were a class than which none has been poorer in outward riches, none so rich in inward. We know not much about them. It is remarkable that we know so much of them as we do. The same is true of the more modern reformers and benefactors of their race. None can be an impartial or wise observer of human life but from the vantage ground of what we should call voluntary poverty. Of a life of luxury the fruit is luxury, whether in agriculture, or commerce, or literature, or art. There are nowadays professors of philosophy, but not philosophers. Yet it is admirable to profess because it was once admirable to live. To be a philosopher is not merely to have subtle thoughts, nor even to found a school, but so to love wisdom as to live according to its dictates, a life of simplicity, independence, magnanimity, and trust. It is to solve some of the problems of life, not only theoretically, but practically. The success of great scholars and thinkers is commonly a courtier-like success, not kingly, not manly. They make shift to live merely by conformity, practically as their fathers did, and are in no sense the progenitors of a noble race of men. But why do men degenerate ever? What makes families run out? What is the nature of the luxury which enervates and destroys nations? Are we sure that there is none of it in our own lives? The philosopher is in advance of his age even in the outward form of his life. He is not fed, sheltered, clothed, warmed, like his contemporaries. How can a man be a philosopher and not maintain his vital heat by better methods than other men? —Walden, "Economy"

How can a man be a wise man, if he doesn't know any better how to live than other men? — if he is only more cunning and intellectually subtle? Does Wisdom work in a treadmill? Does Wisdom fail? or does she teach how to succeed by her example? Is she merely the miller who grinds the finest logic? Did Plato get his *living* in a better way or more successfully than his contemporaries? Did he succumb to the difficulties of life like other men? Did he merely prevail over them by indifference, or by assuming grand airs? or find it easier to live because his aunt remembered him in her will? —Journal, April 21, 1854

At Cliffs, I hear at a distance a wood thrush. It affects us as a part of our unfallen selves. —Journal, April 21, 1855

What is it that makes it so hard sometimes to determine whither we will walk? I believe that there is a subtle magnetism in Nature, which, if we unconsciously yield to it, will direct us aright. It is not indifferent to us which way we walk. There is a right way; but we are very liable from heedlessness and stupidity to take the wrong one. We would fain take that walk, never yet taken by us through this actual world, which is perfectly symbolical of the path which we love to travel in the interior and ideal world; and sometimes, no doubt, we find it difficult to choose our direction, because it does not yet exist distinctly in our idea. —"Walking" (based on a lecture first delivered April 23, 1851)

If the moon looks larger here than in Europe, probably the sun looks larger also. If the heavens of America appear infinitely higher, and the stars brighter, I trust that these facts are symbolical of the height to which the philosophy and poetry and religion of her inhabitants may one day soar. At length, perchance, the immaterial heaven will appear as much higher to the American mind, and the intimations that star it as much brighter. For I believe that climate does thus react on man — as there is something in the mountain air that feeds the spirit and inspires. Will not man grow to greater perfection intellectually as well as physically under these influences? Or is it unimportant how many foggy days there are in his life? I trust that we shall be more imaginative, that our thoughts will be clearer, fresher, and more ethereal, as our sky — our understanding more comprehensive and broader, like our plains — our intellect generally on a grander scale, like our thunder and lightning, our rivers and mountains and forests — and our hearts shall even correspond in breadth and depth and grandeur to our inland seas. Perchance there will appear to the traveller something, he knows not what, of laeta and glabra, of joyous and serene, in our very faces. Else to what end does the world go on, and why was America discovered? —"Walking"

I would not have every man nor every part of a man cultivated, any more than I would have every acre of earth cultivated: part will be tillage, but the greater part will be meadow and forest, not only serving an immediate use, but preparing a mould against a distant future, by the annual decay of the vegetation which it supports. —"Walking"

My desire for knowledge is intermittent, but my desire to bathe my head in atmospheres unknown to my feet is perennial and constant. The highest that we can attain to is not Knowledge, but Sympathy with Intelligence. I do not know that this higher knowledge amounts to anything more definite than a novel and grand surprise on a sudden revelation of the insufficiency of all that we called Knowledge before -- a discovery that there are more things in heaven and earth than are dreamed of in our philosophy. It is the lighting up of the mist by the sun. Man cannot *know* in any higher sense than this, any more than he can look serenely and with impunity in the face of the sun: "You will not perceive that, as perceiving a particular thing," say the Chaldean Oracles.

There is something servile in the habit of seeking after a law which we may obey. We may study the laws of matter at and for our convenience, but a successful life knows no law. It is an unfortunate discovery certainly, that of a law which binds us where we did not know before that we were bound. Live free, child of the mist — and with respect to knowledge we are all children of the mist. The man who takes the liberty to live is superior to all the laws, by virtue of his relation to the lawmaker. "That is active duty," says the Vishnu Purana, "which is not for our bondage; that is knowledge which is for our liberation: all other duty is good only unto weariness; all other knowledge is only the cleverness of an artist." —"Walking"

Above all, we cannot afford not to live in the present. He is blessed over all mortals who loses no moment of the passing life in remembering the past. Unless our philosophy hears the cock crow in every barnyard within our horizon, it is belated. That sound commonly reminds us that we are growing rusty and antique in our employments and habits of thoughts. His philosophy comes down to a more recent time than ours. There is something suggested by it that is a newer testament — the gospel according to this moment. He has not fallen astern; he has got up early and kept up early, and to be where he is is to be in season, in the foremost rank of time. It is an expression of the health and soundness of Nature, a brag for all the world — healthiness as of a spring burst forth, a new fountain of the Muses, to celebrate this last instant of time. Where he lives no fugitive slave laws are passed. Who has not betrayed his master many times since last he heard that note?

The merit of this bird's strain is in its freedom from all plaintiveness. The singer can easily move us to tears or to laughter, but where is he who can excite in us a pure morning joy? —"Walking"

So we saunter toward the Holy Land, till one day the sun shall shine more brightly than ever he has done, shall perchance shine into our minds and hearts, and light up our whole lives with a great awakening light, as warm and

serene and golden as on a bankside in autumn.
—"Walking"

Saw my white-headed eagle again, first at the same place, the outlet of Fair Haven Pond. It was a fine sight, he is mainly — i.e., his wings and body — so black against the sky, and they contrast so strongly with his white head and tail. He was first flying low over the water; then rose gradually and circled westward toward White Pond. Lying on the ground with my glass, I could wach him very easily, and by turns he gave me all possible views of himself. When I observed him edgewise I noticed that the tips of his wings curved upward slightly the more, like a stereotyped undulation. He rose very high at last, till I almost lost him in the clouds, circling or rather looping along westward, high over river and wood and farm, effectually concealed in the sky. We who live this plodding life here below never know how many eagles fly over us.
—Journal, April 23, 1854

It is very rare that I hear one express a strong and imperishable attachment to a particular scenery, or to the whole of nature — I mean such as will control their whole lives and characters. Such seem to have a true home in nature, a hearth in the fields and woods, whatever tenement may be burned. The soil and climate is warm to them. They alone are naturalized, but most are tender and callow creatures that wear a house as their outmost shell and must get their lives insured when they step abroad from it. They are lathed and plastered in from all natural influences, and their delicate lives are a long battle with the dyspepsia. The others are fairly rooted in the soil, and are the noblest plant it bears, more hardy and natural than sorrel. The dead earth seems animated at the prospect of their coming, as if proud to be trodden on by them. It recognizes its lord. Children of the Golden Age. Hospitals and almshouses are not their destiny. When I hear of such

an attachment in a reasonable, a divine, creature to a particular portion of the earth, it seems as if then first the earth succeeded and rejoiced, as if it had been made and existed only for such a use. These various soils and reaches which the farmer plods over, which the traveller glances at and the geologist dryly describes, then first flower and bear their fruit. Does he chiefly own the land who coldly uses it and gets corn and potatoes out of it, or he who loves it and gets inspiration from it? How rarely a man's love for nature becomes a ruling principle with him, like a youth's affection for a maiden, but more enduring! All nature is my bride. That nature which to one is a stark and ghastly solitude is a sweet, tender, and genial society to another.
—Journal, April 23, 1857

I know two species of men. The vast majority are men of society. They live on the surface; they are interested in the transient and fleeting; they are like driftwood on the flood. They ask forever and only the news, the froth and scum of the eternal sea. They use policy; they make up for want of matter with manner. They have many letters to write. Wealth and the approbation of men is to them success. The enterprises of society are something final and sufficing for them. The world advises them, and they listen to its advice. They live wholly the evanescent life, creatures of circumstance. It is of prime importance to them who is the president of the day. They have no knowledge of truth, but by an exceedingly dim and transient instinct, which stereotypes the church and some other institutions. They dwell, they are ever, right in my face and eyes like gnats; they are like motes, so near the eyes that, looking beyond, they appear like blurs; they have their being between my eyes and the end of my nose. The terra firma of my existence lies far beyond, behind them and their improvements. If they write, the best of them deal in "elegant literature." Society, man, has no prize to offer me that can tempt me; not one. That which interests a town or city or any large number of men is always something trivial, as politics. It is impossible for me to be interested in what interests men generally. Their pursuits and interests seem to me frivolous. When I am most myself and see the clearest, men are least to be seen; they are like muscae volitantes, and that they are seen at all is the proof of imperfect vision. These affairs of men are so narrow as to afford no vista, no distance; it is a shallow foreground only, no large extended views to be taken. Men put to me frivolous questions: When did I come? where am I going? That was a more pertinent question - what I lectured for? - which one auditor put to another. What an ordeal it were to make men pass through, to consider how many ever put to you a vital question! Their knowledge of something better gets no further than what is called religion and spiritual knockings. —Journal, April 24, 1852

There is a season for everything, and we do not notice a given phenomenon except at that season, if, indeed, it can be called the same phenomenon at any other season. There is a time to watch the ripples on Ripple Lake, to look for arrowheads, to study the rocks and lichens, a time to walk on sandy deserts; and the observer of nature must improve these seasons as much as the farmer his. So boys fly kites and play ball or hawkie at particular times all over the State. A wise man will know what game to play today, and play it. We must not be governed by rigid rules, as by the almanac, but let the season rule us. The moods and thoughts of man are revolving just as steadily and incessantly as nature's. Nothing must be postponed. Take time by the forelock. Now or never! You must live in the present, launch yourself on every wave, find your eternity in each moment. Fools stand on their island opportunities and look toward another land. There is no other land; there is no other life but this, or the like of this. Where the good husbandman is, there is the good soil. Take any other course, and life will be a succession of regrets. Let us see vessels sailing prosperously before the wind, and not simply stranded barks. There is no world for the penitent and regretful. —Journal, April 24, 1859

As I preferred some things to others, and especially valued my freedom, as I could fare hard and yet succeed well, I did not wish to spend my time in earning rich carpets or other fine furniture, or delicate cookery, or a house in the Grecian or the Gothic style just yet. If there are any to whom it is no interruption to acquire these things, and who know how to use them when acquired, I relinquish to them the pursuit. Some are "industrious," and appear to love labor for its own sake, or perhaps because it keeps them out of worse mischief; to such I have at present nothing to say. Those who would not know what to do with more leisure than they now enjoy, I might advise to work twice as hard as they do — work till they pay for themselves, and get their free papers. For myself I found that the occupation of a day-laborer was the most independent of any, especially as it required only thirty or forty days in a year to support one. The laborer's day ends with the going down of the sun, and he is then free to devote himself to his chosen pursuit, independent of his labor; but his employer, who speculates from month to month, has no respite from one end of the year to the other.

In short, I am convinced, both by faith and experience, that to maintain one's self on this earth is not a hardship but a pastime, if we will live simply and wisely; as the pursuits of the simpler nations are still the sports of the more artificial. It is not necessary that a man should earn his living by the sweat of his brow, unless he sweats easier than I do.

One young man of my acquaintance, who has inherited some acres, told me that he thought he should live as I did, if he had the means. I would not have any one adopt my mode of living on any account; for, beside that before he has fairly learned it I may have found out another for myself, I desire that there may be as many different persons in the world as possible; but I would have each one be very careful to find out and pursue his own way, and not his father's or his mother's or his neighbor's instead. The youth may build or plant or sail, only let him not be hindered from doing that which he tells me he would like to do. It is by a mathematical point only that we are wise, as the sailor or the fugitive slave keeps the polestar in his eye; but that is sufficient guidance for all our life. We may not arrive at our port within a calculable period, but we would preserve the true course. —Walden, "Economy"

How shall we account for our pursuits, if they are original? We get the language with which to describe our various lives out of a common mint. If others have their losses which they are busy repairing, so have I mine, and their hound and horse may *perhaps* be the symbols of some of them. But also I have lost, or am in danger of losing, a far finer and more ethereal treasure which commonly no loss, of which they are conscious, will symbolize. —Letter to B.B Wiley, April 26, 1857

We sit on the shore at Wheeler's fence, opposite Merriam's. At this season still we go seeking the sunniest, most sheltered, and warmest place. C. say this is the warmest place he has been in this year. We are in this like snakes that lie out on banks. In sunny and sheltered nooks we are in our best estate. There our thoughts flow and we flourish most. By and by we shall seek the shadiest and coolest place. How well adapted we are to our climate! In the winter we sit by fires in the house; in spring and fall, in sunny and sheltered nooks; in the summer, in shady and cool groves, or over water where the breeze circulates.

Thus the average temperature of the year just suits us.
—Journal, April 26, 1857

It is only the irresolute and idle who have no leisure for their proper pursuit. Be preoccupied with this, devoted to it, and no accident can befall you, no idle engagements distract you. No man ever had the opportunity to postpone a high calling to a disagreeable *duty*. Misfortunes occur only when a man is false to his Genius. You cannot hear music and noise at the same time. We avoid all the calamities that may occur in a lower sphere by abiding perpetually in a higher. Most men are engaged in business the greater part of their lives, because the soul abhors a vacuum, and they have not discovered any continuous employment for man's nobler faculties. Accordingly they do not pine, because they are not greatly disappointed. A little relaxation in your exertion, a little idleness, will let in sickness and death into your own body, or your family and their attendant duties and distractions. Every human being is the artificer of his own fate in these respects. The well have no time to be sick. Events, circumstances, etc., have their origin in ourselves. They spring from seeds which we have sown. —Journal, April 27, 1854

All men want, not something to do with, but something to do, or rather something to be. —Walden, "Economy"

This may, perhaps, be nearly the order of the world's creation. Thus we have in the spring of the year the spring of the world represented. —Journal, April 28, 1852

Again, as so many times, I am reminded of the advantage to the poet, and philosopher, and naturalist, and whomsoever, of pursuing from time to time some other business than his chosen one — seeing with the side of the eye. The poet will so get visions which no deliberate abandonment can secure. The philosopher is so forced to recognize principles which long study might not detect. And the naturalist even will stumble upon some new and unexpected flower or animal. —Journal, April 28, 1856

How promising a simple, unpretending, quiet, somewhat reserved man, whether among generals or scholars or farmers! How rare an equanimity and serenity which are an encouragement to all observers! —Journal, April 28, 1856

On the 29th of April, as I was fishing from the bank of the river near the Nine-Acre-Corner bridge, standing on the quaking grass and willow roots, where the muskrats lurk, I heard a singular rattling sound, somewhat like that of the sticks which boys play with their fingers, when, looking up, I observed a very slight and graceful hawk, like a nighthawk, alternately soaring like a ripple and tumbling a rod or two over and over, showing the under side of its wings, which gleamed like a satin ribbon in the sun, or like the pearly inside of a shell. This sight reminded me of falconry and what nobleness and poetry are associated with that sport. The Merlin it seemed to me it might be called: but I care not for its name. It was the most ethereal flight I had ever witnessed. It did not simply flutter like a butterfly, nor soar like the larger hawks, but it sported with proud reliance in the fields of air; mounting again and again with its strange chuckle, it repeated its free and beautiful fall, turning over and over like a kite, and then recovering from its lofty tumbling, as if it had never set its foot on terra firma. It appeared to have no companion in the universe — sporting there alone — and to need none but the morning and the ether with which it played. It was not lonely, but made all the earth lonely beneath it. Where was the parent which hatched it, its kindred, and its father in the heavens? The tenant of the air, it seemed related to the earth but by an egg hatched some time in the crevice of a crag — or was its native nest made in the angle of a cloud, woven of the rainbow's trimmings and the sunset sky, and lined with some soft midsummer haze caught up from earth? Its eyry now some cliffy cloud. —Walden, "Spring"

Crossing the Turnpike, we entered Smith's highlands. Dodging behind a swell of land to avoid the men who were plowing, I saw unexpectedly (when I looked to see if we were concealed by the field) the blue mountains' line in the west (the whole intermediate earth and towns being concealed), this greenish field for a foreground sloping upward a few rods, and then those grand mountains seen over it in the background, so blue — seashore, earth-shore — and, warm as it is, covered with snow which reflected the sun. Then when I turned, I saw in the east, just over the woods, the modest, pale, cloud-like moon, two-thirds full, looking spirit-like on these daylight scenes. Such a sight excites me. The earth is worthy to inhabit. The far river-reach from this hill. It is not so placid a blue — as if with a film of azure over it — today, however. The more remote the water, the lighter the blue, perchance. It is like a lake in Tartary; there our camels will find water. Here is a rock made to sit on — large and inviting, which you do not fear to crush. I hear the flicker and the huckleberry-bird. Yet no leaves apparent. This in some measure corresponds to the fine afternoon weather after the leaves have fallen, though there is a different kind of promise now than then. We are now going out into the field to work; then we were going into the house to think.
—Journal, April 30, 1852

May

It is foolish for a man to accumulate material wealth chiefly, houses and land. Our stock in life, our real estate, is that amount of thought which we have had, which we have thought out. The ground we have thus created is forever pasturage for our thoughts. I fall back on to visions which I have had. What else adds to my possessions and makes me rich in all lands? If you have ever done any work with these finest tools, the imagination and fancy and reason, it is a new creation, independent on the world, and a possession forever. You have laid up something against a rainy day. You have to that extent cleared the wilderness. —Journal, May 1, 1857

When I am behind Cheney's this warm and still afternoon, I hear a voice calling to oxen three quarters of a mile distant, and I know it to be Elijah Wood's. It is wonderful how far the *individual* proclaims himself. Out of the thousand millions of human beings on this globe, I know that this sound was made by the lungs and larynx of E. Wood, am as sure of it as if he nudged me with his elbow and shouted in my ear. He can impress himself on the very atmosphere, then, can launch himself a mile on the wind, through trees and rustling sedge and over rippling water, associating with a myriad sounds, and yet arrive distinct at my ear; and yet this creature that is felt so far, that was so noticeable, lives but a short time, quietly dies and makes no more noise that I know of. I can tell him, too, with my eyes by the very gait and motion of him half a mile distant. Far more wonderful his purely spiritual influence — that after the lapse of thousands of years you may still detect the individual in the turn of a sentence or the tone of a thought!! —Journal, May 1, 1858

We accuse the savages of worshipping only the bad spirit, or devil, though they may distinguish both a good and a bad; but they regard only that one which they fear and worship the devil only. We too are savages in this regard, doing precisely the same thing. This occurred to me yesterday as I sat in the woods admiring the beauty of the blue butterfly. We are not chiefly interested in birds and insects, for example, as they are ornamental to the earth and cheering to man, but we spare the lives of the former only on condition that they eat more grubs than they do cherries, and the only account of the insects which the State encourages is of the "Insects *Injurious* to Vegetation." We too admit both a good and a bad spirit, but we worship chiefly the bad spirit, whom we fear. We do not think first of the good but of the harm things will do to us.

The catechism says that the chief end of man is to glorify God and enjoy him forever, which of course is applicable mainly to God as seen in his works. Yet the only account of its beautiful insects — butterflies, etc. — which God has made and set before us which the State ever thinks of spending any money on is the account of those which are injurious to vegetation! This is the way we glorify God and enjoy him forever. Come out here and behold a thousand painted butterflies and other beautiful insects which people the air, then go to the libraries and see what kind of prayer and glorification of God is recorded there. Massachusetts has published her report on "Insects Injurious to Vegetation," and our neighbor the "Noxious Insects of New York." We have attended to the evil and said nothing about the good. This is looking a gift horse in the mouth with a vengeance. Children are attracted by the beauty of butterflies, but their parents and legislators deem it an idle pursuit. The parents remind me of the devil, but the children of God. —Journal, May 1, 1859

How shall we earn our bread is a grave question; yet it is a sweet and inviting question. Let us not shirk it, as is usually done. It is the most important and practical question which is put to man. Let us not answer it hastily. Let us not be content to get our bread in some gross, careless, and hasty manner. Some men go a-hunting, some a-fishing, some a-gaming, some to war; but none have so pleasant a time as they who in earnest seek to earn their bread. It is true actually as it is true really; it is true materially as it is true spiritually, that they who seek honestly and sincerely, with all their hearts and lives and strength, to earn their bread, do earn it, and it is sure to be very sweet to them. A very little bread — a very few crumbs are enough, if it be of the right quality, for it is infinitely nutritious. Let each man, then, earn at least a crumb of bread for his body before he dies, and know the taste of it — that it is identical with the bread of life, and that they both go down at one swallow.

Our bread need not ever be sour or hard to digest. What Nature is to the mind she is also to the body. As she feeds my imagination, she will feed my body; for what she says she means, and is ready to do. She is not simply beautiful to the poet's eye. Not only the rainbow and sunset are beautiful, but to be fed and clothed, sheltered and warmed aright, are equally beautiful and inspiring. —Letter to Harrison Blake, May 2, 1848

Up and down the town, men and boys that are under subjection are polishing their shoes and brushing their go-to-meeting clothes. I, a descendent of Northmen who worshipped Thor, spend my time worshipping neither Thor nor Christ; a descendent of Northmen who sacrificed men and horses, sacrifice neither men nor horses. I care not for Thor nor for the Jews. I sympathize not today with those who go to church in newest clothes and sit quietly in straight-backed pews. I sympathize rather with the boy who has none to look after him, who borrows a boat and paddle and in common clothes sets out to explore these temporary vernal lakes. I meet such a boy paddling along under a sunny bank, with bare feet and his pants rolled up above his knees, ready to leap into the water at a moment's warning. Better for him to read "Robinson Crusoe" than Baxter's "Saint's Rest." —Journal, May 3, 1857

I would not subtract anything from the praise that is due to philanthropy, but merely demand justice for all who by their lives and works are a blessing to mankind. I do not value chiefly a man's uprightness and benevolence, which are, as it were, his stem and leaves. Those plants of whose greenness withered we make herb tea for the sick serve but a humble use, and are most employed by quacks. I want the flower and fruit of a man; that some fragrance be wafted over from him to me, and some ripeness flavor our intercourse. His goodness must not be a partial and transitory act, but a constant superfluity, which costs him nothing and of which he is unconscious. This is a charity that hides a multitude of sins. The philanthropist too often surrounds mankind with the remembrance of his own cast-off griefs as an atmosphere, and calls it sympathy. We should impart our courage, and not our despair, our health and ease, and not our disease, and take care that this does not spread by contagion. —Walden, "Economy"

Your observation, to be interesting, i.e. to be significant, must be *subjective*. The sum of what the writer of whatever class has to report is simply some human experience, whether he be poet or philosopher or man of science. The man of most science is the man most alive, whose life is the greatest event. Senses that take cognizance of outward things merely are of no avail. It matters not whether or how far you travel — the farther commonly the worse — but how much alive you are. If it is possible to conceive of an event outside to humanity, it is not of the slightest significance, though it were the explosion of a planet. Every important worker will report what life there is in him. It makes no odds into what seeming deserts the poet is born. Though all his neighbors pronouce it a Sahara, it will be a paradise to him; for the desert which we see is the result of the barrenness of our experience. No mere willful activity whatever, whether in writing verses or collecting statistics, will produce true poetry or science. If you are really a sick man, it is indeed to be regretted, for you cannot accomplish so much as if you were well. All that a man has to say or do that can possibly concern mankind, is in some shape or other to tell the story of his love — to sing; and, if he is fortunate and keeps alive he will be forever in love. This alone is to be alive to the extremities. It is a pity that this divine creature should ever suffer from cold feet; a still greater pity that the coldness so often reaches to his heart. —Journal, May 6, 1854

I love to see the man, a long-lived child,
As yet uninjured by all worldly taint
As the fresh infant whose whole life is play.
'Tis a serene spectacle for a serene day;
But better still I love to contemplate
The mature soul of lesser innocence,
Who hath travelled far on life's dusty road
Far from the starting point of infancy
And proudly bears his small degen'racy
Blazon'd on his memorial standard high
Who from the sad experience of his fate
Since his bark struck on that unlucky rock
Has proudly steered his life with his own hands.
Though his face harbors less of innocence
Yet there do chiefly lurk within its depths
Furrowed by care, but yet all over spread
With the ripe bloom of a self-wrought content
Noble resolves which do reprove the gods

And it doth more assert man's eminence
Above the happy level of the brute
And more doth advertise me of the heights
To which no natural path doth ever lead
No natural light can ever light our steps,
—But the far-piercing ray that shines
From the recesses of a brave man's eye.
—Manhood (undated poem)

The thinker, he who is serene and self-possessed, is the brave, not the desperate soldier. He who can deal with his thoughts as a material, building them into poems in which future generations will delight, he is the man of the greatest and rarest vigor, not sturdy diggers and lusty polygamists. He is the man of energy, in whom subtle and poetic thoughts are bred. Common men can enjoy partially; they can go a-fishing rainy days; they can *read* poems perchance, but they have not the vigor to beget poems. They can enjoy feebly, but they cannot create. Men talk of freedom! How many are free to think? free from fear, from perturbation, from prejudice? Nine hundred and ninety-nine in a thousand are perfect slaves. How many can exercise the highest human faculties? He is the man truly — courageous, wise, ingeniuous — who can use his thoughts and ecstasies as the material of fair and durable creations. One man shall derive from the fisherman's story more than the fisher has got who tells it. The mass of men do not know how to cultivate the fields they traverse. The mass clear only a scanty pittance where the thinker reaps an abundant harvest. What is all your building, if you do not build with thoughts? No exercise implies more real manhood and vigor than joining thought to thought. How few men can tell what they have thought! I hardly know half a dozen who are not too lazy for this. They cannot get over some difficulty, and therefore they are on the long way round. You conquer fate by thought. If you think the fatal thought of men and institutions, you need never pull the trigger. The consequences of thinking inevitably follow. There is no more Herculean task than to think a thought about this life and then get it expressed.

Horticulturalists think that they make flower-gardens, though in their thoughts they are barren and flower-less, but to the poet the earth is a flower-garden wherever he goes, or thinks. Most men can keep a horse or keep up a certain fashionable style of living, but few indeed can keep up great expectations. They justly think very meanly of themselves. —Journal, May 6, 1858

He is the richest who has most use for nature as raw material of tropes and symbols with which to describe his life. If these gates of golden willows affect me, they correspond to the beauty and promise of some experience on which I am entering. If I am overflowing with life, am rich in experience for which I lack expression, then nature will be my language full of poetry — all nature will *fable*, and every natural phenomenon be a myth. The man of science, who is not seeking for expression but for a fact to be expressed merely, studies nature as a dead language. I pray for such inward experience as will make nature significant. —Journal, May 10, 1853

The value of the mountains in the horizon — would not that be a good theme for a lecture? The text for a discourse in real values, and permanent; a sermon on the mount. They are stepping-stones to heaven — as the rider has a horse-block at his gate — by which to mount when we would commence our pilgrimage to heaven; by which we gradually take our departure from earth, from the time when our youthful eyes first rested on them — from this bare actual earth, which has so little of the hue of heaven. They make it easier to die and easier to live....

They are valuable to mankind as is the iris of the eye to a man. They are the path of the translated. The undisputed territory between earth and heaven. In our travels rising higher and higher, we at length got to where the earth was blue. Suggesting that this earth, unless our conduct curse it, is as celestial as that sky. They are the pastures to which we drive our thoughts on these 20ths of May. —Journal, May 10, 1853

How rarely I meet with a man who can be free, even in thought! We live according to rule. Some men are bedridden; all, world-ridden. I take my neighbor, an intellectual man, out into the woods and invite him to take a new and absolute view of things, to empty clean out of his thoughts all institutions of men and start again; but he can't do it, he sticks to his traditions and his crochets. He thinks that governments, colleges, newspapers, etc., are from everlasting to everlasting. —Journal, May 12, 1857

The best men that I know are not serene, a world in themselves. They dwell in form. They flatter and study effect, only more finely than the rest. The world to me appears uninhabited. My neighbors select granite for the underpinning of their houses and barns; they build their fences of stone; but they do not themselves rest on an underpinning of granite. Their sills are rotten. What stuff is the man made of who is not coexistent in your thought with the purest and subtlest truth? While there are manners and compliments we do not meet. I accuse my finest acquaintances of an immense frivolity. They do not teach me the lessons of honesty and sincerity that the brute beasts do, or of steadiness and solidity that the rocks do. —Journal, May 13, 1852

While dropping beans in the garden at Texas just after sundown (May 13th), I hear from across the fields the note of the bay-wing, *Come here here there there quick quick quick or*

I'm gone (which I have no doubt sits on some fence-post or rail there), and it instantly translates me from the sphere of my work and repairs all the world that we jointly inhabit. It reminds me of so many country afternoons and evenings when this bird's strain was heard far over the fields, as I pursued it from field to field. The spirit of its earth-song, of its serene and true philosophy, was breathed into me, and I saw the world as through a glass, as it lies eternally. Some of its aboriginal contentment, even of its domestic felicity, possessed me. What he suggests is permanently true. As the bay-wing sang many a thousand years ago, so sang he tonight. In the beginning God heard his song and pronounced it good, and hence it has endured. —Journal, May 13, 1857

If you would have the song of the sparrow inspire you a thousand years hence, let your life be in harmony with its strain today. —Journal, May 13, 1857

Most men can be easily transplanted from here there, for they have so little root — no tap-root — or their roots penetrate so little way, that you can thrust a shovel quite under them and take them up, roots and all. —Journal, May 14, 1852

The first cricket's chirrup which I have chanced to hear now falls on my ear and makes me forget all else; all else is a thin and movable crust down to that depth where he resides eternally. He already foretells autumn. Deep under the dry border of some rock in this hillside he sits, and makes the finest singing of birds outward and insignificant, his own song is so much deeper and more significant. His voice has set me thinking, philosophizing, moralizing at once. It is not so wildly melodious, but it is wiser and more mature than that of the wood thrush. With this elixir I see clear through the summer now to autumn, and any summer work seems frivolous. I am disposed to ask this humblebee that hurries humming past so busily, if he knows what he is about. At one leap I go from the just opened buttercup to the life-everlasting. This singer has antedated autumn. His strain is superior to seasons. It annihilates time and space; the summer is for time-servers. —Journal, May 15, 1853

Now the sun has come out after the May storm, how bright, how full of freshness and tender promise and fragrance is the new world! The woods putting forth new leaves; it is a memorable season. So hopeful! These young leaves have the beauty of flowers. —Journal, May 17, 1852

I sit now on a rock on the west slope of Fair Haven orchard, an hour before sunset, this warm, almost sultry evening, the air filled with the sweetness of apple blossoms (this is blossom week) — or I think it is mainly that meadow fragrance still — the sun partly concealed behind a low cloud in the west, the air cleared by last evening's thunder-shower, the river now beautifully smooth (though a warm, bland breeze blows up here), full of light and reflecting the placid western sky and the dark woods which overhang it. I was surprised, on turning round, to behold the serene and everlasting beauty of the world, it was so soothing, I saw that I could not go home to supper and lose it. It was so much fairer, serener, more beautiful, than my mood had been. The fields beyond the river have unexpectedly a smooth, lawn-like beauty, and in beautiful curves sweep round the edge of the woods. The rapidly expanding foliage of the deciduous trees (last evening's rain or moisture has started them) lights up with a lively yellow green the dark pines which we have so long been used to. Some patches (I speak of woods half a mile or more off) are a lively green, some gray or reddish-gray still, where white oaks stand. With the stillness of the air comes the stillness of the water. The sweetest singers among the birds are heard more distinctly now, as the reflections are seen more distinctly in the water — the veery constantly now. Methinks this serene, ambrosial beauty could hardly have been but for last evening's thunder-shower, which, to be sure, barely touched us, but cleared the air and gave a start to vegetation. The elm on the opposite side of the river has now a thin but dark verdure, almost as dark as the pines, while, as I have said, the prevailing color of the deciduous woods is a light yellowish and sunny green. The woods rarely if ever present a more beautiful aspect from afar than now. Methinks the black oak at early leafing is more red than the red oak. Ah, the beauty of this last hour of the day — when a power stills the air and smooths all waters and all minds — that partakes of the light of the day and the stillness of the night! —Journal, May 17, 1853

The shrub oaks are now blossoming. The scarlet tanagers are come. The oak leaves of all colors are just expanding, and are more beautiful than most flowers. The hickory buds are almost leaves. The landscape has a new life and light infused into it. The deciduous trees are springing, to countenance the pines, which are evergreen. It seems to take but one summer day to fetch the summer in. The turning-point between winter and summer is reached. —Journal, May 18, 1851

There is, no doubt, a perfect analogy between the life of the human and that of the vegetable, both of the body and the mind. The botanist Gray says:

The organs of plants are of two sorts: —1. Those of *Vegetation*, which are concerned in growth — by which the plant takes in the aërial and earthy matters on which it lives, and elaborates them into the materials of its own organized substance; 2. Those of *Fructification* or *Reproduction*, which are concerned with the propagation of the species.

So it is with the human being. I am concerned first to come to my *Growth*, intellectually and morally (and physically, of course, as a means to this, for the body is the symbol of the soul), and then to bear my *Fruit*, do my *Work*, *propagate*, not only physically but *morally*, not only in body but in mind.

The organs of vegetation are the *Root*, *Stem*, and *Leaves*. The *Stem* is the axis and original basis of the plant. The first point of the stem preëxists in the embryo (i.e. in the rudimentary plantlet contained within the seed): it is here called the radicle.

Such is the rudiment of mind, already partially developed, more than a bud, but pale, never having been exposed to the light, and slumbering coiled up, packed away in the seed, unfolded.

Consider the still pale, rudimentary, infantine, radicle-like thoughts of some students, which who knows what they might expand to, if they should ever come to the light and air, if they do not become rancid and perish in the seed. It is not every seed that will survive a thousand years. Other thoughts, further developed, but yet pale and languid, like shoots grown in a cellar.

The plant . . . develops from the first in two opposite directions, viz. upwards [to expand in the light and air] to produce and continue the stem (or *ascending axis*), and downwards [avoiding the light] to form the root (or *descending* axis). The former is ordinarily or in great part aërial, the latter subterranean.

So the mind develops from the first in two opposite directions: upwards to expand in the light and air; and downwards avoiding the light to form the root. One half is aërial, the other subterranean. The mind is not well balanced and firmly planted, like the oak, which has not as much root as branch, whose roots like those of the white pine are slight and near the surface. One half of the mind's development must still be root — in the embryonic state, in the womb of nature, more unborn than at first. For each successive new idea or bud, a new rootlet in the earth. The growing man penetrates yet deeper by his roots into the womb of things. The infant is comparatively near the surface, just covered from the light; but the man sends down a tap-root to the centre of things.

The mere logician, the mere reasoner, who weaves his arguments as a tree its branches in the sky — nothing equally developed in the roots — is overthrown by the first wind.

As with the roots of the plant, so with the roots of the mind, the branches and branchlets of the root "are mere repetitions for the purpose of multiplying the absorbing points, which are chiefly the growing or newly formed extremities, sometimes termed *spongelets*. It bears no other organs."

So this organ of the mind's development, the *Root*, bears no organs but spongelets or absorbing points.

Annuals, which perish root and all the first season, especially have slender and thread-like fibrous roots. But biennials are particularly characterized by distended, fleshy roots containing starch, a stock for future growth, to be consumed during their second or flowering season — as carrots, radishes, turnips. Perennials frequently have many thickened roots clustered together, tuberous or palmate roots, fasciculated or clustered as in the dahlia, peony, etc.

Roots may spring from any part of the stem under favorable circumstances; "that is to say in darkness and moisture, as when covered by the soil or resting on its surface."

That is, the most clear and ethereal ideas (Antaeus-like) readily ally themselves to the earth, to the primal womb of things. They put forth roots as soon as branches; they are eager to be *soiled*. No thought soars so high that it sunders these apron-strings of its mother. The thought that comes to light, that pierces the empyrean on the other side, is wombed and rooted in darkness, a moist and fertile darkness — its roots in Hades like the tree of life. No idea is so soaring but it will readily put forth roots. Wherever there is an air-and-light-seeking bud about to expand, it may become in the earth a darkness-seeking root. Even swallows and birds-of-paradise *can* walk on the ground. To quote the sentence from Gray entire: "Roots not only spring from the root-end of the primary stem in germination, but also from any subsequent part of the stem under favorable circumstances, that is to say, in darkness and moisture, as when covered by the soil or resting on its surface."

No thought but is connected as strictly as a flower, with the earth. The mind flashes not so far on one side but its rootlets, its spongelets, find their way instantly on the other side into a moist darkness, uterine — a low bottom in the heavens, even miasma-exhaling to such immigrants as are not acclimated. A cloud is uplifted to sustain its roots. Imbosomed in clouds as in a chariot, the mind drives through the boundless fields of space. Even there is the dwelling of Indra.

I might here quote the following, with the last — of roots:

They may even strike in the open air and light, as is seen in the copious aërial rootlets by which the Ivy, the Poison Ivy, and the Trumpet Creeper climb and adhere to the trunks of trees or other bodies; and also in Epiphytes or Air-plants, of most warm regions, which have no connection whatever with the soil, but germinate and grow high in air on the trunks or branches of trees, etc.; as well as in some terrestrial plants, such as the Banian and Mangrove, that send off aërial roots from their trunks or branches, which finally reach the ground.

So, if our light-and-air-seeking tendencies extend too widely for our original root or stem, we must send downward new roots to ally us to the earth.

Also there are parasitic plants which have their roots in the branches or roots of other trees, as the mistletoe, the beech-drops, etc. There are minds which so have their roots in other minds as in the womb of nature — if, indeed, most are not such?! —Journal, May 20, 1851

Who knows how incessant a surveillance a strong man may maintain over himself — how far subject passion and appetite to reason, and lead the life his imagination paints? —Journal, May 21, 1839

You must not only aim aright,
But draw the bow with all your might.
—(undated)

In the long run men hit only what they aim at. Therefore, though they should fail immediately, they had better aim at something high. —Walden, "Economy"

As for the dispute about solitude and society, any comparison is impertinent. It is an idling down on the plain at the base of a mountain, instead of climbing steadily to its top. Of course you will be glad of all the society you can get to go up with. Will you go to glory with me? is the burden of the song. I love society so much that I swallowed it all at a gulp — that is, all that came in my way. It is not that we love to be alone, but that we love to soar, and when we do soar, the company grows thinner and thinner till there is none at all. It is either the *Tribune* on the plain, a sermon on the mount, or a very private ecstasy still higher up. We are not the less to aim at the summits, though the multitude does not ascend them. Use all the society that will abet you. —Letter to Harrison Blake, May 21, 1856

First observe the creak of crickets. It is quite general amid these rocks. The song of only one is more interesting to me. It suggests lateness, but only as we come to a knowledge of eternity after some acquaintance with time. It is only late for all trivial and hurried pursuits. It suggests a wisdom mature, never late, being above all temporal considerations, which possesses the coolness and maturity of autumn amidst the aspiration of spring and the heats of summer. To the birds they say: "Ah! you speak like children from impulse; Nature speaks through you; but with us it is ripe knowledge. The seasons do not revolve for us; we sing their lullaby." So they chant, eternal, at the roots of the grass. It is heaven where they are, and their dwelling need not be *heaved* up. Forever the same, in May and in November. Serenely wise, their song has the security of prose. They have drunk no wine but the dew. It is no transient love-strain, hushed when the incubating season is past, but a glorifying of God and enjoying him forever. They sit aside from the revolution of the seasons. Their strain is as unvaried as Truth. Only in their saner moments do men hear the crickets. It is balm to the philosopher. It tempers his thoughts. They dwell forever in a temperate latitude. By listening to whom, all voices are tuned. In their song they ignore our accidents. They are not concerned about the news. A quire has begun which

pauses not for any news, for it knows only the eternal.
—Journal, May 22, 1854

This earth which is spread out like a map around me is but the lining of my inmost soul exposed. —Journal, May 23, 1854

There was a time when the beauty and the music were all within, and I sat and listened to my thoughts, and there was a song in them. I sat for hours on rocks and wrestled with the melody which possessed me. I sat and listened by the hour to a positive though faint and distant music, not sung by any bird, nor vibrating any earthly harp. When you walked with a joy which knew not its own origin. When you were an organ of which the world was but one poor broken pipe. I lay long on the rocks, foundered like a harp on the seashore, that knows not how it is dealt with. You sat on the earth, but which ruled and arranged it. Man *should be* the harp articulate. When your cords were tense.

Think of going abroad out of one's self to hear music — to Europe or Africa! Instead of so living as to be the lyre which the breath of the morning causes to vibrate with that melody which creates worlds. —Journal, May 23, 1854

Our most glorious experiences are a kind of regret. Our regret is so sublime that we may mistake it for triumph. It is the painful, plaintively sad surprise of our Genius remembering our past lives and contemplating what is possible. It is remarkable that men commonly never refer to, never hint at, any crowning experiences when the common laws of their being were unsettled and the divine and eternal laws prevailed in them. Their lives are not revolutionary; they never recognize any other than the local and temporal authorities. It is a regret so divine and inspiring, so genuine, based on so true and distinct a contrast, that it surpasses our proudest boasts and the fairest expectations.

My most sacred and memorable life is commonly on awaking in the morning. I frequently awake with an atmosphere about me as if my unremembered dreams had been divine, as if my spirit had journeyed to its native place, and, in the act of reentering its native body, had diffused an elysian fragrance around. —Journal, May 24, 1851

I am struck by the fact that, though any important individual experience is rare, though it is so rare that the individual is conscious of a relation to his maker transcending time and space and earth, though any knowledge or, or communication from, "Providence" is the rarest thing in the world, yet men very easily, regarding themselves in the gross, speak of carrying out the designs of Providence as nations. —Journal, May 24, 1855

Heard one speak today of his sense of awe at the thought of God, and suggested to him that awe was the cause of the potato-rot. The same speaker dwelt on the sufferings of life, but my advice was to go about one's business, suggesting that no ecstasy was ever interrupted, nor its fruit blasted. As for completeness and roundness, to be sure, we are each like one of the laciniae of a lichen, a torn fragment, but not the less cheerfully we expand in a moist day and assume unexpected colors. We want no completeness but intensity of life. —Journal, May 24, 1857

How rapidly the young twigs shoot — the herbs, trees, shrubs no sooner leaf out than they shoot forward surprisingly, as if they had acquired a head by being repressed so long. They do not grow nearly so rapidly at any other season. Many do most of their growing for the year in a week or two at this season. They *shoot* — they *spring* — and the rest of the year they harden and mature, and perhaps have a second spring in the latter part of summer or in the fall. —Journal, May 25, 1853

A peculiarity of these days is the first hearing of the crickets' creak, suggesting philosophy and thought. No greater event transpires now. It is the most interesting piece of news to be communicated, yet it is not in any newspaper. —Journal, May 27, 1859

For rural interest, give me the houses of the poor, with simply a cool spring, a good deal of weather-stained wood, and a natural door-stone; a house standing somewhere in nature, and not merely in an atmosphere of art, on a measured lot; on a hillside, perchance, obviously not made by any gardener, amid rocks not placed there by a landscape gardener for effect; with nothing "pretty" about it, but life reduced to its lowest terms yet found to be beautiful. This is a good foundation or board to spring from. All that the natives erect themselves above that will be a genuine growth. —Journal, May 27, 1859

Some absorbing employment on your higher ground — your upland farm — whither no cart-path leads, but where you mount alone with your hoe — where the life everlasting grows; there you raise a crop which needs not to be brought down into the valley to a market; which you barter for heavenly products.

Do you separate distinctly enough the support of your body from that of your essence? By how distinct a course commonly are these two ends attained! Not that they should not be attained by one and the same means — that, indeed, is the rarest success — but there is no half and half about it. —Letter to Harrison Blake, May 28, 1850

The morning wind forever blows; the poem of the world is uninterrupted, but few are the ears that hear it. Forever that strain of the harp which soothed the Cerberus and called me back to life is sounding. Olympus is outside of the earth everywhere. —Journal, May 30, 1853

Some incidents in my life have seemed far more allegorical than actual; they were so significant that they plainly served no other use. That is, I have been more impressed by their allegorical significance and fitness; they have been like myths or passages in a myth, rather than mere incidents or history which have to wait to become significant. Quite in harmony with my subjective philosophy. This, for instance: that, when I thought I knew the flowers so well, the beautiful purple azalea or pinxter-flower should be shown to me by the hunter who found it. Such facts are quite above the level of the actual. They are all just such events as my imagination prepares me for, no matter how incredible. Perfectly in keeping with my life and characteristic. Ever and anon something will occur which my philosophy has not dreamed of. The limits of the actual are set some thoughts further off. That which had seemed a rigid wall of vast thickness unexpectedly proves a thin and undulating drapery. The boundaries of the actual are no more fixed and rigid than the elasticity of our imaginations. The fact that a rare and beautiful flower which we never saw, perhaps never heard of, for which therefore there was no place in our thoughts, may at length be found in our immediate neighborhood, is very suggestive. —Journal, May 31, 1853

SUMMER

June

Summer begins now about a week past, with the expanded leaves, the shade and warm weather. Cultivated fields also are *leaving* out, i.e., corn and potatoes coming up. Most trees have bloomed and are now forming their fruit. Young berries, too, are forming, and birds are being hatched. Dor-bugs and other insects have come forth the first warm evening after showers.

The birds have now all come and no longer fly in flocks. The hylodes are no longer heard. The bullfrog begins to trump. Thick and extensive fogs in the morning begin. Plants are rapidly growing — *shooting*. Hoeing has commenced (June 1st). It is now the season of growth. The first bloom of the year is over. Have not wild animals now henceforth their young? and fishes too?

The pincushion galls on young white oaks are now among the most beautiful objects in the woods, coarse woolly white to appearance, spotted with bright red or crimson on the exposed side. It is remarkable that a mere gall, which at first we are inclined to regard as something abnormal, should be made so beautiful, as if it were the *flower* of the tree; that a disease, an excrescence, should prove, perchance, the greatest beauty — as the tear of the pearl. Beautiful scarlet sins they may be. Through our temptations — aye, and our falls — our virtues appear. As in many a character — many a poet — we see that beauty exhibited in a gall, which was meant to have bloomed in a flower, unchecked. Such, however, is the accomplishment of the world. The poet cherishes his chagrins and sets his sighs to music. This gall is the tree's "Ode to Dejection." How oft it chances that the apparent fruit of a shrub, its apple, is merely a gall or blight! How many men meet with

some blast in the moist growing days of their youth, and what should have been a sweet and palatable fruit in them becomes a mere puff and excrescence, ripening no kernel, and they say that they have experienced religion! For the hardening of the seed is the crisis. Their fruit is a gall, a puff, an excrescence, for want of moderation and continence. So many plants never ripen their fruit.
—Journal, June 1, 1853

Now I see gentlemen and ladies sitting at anchor in boats on the lakes in the calm afternoons, under parasols, making use of nature, not always accumulating money. The farmer hoeing is wont to look with scorn and pride on a man sitting in a motionless boat a whole half-day, but he does not realize that the object of his own labor is perhaps merely to add another dollar to his heap, nor through what coarseness and inhumanity to his family and servants he often accomplishes this. He has an Irishman or a Canadian working for him by the month; and what, probably, is the lesson that he is teaching him by precept and example? Will it make that laborer more of a man? this earth more like heaven? —Journal, June 1, 1854

When I awake I hear the low universal chirping or twittering of the chip-birds, like the bursting bead on the surface of the uncorked day. First come, first served! You must taste the first glass of the day's nectar, if you would get all the spirit of it. —Journal, June 2, 1853

The song of birds is more lively and seems to have a new character; a new season has commenced. —Journal, June 4, 1857

One thing that chiefly distinguishes this season from three weeks ago is that fine serene undertone or earthsong as we go by sunny banks and hillsides, the creak of crickets, which affects our thoughts so favorably, imparting its own serenity. It is time now to bring our philosophy out of doors. Our thoughts pillow themselves unconsciously in the troughs of this serene, rippling sea of sound. Now first we begin to be peripatetics. No longer our ears come in contact with the bold echoing earth, but everywhere recline on the spring cushion of a cricket's chirp. These rills that ripple from every hillside become at length a universal sea of sound, nourishing our ears when we are most unconscious. —Journal, June 4, 1857

You may say that now, when most trees have fully expanded leaves and the black ash fairly shows green, the leafy season has fairly commenced. —Journal, June 4, 1860

The constant inquiry which nature puts is: "Are you virtuous? Then you can behold me." Beauty, fragrance, music, sweetness, and joy of all kinds are for the virtuous. —Journal, June 5, 1852

I have come to this hill to see the sun go down, to recover sanity and put myself again in relation with Nature. I would fain drink a draft of Nature's serenity. Let deep answer to deep. —Journal, June 5, 1854

This is June, the month of grass and leaves. The deciduous trees are investing the evergreens and revealing how dark they are. Already the aspens are trembling again, and a new summer is offered me. I feel a little fluttered in my thoughts, as if I might be too late. Each season is but an infinitesimal point. It no sooner comes than it is gone. It has no duration. It simply gives a tone and hue to my thought. Each annual phenomenon is a reminiscence and prompting. Our thoughts and sentiments answer to the revolutions of the seasons, as two cog-wheels fit into each other. We are conversant with only one point of contact at a time, from which we receive a prompting and impulse and instantly pass to a new season or point of contact. A year is made up of a certain series and number of sensations and thoughts which have their language in nature. Now I am ice, now I am sorrel. Each experience reduces itself to a mood of the mind. —Journal, June 6, 1857

My practicalness is not to be trusted to the last. To be sure, I go upon my legs for the most part, but, being hard-pushed and dogged by a superficial common sense which is bound to near objects by beaten paths, I am off the handle, as the phrase is — I begin to be transcendental and show where my heart is. —Journal, June 7, 1851

It is but a step from flowers to fruit. —Journal, June 7, 1854

The life in us is like the water in the river; it may rise this year higher than ever it was known to before and flood the uplands — even this may be the eventful year — and drown out all our muskrats.

There are as many strata at different levels of life as there are leaves in a book. When on the higher levels we can remember the lower levels, but when on the lower we cannot remember the higher. —Journal, June 8, 1850

Herndon, in his "Exploration of the Amazon," says that "there is wanting an industrious and active population, who know what the comforts of life are, and who have artificial wants to draw out the great resources of the country." But what are the "artificial wants," to be encouraged, and the "great resources" of a country? Surely not the love of luxuries like the tobacco and slaves of his native Virginia, or that fertility of soil which produces these. The chief want is ever a life of deep experiences – that is, character – which alone draws out "the great resources" of Nature. When our wants cease to be chiefly superficial and trivial, which is commonly meant by artificial, and begin to be wants of character, then the great resources of a country are taxed and drawn out, and the result, the staple production, is poetry. Have the "great resources" of Virginia been drawn out by such "artificial wants" as there exist? Was that country really designed by its Maker to produce slaves and tobacco, or something more even than freemen and food for freemen? Wants of character, aspirations — this is what is wanted; but what is called civilization does not always substitute this for the barren simplicity of the savage. —Journal, June 8, 1854

There are some large cumuli with glowing downy cheeks floating about. Now I notice where an elm is in the shadow of a cloud — the black elm-tops and shadows of June. It is a dark eyelash which suggests a flashing eye beneath. It suggests houses that lie under the shade, the repose and siesta of summer noons, the thunder-cloud, bathing, and all that belongs to summer. These veils are now spread here and there over the village. It suggests also the creak of crickets, a June sound now fairly begun, inducing contemplation and philosophic thoughts — the sultry hum of insects. —Journal, June 9, 1856

In Julius Smith's yard, a striped snake (so called) was running about this forenoon, and in the afternoon it was found to have shed its slough, leaving it half-way out a hole, which probably it used to confine it in. It was about in its new skin. Many creatures — devil's-needles, etc., etc. — cast their sloughs now. Can't I? —Journal, June 10, 1857

Ah, that life that I have known! How hard it is to remember what is most memorable! We remember how we itched, not how our hearts beat. I can sometimes recall to mind the quality, the immortality, of my youthful life, but in memory only relation to it. —Journal, June 11, 1851

No one, to my knowledge, has observed the minute differences in the seasons. Hardly two nights are alike. The rocks do not feel warm tonight, for the air is warmest; nor does the sand particularly. A book of the seasons, each page of which should be written in its own season and out-of-doors, or in its own locality wherever it may be. —Journal, June 11, 1851

What if we feel a yearning to which no breast answers? I walk alone. My heart is full. Feelings impede the current of my thoughts. I knock on the earth for my friend. I expect to meet him at every turn; but no friend appears, and perhaps none is dreaming of me. I am tired of frivolous society, in which silence is forever the most natural and the best manners. I would fain walk on the deep waters, but my companions will only walk on shallows and puddles. I am naturally silent in the midst of twenty from day to day, from year to year. I am rarely reminded of their presence. Two yards of politeness do not make society for me. One complains that I do not take his jokes. I took them before he had done uttering them, and went my way. One talks to me of his apples and pears, and I depart with my secret untold. His are not the apples that tempt me. —Journal, June 11, 1855

All things in this world must be seen with the morning dew on them, must be seen with youthful, early-opened, hopeful eyes. —Journal, June 13, 1852

The note of the wood thrush answers to some cool unexhausted morning vigor in the hearer. —Journal, June 12, 1853

This seems to be the true hour to be abroad sauntering far from home. Your thoughts being already turned toward home, your walk in one sense ended, you are in that favorable frame of mind described by De Quincey, open to great impressions, and you see those rare sights with the unconscious side of the eye, which you could not see by a direct gaze before. Then the dews begin to descend in your mind, and its atmosphere is strained of all impurities; and home is farther away than ever. Here is home; the beauty of the world impresses you. There is coolness in your mind as in a well. Life is too grand for supper. —Journal, June 14, 1853

The motive of the laborer should be not to get his living, to get a good job, but to perform well a certain work. A town must pay its engineers so well that they shall not feel that they are working for low ends, as for a livelihood merely, but for scientific ends. Do not hire a man who does your work for money, but him who does it for love, and pay him well. —Journal, June 15, 1852

By and by the bidens (marigold) will stand in the river, as now the ranunculus. The summer's vervor will have sunk into it. The spring yellows are faint, cool, innocent as the saffron of the morning compared with the blaze of noon. The autumnal, methinks, are the fruit of the dog-days, heats of manhood or age, not of youth. The former are pure, transparent, crystalline, viz. the willow catkins and the early cinquefoils. —Journal, June 16, 1852

Again I scent the white water-lily, and a season I had waited for is arrived. How indispensible all these experiences to make up the summer! It is the emblem of purity, and its scent suggests it. Growing in stagnant and muddy water, it bursts up so pure and fair to the eye and so sweet to the scent, as if to show us what purity and sweetness reside in, and can be extracted from, the slime and muck of earth. I think I have plucked the first one that has opened for a mile at least. What confirmation of our hopes is the fragrance of the water-lily! I shall not so soon despair of the world for it, notwithstanding slavery, and

the cowardice and want of principle of the North. It suggests that the time may come when man's deeds will smell as sweet. Such, then, is the odor our planet emits. Who can doubt, then, that Nature is young and sound? If Nature can compound this fragrance still annually, I shall believe her still full of vigor, and that there is virtue in man, too, who perceives and loves it. It is as if all the pure and sweet and virtuous was extracted from the slime and decay of earth and presented thus in a flower. The resurrection of virtue! It reminds me that Nature has been partner to no Missouri compromise. I scent no compromise in the fragrance of the white water-lily. In it, the sweet, and pure, and innocent are wholly sundered from the obscene and the baleful. I do not scent in this the time-serving irresolution of a Massachusetts Governor, nor of a Boston Mayor. All good actions have contributed to this fragrance. So behave that the odor of your actions may enhance the general sweetness of the atmosphere, that, when I behold or scent a flower, I may not be reminded how inconsistent are your actions with it; for all odor is but one form of advertisement of a moral quality.
—Journal, June 16, 1854

Perhaps these mornings are the most memorable in the year — after a sultry night and before a sultry day — when, especially, the morning is the most glorious season of the day, when its coolness is most refreshing and you enjoy the glory of the summer gilded or silvered with dews, without the torrid summer's sun or the obscuring haze. The sound of crickets at dawn after these first sultry nights seems like the dreaming of the earth still continued into the daylight. I love that early twilight hour when the crickets still creak right on with such dewy faith and promise, as if it were still night — expressing the innocence of morning — when the creak of the cricket is fresh and bedewed. While the creak of the cricket has that ambrosial sound, no crime can be committed. It buries

Greece and Rome past resurrection. The earth-song of the cricket! Before Christianity was, it is. Health! health! health! is the burden of its song. It is, of course, that man, refreshed with sleep, is thus innocent and healthy and hopeful. When we hear that sound of the crickets in the sod, the world is not so much with us. —Journal, June 16, 1852

The season of hope and promise is past; already the season of small fruits has arrived. The Indian marked the midsummer as the season when berries were ripe. We are a little saddened, because we begin to see the interval between our hopes and their fulfillment. The prospect of the heavens is taken away, and we are presented only with a few small berries. —Journal, June 17, 1854

What subtile differences between one season and another! The warmest weather has, perchance, arrived and the longest days, but not the driest. When I remember gathering ripe blackberries on sandy fields or stones by the roadside, the very berries warmed by the sun, I am convinced of this. The seasons admit of infinite degrees in their revolutions. —Journal, June 19, 1852

If we only see clearly enough how mean our lives are, they will be splendid enough. Let us remember not to strive upwards too long, but sometimes drop plumb down the other way, and wallow in meanness. From the deepest pit we may see the stars, if not the sun. Let us have presence of mind enough to sink when we can't swim. At any rate, a carcass had better lie on the bottom than float an offense to all nostrils. It will not be falling, for we shall ride wide of the earth's gravity as a star, and always be drawn upward still — *semper cadendo nunquam cadit* — and so, by yielding to universal gravity, at length become fixed stars. —Journal, June 21, 1840

It is wisest to live without any definite and recognized object from day to day — any particular object — for the world is round, and we are not to live on a tangent or a radius to the sphere. As an old poet says, "though man proposeth, God disposeth all." —Journal, June 1850

I too revise as does the grass after rain. We are never so flourishing, our day is never so fair, but that the sun may come out a little brighter through mists and we yearn to live a better life. —Journal, June 1850

When I see the dense, shady masses of weeds about water — already an unexplorable maze — I am struck with the contrast between this and the spring, when I wandered about in search of the first faint greenness along the borders of the brooks. Then an inch or two of green was something remarkable and obvious afar. Now there is a dense mass of weeds along the waterside, where the muskrats lurk, and overhead a canopy of leaves conceals the birds and shuts out the sun. It is hard to realize that the seeds of all this growth were buried in that bare, frozen earth. —Journal, June 21, 1854

That solitude was sweet to me as a flower. I sat down on the boundless level and enjoyed the solitude, drank it in, the medicine for which I had pined, worth more than the bear-berry so common on the Cape. —Journal, June 21, 1857

I am sane only when I have risen above my common sense, when I do not take the foolish view of things which is commonly taken, when I do not live for the low ends for which men commonly live. Wisdom is not common. To what purposes have I senses, if I am thus absorbed in affairs? My pulse must beat with nature. After a hard day's work without a thought, turning my very brain into a mere tool, only in the quiet of evening do I so far recover my senses as to hear the cricket, which in fact has been chirping all day. In my better hours I am conscious of the influx of a supreme and unquestionable wisdom which partly unfits, and if I yielded to it more rememberingly would wholly unfit me, for what is called the active business of life, for that furnishes nothing on which the eye of reason can rest. What is that other kind of life to which I am thus continually allured? which alone I love? Is it a life for this world? Can a man feed and clothe himself gloriously who keeps only the truth steadily before him? who calls me in no evil to his aid? Are there duties which necessarily interfere with the serene perception of truth? Are our serene moments mere foretastes of heaven — joys gratuitously vouchsafed to us as a consolation — or simply a transient realization of what might be the whole tenor of our lives?

To be calm, to be serene! There is the calmness of the lake when there is not a breath of wind; there is the calmness of a stagnant ditch. So it is with us. Sometimes we are clarified and calmed healthily, as we never were before in our lives, not by an opiate, but by some unconscious obedience to the all-just laws so that we become like a still lake of purest crystal and without an effort our depths are revealed to ourselves. All the world goes by us and is reflected in our deeps. Such clarity! obtained by such pure means! by simple living, by honesty of purpose. We live and rejoice. I awoke into a music which no one about me heard. Whom shall I thank for it? The luxury of wisdom! the luxury of virtue! Are there any intemperate in these things? I feel my Maker blessing me. To the sane man the world is a musical instrument. The very touch affords an exquisite pleasure. —Journal, June 22, 1851

As I come over the hill, I hear the wood thrush singing his evening lay. This is the only bird whose note affects me like music, affects the flow and tenor of my thought, my fancy and imagination. It lifts and exhilarates me. It is inspiring. It is a medicative draught to my soul. It is an elixir to my eyes and a fountain of youth to all my senses. It changes all hours to an eternal morning. It banishes all trivialness. It reinstates me in my dominion, makes me the lord of creation, is chief musician of my court. This minstrel sings in a time, a heroic age, with which no event in the village can be contemporary. How can they be contemporary when only the latter is temporary at all? How can the infinite and eternal be contemporary with the finite and temporal? So there is something in the music of the cow-bell, something sweeter and more nutritious than in the milk which the farmers drink. This thrush's song is a *ranz des vaches* to me. I long for wildness, a nature which I cannot put my foot through, woods where the wood thrush forever sings, where the hours are early morning ones, and there is dew on the grass, and the day is forever unproved, where I might have a fertile unknown for a soil about me. I would go after the cows, I would watch the flocks of Admetus therefore forever, only for my board and clothes. A New Hampshire everlasting and unfallen.

How wonderfully moral our whole life! There is never an instant's truce between virtue and vice. Goodness is the only investment that never fails. It is sung of in the music of the harp. —Journal, June 22, 1853

I cannot see the bottom of the sky, because I cannot see to the bottom of myself. It is the symbol of my own infinity. My eye penetrates as far into the ether as that depth is inward from which my contemporary thought springs.

Not by constraint or severity shall you have access to true wisdom, but by abandonment, and childlike mirthfulness.
—Journal, June 23, 1840

The *Convolvulus sepium*, bindweed; morning-glory is the best name. It always refreshes me to see it. Some saw it the 19th. In the morning and cloudy weather, says Gray. I associate it with the holiest morning hours. It may preside over my morning walks and thoughts. There is a flower for every mood of the mind.

Methinks roses oftenest display their high colors, colors which invariably attract all eyes and betray them, against a dark ground, as the dark green or the shady recesses of the bushes and copses, where they show to best advantage. Their enemies do not spare the open flower for an hour. Hence, if for no other reason, their buds are most beautiful. Their promise of perfect and dazzling beauty, when their buds are just beginning to expand — beauty which they can hardly contain — as in most youths, commonly surpasses their expanded flowers. —Journal, June 25, 1852

Now his day's work is done, the laborer plays his flute — only possible at this hour. Contrasted with his work, what an accomplishment! Some drink and gamble. He plays some well-known march. But the music is not in the tune; it is in the sound. It does not proceed from the trading nor political world. He practices this ancient art. —Journal, June 25, 1852

The highest condition of art is artlessness.

Truth is always paradoxical.

He will get to the goal first who stands stillest.

There is one let better than any help, and that is — Let-alone.

By sufferance you may escape suffering.

He who resists not at all will never surrender.

When a dog runs at you, whistle for him.

Say, Not so, and you will outcircle the philosophers.

Stand outside the wall, and no harm can reach you. The danger is that you be walled in with it.

—Journal, June 26, 1840

I love to see the firm earth mingled with the sky, like the spray of the sea tossed up. Is there not always, whenever an arch is constructed, a latent reference to its beauty? The arch supports itself, like the stars, by gravity — by always falling never falls. But it should not be by their architecture but by their abstract thoughts that a nation should seek to commemorate itself. How much more admirable the Bhagavat Geeta than all the ruins of the East! Methinks there are few specimens of architecture so perfect as a verse of poetry. Architectural remains are beautiful not intrinsically and absolutely, but from association. They are the luxury of princes. A simple and independent mind does not toil at the bidding of any prince, nor is its material silver and gold, or marble. —Journal, June 26, 1852

A man's life should be a stately march to a sweet but unheard music, and when to his fellows it shall seem irregular and inharmonious, he will only be stepping to a livelier measure, or his nicer ear hurry him into a thousand symphonies and concordant variations. There will be no halt ever, but at most a marching on his post, or such a pause as is richer than any sound, when the melody runs

into such depth and wildness as to no longer be heard, but simply consented to with the whole life and being. He will take a false step never, even in the most arduous times, for then the music will not fail to swell into greater sweetness and volume, and itself rule the movement it inspired.
—Journal, June 30, 1840

SEASONS OF THOREAU

July

Occasionally, in still summer forenoons — when perhaps a mantua-maker was to be dined and a huckleberry pudding had been decided on — I, a lad of ten, was despatched to a neighboring hill alone. My scholastic education could be thus far tampered with, and an excuse might be found....

I well remember with what a sense of freedom and spirit of adventure I used to take my way across the fields with my pail, some years later, toward some distant hill or swamp, when dismissed for all day, and I would not now exchange such an expansion of all my being for all the learning in the world. Liberation and enlargement — such is the fruit which all culture aims to secure.
—"Huckleberries"

Many an object is not seen, though it falls within the range of our visual ray, because it does not come within the range of our intellectual ray, i.e., we are not looking for it. So, in the largest sense, we find only the world we look for.
—Journal, July 2, 1857

The last sunrise I witnessed seemed to outshine the splendor of all the preceding ones, and I was convinced that it behooved man to dawn as freshly, and with equal promise and steadiness advance into the career of life, with as lofty and serene a countenance to move onward through his midday to a yet fairer and more promising setting. Has the day grown old when it sets? and shall man wear out sooner than the sun? In the crimson colors of the west I discern the budding hues of dawn. To my western brother it is rising pure and bright as it did to me, but the evening exhibits in the still rear of the day the beauty which through morning and noon escaped me. When we

are oppressed by the heat and turmoil of the noon, let us
remember that the sun which scorches us with brazen
beams is gilding the hills of morning and awaking the
woodland quires for other men.

We will have a dawn, and noon, and serene sunset in
ourselves.

What we call the gross atmosphere of evening is the
accumulated deed of the day, which absorbs the rays of
beauty, and shows more richly than the naked promise of
the dawn. By earnest toil in the heat of the noon, let us get
ready a rich western blaze against the evening of our lives.
—Journal, July 3, 1840

Every morning was a cheerful invitation to make my life of
equal simplicity, and I may say innocence, with Nature
herself. I have been as sincere a worshipper of Aurora as
the Greeks. I got up early and bathed in the pond; that was
a religious exercise, and one of the best things which I did.
They say that characters were engraven on the bathing tub
of King Tchingthang to this effect: "Renew thyself
completely each day; do it again, and again, and forever
again." I can understand that. Morning brings back the
heroic ages. I was as much affected by the faint hum of a
mosquito making its invisible and unimaginable tour
through my apartment at earliest dawn, when I was sitting
with door and windows open, as I could be by any trumpet
that ever sang of fame. It was Homer's requiem; itself an
Iliad and Odyssey in the air, singing its own wrath and
wanderings. There was something cosmical about it; a
standing advertisement, till forbidden, of the everlasting
vigor and fertility of the world. The morning, which is the
most memorable season of the day, is the awakening hour.
Then there is least somnolence in us; and for an hour, at
least, some part of us awakes which slumbers all the rest of
the day and night. Little is to be expected of that day, if it

can be called a day, to which we are not awakened by our Genius, but by the mechanical nudgings of some servitor, are not awakened by our own newly acquired force and aspirations from within, accompanied by the undulations of celestial music, instead of factory bells, and a fragrance filling the air — to a higher life than we fell asleep from; and thus the darkness bear its fruit, and prove itself to be good, no less than the light. That man who does not believe that each day contains an earlier, more sacred, and auroral hour than he has yet profaned, has despaired of life, and is pursuing a descending and darkening way. After a partial cessation of his sensuous life, the soul of man, or its organs rather, are reinvigorated each day, and his Genius tries again what noble life it can make. All memorable events, I should say, transpire in morning time and in a morning atmosphere. The Vedas say, "All intelligences awake with the morning." Poetry and art, and the fairest and most memorable of the actions of men, date from such an hour. All poets and heroes, like Memnon, are the children of Aurora, and emit their music at sunrise. To him whose elastic and vigorous thought keeps pace with the sun, the day is a perpetual morning. It matters not what the clocks say or the attitudes and labors of men. Morning is when I am awake and there is a dawn in me. Moral reform is the effort to throw off sleep. Why is it that men give so poor an account of their day if they have not been slumbering? They are not such poor calculators. If they had not been overcome with drowsiness, they would have performed something. The millions are awake enough for physical labor; but only one in a million is awake enough for effective intellectual exertion, only one in a hundred millions to a poetic or divine life. To be awake is to be alive. I have never yet met a man who was quite awake. How could I have looked him in the face?

We must learn to reawaken and keep ourselves awake, not by mechanical aids, but by an infinite expectation of the dawn, which does not forsake us in our soundest sleep. I know of no more encouraging fact than the unquestionable ability of man to elevate his life by a conscious endeavor. It is something to be able to paint a particular picture, or to carve a statue, and so to make a few objects beautiful; but it is far more glorious to carve and paint the very atmosphere and medium through which we look, which morally we can do. To affect the quality of the day, that is the highest of arts. Every man is tasked to make his life, even in its details, worthy of the contemplation of his most elevated and critical hour. If we refused, or rather used up, such paltry information as we get, the oracles would distinctly inform us how this might be done.

I went to the woods because I wished to live deliberately, to front only the essential facts of life, and see if I could not learn what it had to teach, and not, when I came to die, discover that I had not lived. I did not wish to live what was not life, living is so dear; nor did I wish to practise resignation, unless it was quite necessary. I wanted to live deep and suck out all the marrow of life, to live so sturdily and Spartan-like as to put to rout all that was not life, to cut a broad swath and shave close, to drive life into a corner, and reduce it to its lowest terms, and, if it proved to be mean, why then to get the whole and genuine meanness of it, and publish its meanness to the world; or if it were sublime, to know it by experience, and be able to give a true account of it in my next excursion. For most men, it appears to me, are in a strange uncertainty about it, whether it is of the devil or of God, and have somewhat hastily concluded that it is the chief end of man here to "glorify God and enjoy him forever." —Walden, "Where I Lived, and What I Lived For"

Many fields have now received their last hoeing, and the farmers' work seems to be soon over with them. What a pleasant interview he must have had with them! What a liberal education with these professors! Better than a university. It is pleasing to consider man's cultivating this plant thus assiduously, without reference to any crop it may yield him, as if he were to cultivate johnswort in like manner. What influences does he receive from this long intercourse. —Journal, July 5, 1851

The deep places in the river are not so obvious as the shallow ones and can only be found by carefully probing it. So perhaps it is with human nature. —Journal, July 5, 1859

Still we live meanly, like ants; though the fable tells us that we were long ago changed into men; like pygmies we fight with cranes; it is error upon error, and clout upon clout, and our best virtue has for its occasion a superfluous and evitable wretchedness. Our life is frittered away by detail. An honest man has hardly need to count more than his ten fingers, or in extreme cases he may add his ten toes, and lump the rest. Simplicity, simplicity, simplicity! I say, let your affairs be as two or three, and not a hundred or a thousand; instead of a million count half a dozen, and keep your accounts on your thumb-nail. In the midst of this chopping sea of civilized life, such are the clouds and storms and quicksands and thousand-and-one items to be allowed for, that a man has to live, if he would not founder and go to the bottom and not make his port at all, by dead reckoning, and he must be a great calculator indeed who succeeds. Simplify, simplify. Instead of three meals a day, if it be necessary eat but one; instead of a hundred dishes, five; and reduce other things in proportion. Our life is like a German Confederacy, made up of petty states, with its boundary forever fluctuating, so that even a German cannot tell you how it is bounded at any moment. The nation itself, with all its so-called internal improvements, which, by the way are all external and superficial, is just such an unwieldy and overgrown establishment, cluttered with furniture and tripped up by its own traps, ruined by luxury and heedless expense, by want of calculation and a worthy aim, as the million households in the land; and the only cure for it, as for them, is in a rigid economy, a stern and more than Spartan simplicity of life and elevation of purpose. —Walden, "Where I Lived, and What I Lived For"

The intimations of the night are divine, methinks. Men might meet in the morning and report the news of the night — what divine suggestions have been made to them. I find that I carry with me into the day often some such hint derived from the gods — such impulses to purity, to heroism, to literary effort even, as are never day-born....

There is inspiration, the divine gossip which comes to the ear of the attentive mind from the courts of heaven; there is the profane and stale revelation of the bar-room and the police court. The same ear is fitted to receive both communications. Only the character of the individual determines to which source chiefly it shall be open and to which closed. I believe that the mind can be profaned by the habit of attending to trivial things, so that all our thoughts shall be tinged with triviality....

Every thought that passes through the mind helps to wear and tear it, and to deepen the ruts, which, as in the streets of Pompeii, evince how much it has been used. How many things there are concerning which we might well deliberate whether we had better know them! Routine, conventionality, manners, etc., etc. — how insensibly an undue attention to these dissipates and impoverishes the mind, robs it of its strength and simplicity, emasculates it! —Journal, July 7, 1851

I came near awaking this morning. I am older than last year; the mornings are further between; the days are fewer. Any excess — to have drunk too much water, even, the day before — is fatal to the morning's clarity, but in health the sound of a cow-bell is celestial music. Oh, might I always wake to thought and poetry — regenerated! Can it be called a morning, if our senses are not clarified so that we perceive more clearly, if we do not rise with elastic vigor? —Journal, July 7, 1852

Staying at home is the heavenly way. —Letter to Ralph Waldo Emerson, July 8, 1843

Shams and delusions are esteemed for soundest truths, while reality is fabulous. If men would steadily observe realities only, and not allow themselves to be deluded, life, to compare it with such things as we know, would be like a fairy tale and the Arabian Nights' Entertainments. If we respected only what is inevitable and has a right to be, music and poetry would resound along the streets. When we are unhurried and wise, we perceive that only great and worthy things have any permanent and absolute existence, that petty fears and petty pleasures are but the shadow of the reality. This is always exhilarating and sublime. By closing the eyes and slumbering, and consenting to be deceived by shows, men establish and confirm their daily life of routine and habit everywhere, which still is built on purely illusory foundations. Children, who play life, discern its true law and relations more clearly than men, who fail to live it worthily, but who think that they are wiser by experience, that is, by failure. I have read in a Hindoo book, that "there was a king's son, who, being expelled in infancy from his native city, was brought up by a forester, and, growing up to maturity in that state, imagined himself to belong to the barbarous race with which he lived. One of his father's ministers having discovered him, revealed to him what he was, and the misconception of his character was removed, and he knew himself to be a prince. So soul," continues the Hindoo philosopher, "from the circumstances in which it is placed, mistakes its own character, until the truth is revealed to it by some holy teacher, and then it knows itself to be Brahme." I perceive that we inhabitants of New England live this mean life that we do because our vision does not penetrate the surface of things. We think that that is which appears to be. If a man should walk through this town and see only the reality, where, think you, would the "Mill-dam" go to? If he should give us an account of the realities he beheld there, we should not recognize the place in his description. Look at a meeting-house, or a court-house, or a jail, or a shop, or a dwelling-house, and say what that thing really is before a true gaze, and they would all go to pieces in your account of them. Men esteem truth remote, in the outskirts of the system, behind the farthest star, before Adam and after the last man. In eternity there is indeed something true and sublime. But all these times and places and occasions are now and here. God himself culminates in the present moment, and will never be more divine in the lapse of all the ages. And we are enabled to apprehend at all what is sublime and noble only by the perpetual instilling and drenching of the reality that surrounds us. The universe constantly and obediently answers to our conceptions; whether we travel fast or slow, the track is laid for us. Let us spend our lives in conceiving then. The poet or the artist never yet had so fair and noble a design but some of his posterity at least could accomplish it.

Let us spend one day as deliberately as Nature, and not be thrown off the track by every nutshell and mosquito's wing that falls on the rails. Let us rise early and fast, or break fast, gently and without perturbation; let company come and let company go, let the bells ring and the children cry — determined to make a day of it. Why should we knock under and go with the stream? Let us not be upset and overwhelmed in that terrible rapid and whirlpool called a dinner, situated in the meridian shallows. Weather this danger and you are safe, for the rest of the way is down hill. With unrelaxed nerves, with morning vigor, sail by it, looking another way, tied to the mast like Ulysses. If the engine whistles, let it whistle till it is hoarse for its pains. If the bell rings, why should we run? We will consider what kind of music they are like. Let us settle ourselves, and work and wedge our feet downward through the mud and slush of opinion, and prejudice, and tradition, and delusion, and appearance, that alluvion which covers the globe, through Paris and London, through New York and Boston and Concord, through Church and State, through poetry and philosophy and religion, till we come to a hard bottom and rocks in place, which we can call reality, and say, This is, and no mistake; and then begin, having a point d'appui, below freshet and frost and fire, a place where you might found a wall or a state, or set a lamp-post safely, or perhaps a gauge, not a Nilometer, but a Realometer, that future ages might know how deep a freshet of shams and appearances had gathered from time to time. If you stand right fronting and face to face to a fact, you will see the sun glimmer on both its surfaces, as if it were a cimeter, and feel its sweet edge dividing you through the heart and marrow, and so you will happily conclude your mortal career. Be it life or death, we crave only reality. If we are really dying, let us hear the rattle in our throats and feel cold in the extremities; if we are alive, let us go about our business. —Walden, "Where I Lived, and What I Lived For"

What is called genius is the abundance of life or health, so that whatever addresses the senses, as the flavor of these berries, or the lowing of that cow, which sounds as if it echoed along a cool mountain-side just before night, where odiferous dews perfume the air and there is everlasting vigor, serenity, and expectation of perpetual untarnished morning — each sight and sound and scent and flavor — intoxicates with a healthy intoxication. The shrunken stream of live overflows its banks, makes and fertilizes broad intervals, from which generations derive their sustenances. This is the true overflowing of the Nile. So exquisitely sensitive are we, it makes us embrace our fates, and, instead of suffering or indifference, we enjoy and bless. —Journal, July 11, 1852

I look at a young fox at Derby's. You would say from his step and motions that his legs were as elastic as india-rubber — all springs, ready at an instant to bound high into the air. Gravity seems not enough to keep him in contact with the earth. There seems to be a peculiar principle of resiliency constantly operating in him.
—Journal, July 11, 1860

I sometimes awake in the night and think of friendship and its possibilities, a new life and revelation to me, which perhaps I had not experienced for many months. Such transient thoughts have been my nearest approach to realization of it, thoughts which I know of no one to communicate to. I suddenly erect myself in my thoughts, or find myself erected, infinite degrees above the possibility of ordinary endeavors, and see for what grand stakes the game of life may be played. Men, with their indiscriminate attentions and ceremonious good-will, offer you trivial baits, which do not tempt; they are not serious enough either for success or failure. I wake up in the night to these higher levels of life, as to a day that begins to dawn, as if my intervening life had been a long night. I catch an echo of the great strain of Friendship played somewhere, and feel compensated for months and years of commonplace. I rise into a diviner atmosphere, in which simply to exist and breath is a triumph, and my thoughts inevitably tend toward the grand and infinite, as aeronauts report that there is ever an upper current hereabouts which sets toward the ocean. If they rise high enough they go out to sea, and behold the vessels seemingly in mid-air like themselves. It is as if I were serenaded, and the highest and truest compliments were paid me. The universe gives me three cheers.

Friendship is the fruit which the year should bear; it lends its fragrance to the flowers, and it is in vain if we get only a large crop of apples without it. —Journal, July 13, 1857

What sweet and tender, the most innocent and divinely encouraging society there is in every natural object, and so in universal nature, even for the poor misanthrope and most melancholy man. There can be no really black melancholy to him who lives in the midst of nature and has still his senses. There never was yet such a storm but it was Aeolian music to the innocent ear. Nothing can compel to a vulgar sadness a simple and brave man. While I enjoy the sweet friendship of the seasons I trust that nothing can make life a burden to me. —Journal, July 14, 1845

The youth gets together his materials to build a bridge to the moon, or perchance a palace or a temple on the earth, and at length the middle-aged man concludes to build a wood-shed with them.

Trees have commonly two growths in a year, a spring and a fall growth, and you can see where the first was checked whether by cold or drouth, and wonder what there was in the summer to produce this check, this blight. So it is with man; most have a spring growth only, and never get over this first check to their youthful hopes; but plants of hardier constitution, or perchance planted in a more genial soil, speedily recover themselves, and, though they bear the scar or knot in remembrance of their disappointment, they push forward again and have a vigorous fall growth which is equivalent to a new spring. —Journal, July 14, 1852

Health is a sound relation to nature. —Journal, July 14, 1854

This cooler, still, cloudy weather after the rain is very autumnal and restorative to our spirits. The robin sings still, but the goldfinch twitters over oftener, and I hear the *link link* of the bobolink (one perfect strain!), and the crickets creak more as in the fall. All these sounds dispose our minds to serenity. Perhaps the mosquitoes are most troublesome such days in the woods, if it is warm enough. We seem to be passing, or to have passed, a dividing line between spring and autumn, and begin to descend the long slope toward winter. —Journal, July 14, 1854

Let us consider for a moment what most of the trouble and anxiety which I have referred to is about, and how much it is necessary that we be troubled, or at least careful. It would be some advantage to live a primitive and frontier life, though in the midst of an outward civilization, if only to learn what are the gross necessaries of life and what methods have been taken to obtain them; or even to look over the old day-books of the merchants, to see what it was that men most commonly bought at the stores, what they stored, that is, what are the grossest groceries. For the improvements of ages have had but little influence on the essential laws of man's existence; as our skeletons, probably, are not to be distinguished from those of our ancestors....

When a man is warmed by the several modes which I have described, what does he want next? Surely not more warmth of the same kind, as more and richer food, larger and more splendid houses, finer and more abundant clothing, more numerous, incessant, and hotter fires, and the like. When he has obtained those things which are necessary to life, there is another alternative than to obtain the superfluities; and that is, to adventure on life now, his vacation from humbler toil having commenced. The soil, it appears, is suited to the seed, for it has sent its radicle downward, and it may now send its shoot upward also with confidence. Why has man rooted himself thus firmly in the earth, but that he may rise in the same proportion into the heavens above? — for the nobler plants are valued for the fruit they bear at last in the air and light, far from the ground, and are not treated like the humbler esculents, which, though they may be biennials, are cultivated only till they have perfected their root, and often cut down at top for this purpose, so that most would not know them in their flowering season. —Walden, "Economy"

It is said that Mirabeau took to highway robbery "to ascertain what degree of resolution was necessary in order to place one's self in formal opposition to the most sacred laws of society." He declared that "a soldier who fights in the ranks does not require half so much courage as a footpad" — "that honor and religion have never stood in the way of a well-considered and a firm resolve." This was manly, as the world goes; and yet it was idle, if not desperate. A saner man would have found himself often enough "in formal opposition" to what are deemed "the most sacred laws of society," through obedience to yet more sacred laws, and so have tested his resolution without going out of his way. It is not for a man to put himself in such an attitude to society, but to maintain himself in whatever attitude he find himself through obedience to the laws of his being, which will never be one of opposition to a just government, if he should chance to meet with such....

I learned this, at least, by my experiment: that if one advances confidently in the direction of his dreams, and endeavors to live the life which he has imagined, he will meet with a success unexpected in common hours. He will put some things behind, will pass an invisible boundary; new, universal, and more liberal laws will begin to establish themselves around and within him; or the old laws be expanded, and interpreted in his favor in a more liberal sense, and he will live with the license of a higher order of beings. In proportion as he simplifies his life, the laws of the universe will appear less complex, and solitude will not be solitude, nor poverty poverty, nor weakness weakness. If you have built castles in the air, your work need not be lost; that is where they should be. Now put the foundations under them. —Walden, "Conclusion"

Methinks my present experience is nothing; my past experience is all in all. I think that no experience which I have today comes up to, or is comparable with, the experiences of my boyhood. And not only this is true, but as far back as I can remember I have unconsciously referred to the experiences of a previous state of existence. "For life is a forgetting," etc. Formerly, methought, nature developed as I developed, and grew up with me. My life was ecstasy. In youth, before I lost any of my senses, I can remember that I was all alive, and inhabited my body with inexpressible satisfaction; both its weariness and its refreshment were sweet to me. This earth was the most glorious musical instrument, and I was audience to its strains. To have such sweet impressions made on us, such ecstasies begotten of the breezes! I can remember how I was astonished. I said to myself — I said to others — "There comes into my mind such an indescribable, infinite, all-absorbing, divine, heavenly pleasure, a sense of elevation and expansion, and I have had nought to do with it. I perceive that I am dealt with by superior powers. This is a pleasure, a joy, an existence which I have not procured myself. I speak as a witness on the stand and tell what I have perceived." The morning and the evening were sweet to me, and I led a life aloof from society of men. I wondered if a mortal had ever known what I knew. I looked in books for some recognition of a kindred experience — but strange to say, I found none. Indeed I was slow to discover that other men had had this experience — for it had been possible to read books and to associate with men on other grounds. The maker of me was improving me. When I detected this interference I was profoundly moved. For years I marched as to a music in comparison with which the military music of the streets is noise and discord. I was daily intoxicated, and yet no man would call me intemperate. With all your science can you tell how it is, and whence it is, that light comes into the soul? —Journal, July 16, 1851

What more glorious condition of being can we imagine than from impure to be becoming pure? It is almost desirable to be impure that we may be the subject of this improvement. That I am innocent to myself! That I love and reverence my life! That I am better fitted for a lofty society today than I was yesterday! To make my life a sacrament! What is nature without this lofty tumbling? May I treat myself with more and more respect and tenderness. May I not forget that I am impure and vicious. May I not cease to love purity. May I go to my slumbers as expecting to arise to a new and more perfect day. May I so live and refine my life as fitting myself for a society ever higher than I actually enjoy. May I treat myself tenderly as I would treat the most innocent child whom I love; may I treat children and my friends as my newly discovered self. Let me forever go in search of myself; never for a moment think that I have found myself; be as a stranger to myself, never a familiar, seeking acquaintance still. May I be to myself as one is to me whom I love, a dear and cherished object. What temple, what fane, what sacred place can there be but the innermost part of my own being? The possibility of my own improvement, that is to be cherished. As I regard myself, so I am. O my dear friends, I have not forgotten you. I will know you tomorrow. I associate you with my ideal self. I had ceased to have faith in myself. I thought I was grown up and become what I was intended to be, but it is earliest spring with me. In relation to virtue and innocence the oldest man is in the beginning spring and vernal season of life. It is the love of virtue makes us young ever. That is the fountain of youth, the very aspiration after the perfect. I love and worship myself with a love which absorbs my love for the world. The lecturer suggested to me that I might become better than I am. Was it not a good lecture then? May I dream not that I shunned vice; may I dream that I loved and practiced virtue. —Journal, July 16, 1851

The mass of men lead lives of quiet desperation. What is called resignation is confirmed desperation. From the desperate city you go into the desperate country, and have to console yourself with the bravery of minks and muskrats. A stereotyped but unconscious despair is concealed even under what are called the games and amusements of mankind. There is no play in them, for this comes after work. But it is a characteristic of wisdom not to do desperate things. When we consider what, to use the words of the catechism, is the chief end of man, and what are the true necessaries and means of life, it appears as if men had deliberately chosen the common mode of living because they preferred it to any other. Yet they honestly think there is no choice left. But alert and healthy natures remember that the sun rose clear. It is never too late to give up our prejudices. No way of thinking or doing, however ancient, can be trusted without proof. —Walden, "Economy"

Why should we be in such desperate haste to succeed and in such desperate enterprises? If a man does not keep pace with his companions, perhaps it is because he hears a different drummer. Let him step to the music which he hears, however measured or far away. It is not important that he should mature as soon as an apple tree or an oak. Shall he turn his spring into summer? If the condition of things which we were made for is not yet, what were any reality which we can substitute? We will not be shipwrecked on a vain reality. Shall we with pains erect a heaven of blue glass over ourselves, though when it is done we shall be sure to gaze still at the true ethereal heaven far above, as if the former were not? —Walden, "Conclusion"

Here I am thirty-four years old, and yet my life is almost wholly unexpanded. How much is in the germ! There is such an interval between my ideal and the actual in many instances that I may say I am unborn. There is the instinct for society, but no society. Life is not long enough for one success. Within another thirty-four years that miracle can hardly take place. Methinks my seasons revolve more slowly than those of nature; I am differently timed. I am contented. This rapid revolution of nature, even of nature in me, why should it hurry me? Let a man step to the music which he hears, however measured. Is it important that I should mature as soon as an apple tree? aye, as soon as an oak? May not my life in nature, in proportion as it is supernatural, be only the spring and infantile portion of my spirit's life? Shall I turn my spring to summer? May I not sacrifice a hasty and petty completeness here to entireness there? If my curve is large, why bend it to a smaller circle? My spirit's unfolding observes not the pace of nature. The society which I was made for is not here. Shall I, then, substitute for the anticipation of that this poor reality? I would rather have the unmixed expectation of that than this reality. If life is a waiting, so be it. I will not be shipwrecked on a vain reality. —Journal, July 19, 1851

The gentle susurrus from the leaves of the trees on shore is very enlivening, as if Nature were freshening, awakening to some enterprise. There is but little wind, but its sound, incessantly stirring the leaves at a little distance along the shore, heard not seen, is very inspiriting. It is like an everlasting dawn or awakening of nature to some great purpose. —Journal, July 20, 1853

There is, however, this consolation to the most way-worn traveller, upon the dustiest road, that the path his feet describe is so perfectly symbolical of human life — now climbing the hills, now descending into the vales. From the summits he beholds the heavens and the horizon, from the vales he looks up to the heights again. He is treading his old lessons still, and though he may be very weary and travel-worn, it is yet sincere experience.

Leaving the Nashua, we changed our route a little, and arrived at Stillriver Village, in the western part of Harvard, just as the sun was setting. From this place, which lies to the northward, upon the western slope of the same range of hills on which we had spent the noon before, in the adjacent town, the prospect is beautiful, and the grandeur of the mountain outlines unsurpassed. There was such a repose and quiet here at this hour, as if the very hill-sides were enjoying the scene, and we passed slowly along, looking back over the country we had traversed, and listening to the evening song of the robin, we could not help contrasting the equanimity of nature with the bustle and impatience of man. His words and actions presume always a crisis near at hand, but she is forever silent and unpretending.

We rested that night at Harvard, and the next morning, while one bent his steps to the nearer village of Groton, the other took his separate and solitary way to the peaceful meadows of Concord; but let him not forget to record the brave hospitality of a farmer and his wife, who generously entertained him at their board, though the poor wayfarer could only congratulate the one on the continuance of hayweather, and silently accept the kindness of the other. Refreshed by this instance of generosity, no less than by the substantial viands set before him, he pushed forward with new vigor, and reached the banks of the Concord before the sun had climbed many degrees into the heavens.

And now that we have returned to the desultory life of the plain, let us endeavor to import a little of that mountain grandeur into it. We will remember within what walls we lie, and understand that this level life too has its summit, and why from the mountain-top the deepest valleys have a tinge of blue; that there is elevation in every hour, as no part of the earth is so low that the heavens may not be seen from, and we have only to stand on the summit of our hour to command an uninterrupted horizon.
—"A Walk to Wachusett" (describing an excursion taken in mid-July 1842)

Now I yearn for one of those old, meandering, dry, uninhabited roads, which lead away from towns, which lead us away from temptation, which conduct to the outside of earth, over its uppermost crust; where you may forget in what country you are travelling; where no farmer can complain that you are treading down his grass, no gentleman who has recently constructed a seat in the country that you are trespassing; on which you can go off at half-cock and wave adieu to the village; along which you may travel like a pilgrim, going nowhither; where travellers are not too often to be met; where my spirit is free; where the walls and fences are not cared for; where your head is more in heaven than your feet are on earth; which have long reaches where you can see the approaching traveller half a mile off and be prepared for him; not so luxuriant a soil as to attract men; some root and stump fences which

do not need attention; where travellers have no occasion to stop, but pass along and leave you to your thoughts; where it makes no odds which way you face, whether you are going or coming, whether it is morning or evening, mid-noon or midnight; where earth is cheap enough by being public; where you can walk and think with least obstruction, there being nothing to measure progress by; where you can pace when your breast is full, and cherish your moodiness; where you are not in false relations with men, are not dining nor conversing with them; by which you may go to the uttermost parts of the earth. It is wide enough, wide as the thoughts it allows to visit you. Sometimes it is some particular half-dozen rods which I wish to find myself pacing over, as where certain airs blow; then my life will come to me, methinks; like a hunter I walk in wait for it. When I am against this bare promontory of a huckleberry hill, then forsooth my thoughts will expand. Is it some influence, as a vapor which exhales from the ground, or something in the gales which blow there, or in all things there brought together agreeably to my spirit? The walls must not be too high, imprisoning me, but low, with numerous gaps. The trees must not be too numerous, nor the hills too near, bounding the view, nor the soil too rich, attracting the attention to the earth. It must simply be the way and the life — a way that was never known to be repaired, nor to need repair, within the memory of the oldest inhabitant.
—Journal, July 21, 1851

All the world complain nowadays of a press of trivial duties and engagements, which prevents their employing themselves on some higher ground they know of; but, undoubtedly, if they were made of the right stuff to work on that higher ground, provided they were released from all those engagements, they would now at once fulfill the superior engagement, and neglect all the rest, as naturally as they breathe. They would never be caught saying that they had no time for this, when the dullest man knows that this is all that he has time for. No man who acts from a sense of duty ever puts the lesser duty above the greater. No man has the desire and the ability to work on high things, but he has also the ability to build himself a high staging. —Letter to Harrison Blake, July 21, 1852

He who passes over a lake at noon, when the waves run, little imagines its serene and placid beauty at evening, as little as he anticipates his own serenity. —Journal, July 21, 1853

Nature is beautiful only as a place where a life is to be lived. It is not beautiful to him who has not resolved on a beautiful life. —Journal, July 21, 1853

Most men, even in this comparatively free country, through mere ignorance and mistake, are so occupied with the factitious cares and superfluously coarse labors of life that its finer fruits cannot be plucked by them. Their fingers, from excessive toil, are too clumsy and tremble too much for that. Actually, the laboring man has not leisure for a true integrity day by day; he cannot afford to sustain the manliest relations to men; his labor would be depreciated in the market. He has no time to be anything but a machine. How can he remember well his ignorance — which his growth requires — who has so often to use his knowledge? We should feed and clothe him gratuitously sometimes, and recruit him with our cordials, before we judge of him. The finest qualities of our nature, like the bloom on fruits, can be preserved only by the most delicate handling. Yet we do not treat ourselves nor one another thus tenderly. —Walden, "Economy"

The life in us is like the water in the river. It may rise this year higher than man has ever known it, and flood the parched uplands; even this may be the eventful year, which will drown out all our muskrats. It was not always dry land where we dwell. I see far inland the banks which the stream anciently washed, before science began to record its freshets. Every one has heard the story which has gone the rounds of New England, of a strong and beautiful bug which came out of the dry leaf of an old table of apple-tree wood, which had stood in a farmer's kitchen for sixty years, first in Connecticut, and afterward in Massachusetts — from an egg deposited in the living tree many years earlier still, as appeared by counting the annual layers beyond it; which was heard gnawing out for several weeks, hatched perchance by the heat of an urn. Who does not feel his faith in a resurrection and immortality strengthened by hearing of this? Who knows what beautiful and winged life, whose egg has been buried for ages under many concentric layers of woodenness in the dead dry life of society, deposited at first in the alburnum of the green and living tree, which has been gradually converted into the semblance of its well-seasoned tomb — heard perchance gnawing out now for years by the astonished family of man, as they sat round the festive board — may unexpectedly come forth from amidst society's most trivial and handselled furniture, to enjoy its perfect summer life at last! —Walden, "Conclusion"

There is no remedy for love but to love more.—Journal, July 24, 1839

How far behind the spring seems now — farther off, perhaps, than ever, for this heat and dryness is most opposed to spring. Where most I sought for flowers in April and May I do not think to go now; it is either drought or barrenness or fall there now. The reign of moisture is long since over. For a long time the year feels the influence of the snows of winter and the long rains of spring, but now how changed! It is like another and a fabulous age to look back on, when earth's veins were full of moisture, and violets burst out on every hillside. Spring is the reign of water; summer, of heat and dryness; winter, of cold. —Journal, July 24, 1853

The berries of *Vaccinium vacillans* are very abundant and large this year at Fair Haven, where I am now. Indeed these and huckleberries and blackberries are very abundant in this part of the town. Nature does her best to feed man. The traveller need not go out of the road to get as many as he wants; every bush and vine teems with palatable fruit. Man for once stands in such relation to Nature as the animals that pluck and eat as they go. The fields and hills are a table constantly spread. Wines of all kinds and qualities, of noblest vintage, are bottled up in the skins of countless berries, for the taste of men and animals. To men they seem offered not so much for food as for sociality, that they may picnic with Nature – diet drinks, cordials, wines. We pluck and eat in remembrance of Her. It is a sacrament, a communion. The not-forbdden fruits, which no serpent tempts us to taste. Slight and innocent savors, which relate us to Nature, make us her guests and entitle us to her regard and protection. It is a Saturnalia, and we quaff her wines at every turn. —Journal, July 24, 1853

By intimacy with nature I find myself withdrawn from man. My interest in the sun and the moon, in the morning and the evening, compels me to solitude.

The grandest picture in the world is the sunset sky. In your higher moods what man is there to meet? You are of necessity isolated. The mind that perceives clearly any natural beauty is in that instant withdrawn from human society. My desire for society is infinitely increased; my fitness for any actual society is diminished. —Journal, July 26, 1852

I mark again the sound of crickets or locusts about alders, etc., about this time when the first asters open, which makes you fruitfully meditative, helps condense your thoughts, like the *mel*dews in the afternoon. This the afternoon of the year. How apt we are to be reminded of lateness, even before the year is half spent! Such little objects check the diffuse tide of our thoughts and bring it to a head, which thrills us. They are such fruits as music, poetry, love, which humanity bears. —Journal, July 26, 1853

We should think sacredly, with devotion. That is one thing, at least, we may do magnanimously. May not every man have some private affair which he can conduct greatly, unhurriedly? —Journal, July 27, 1852

Methinks the season culminated about the middle of this month — that the year was of indefinite promise before, but that, after the first intense heats, we postponed the fulfillment of many of our hopes for this year, and, having as it were attained the ridge of the summer, commenced to descend the long slope toward winter, the afternoon and down-hill of the year. —Journal, July 28, 1854

Do not all flowers that blossom after mid-July remind us of the fall? After midsummer we have a belated feeling as if we had all been idlers, and are forward to see in each sight and hear in each sound some presage of the fall, just as in middle age man anticipates the end of life. —Journal, July 30, 1852

August

I never met a man who cast a free and healthy glance over life, but the best live in a sort of Sabbath light, a Jewish gloom. The best thought is not only without sombreness, but even without morality. The universe lies outspread in floods of white light to it. The moral aspect of nature is a jaundice reflected from man. To the innocent there are no cherubim nor angels. Occasionally we rise above the necessity of virtue into an unchangeable morning light, in which we have not to choose in a dilemma between right and wrong, but simply to live right on and breathe the circumambient air. There is no name for this life unless it be the very vitality of *vita*. Silent is the preacher about this, and silent must ever be, for he who knows it will not preach. —Journal, August 1, 1841

This is a delicious evening, when the whole body is one sense, and imbibes delight through every pore. I go and come with a strange liberty in Nature, a part of herself. As I walk along the stony shore of the pond in my shirt-sleeves, though it is cool as well as cloudy and windy, and I see nothing special to attract me, all the elements are unusually congenial to me. The bullfrogs trump to usher in the night, and the note of the whip-poor-will is borne on the rippling wind from over the water. Sympathy with the fluttering alder and poplar leaves almost takes away my breath; yet, like the lake, my serenity is rippled but not ruffled....

I find it wholesome to be alone the greater part of the time. To be in company, even with the best, is soon wearisome and dissipating. I love to be alone. I never found the companion that was so companionable as solitude. We are for the most part more lonely when we go abroad among men than when we stay in our chambers. A man thinking or working is always alone, let him be where he will. Solitude is not measured by the miles of space that intervene between a man and his fellows. The really diligent student in one of the crowded hives of Cambridge College is as solitary as a dervish in the desert. The farmer can work alone in the field or the woods all day, hoeing or chopping, and not feel lonesome, because he is employed; but when he comes home at night he cannot sit down in a room alone, at the mercy of his thoughts, but must be where he can "see the folks," and recreate, and, as he thinks, remunerate himself for his day's solitude; and hence he wonders how the student can sit alone in the house all night and most of the day without ennui and "the blues"; but he does not realize that the student, though in the house, is still at work in his field, and chopping in his woods, as the farmer in his, and in turn seeks the same recreation and society that the latter does, though it may be a more condensed form of it. —Walden, "Solitude"

I feel the necessity of deepening the stream of my life; I must cultivate privacy. It is very dissipating to be with people too much. As C. says, it takes the edge off a man's thoughts to have been much in society. I cannot spare my moonlight and my mountains for the best of man I am likely to get in exchange.

I am inclined now for a pensive evening walk.... As I go up the hill, surrounded by its shadow, while the sun is setting, I am soothed by the delicious stillness of the evening, save that on the hills the wind blows. I was surprised by the sound of my own voice. It is an atmosphere burdensome with thought. For the first time for a month, at least, I am reminded that thought is possible. The din of trivialness is silenced. I float over or through the deeps of silence. It is the first silence I have heard for a month. My life had been a River Platte, tinkling over its sands but useless for all great navigation, but now it suddenly became a fathomless ocean. It shelved off to unimagined depths. —Journal, August 2, 1851

That fine z-ing of locusts in the grass which I have heard for three or four days is, methinks, an August sound and is very inspiriting. It is a certain maturity in the year which it suggests. My thoughts are less crude for it. There is a certain moral and physical sluggishness and standstill at midsummer. —Journal, August 2, 1859

I hear a cricket creak in the shade; also the sound of a distant piano. The music reminds me of imagined heroic ages; it suggests such ideas of human life and the field which it affords as the few noblest passages of poetry. Those few interrupted strains which reach me through the trees suggest the same thoughts and aspirations that all melody, by whatever sense appreciated, has ever done. I am affected. What coloring variously fair and intense our life admits of! How a thought will mould and paint it. Impressed by some vague vision, as it were, elevated into a more glorious sphere of life, we no longer know this, and we can deny its existence. We say we are enchanted, perhaps. But what I am impressed by is the fact that this enchantment is no delusion. So far as truth is concerned, it is a fact such as what we *call* our actual existence, but it is a far higher and more glorious fact. It is evidence of such a sphere, of such possibilities. It is its truth and reality that affect me. A thrumming of piano-strings beyond the gardens and through the elms. At length the melody steals into my being. I know not when it began to occupy me. By some fortunate coincidence of thought or circumstance I am attuned to the universe, I am fitted to hear, my being moves in a sphere of melody, my fancy and imagination are excited to an inconceivable degree. This is no longer the dull earth on which I stood. It is possible to live a grander life here; already the steed is stamping, the knights are prancing; already our thoughts bid a proud farewell to the so-called actual life and its humble glories. Now this is the verdict of a soul in health. But the soul diseased says that its own vision and life alone is true and sane. What a different aspect will courage put upon the face of things! This suggests what a perpetual flow of spirit would produce. —Journal, August 3, 1852

Elder-berries begin to be ripe, bending their stems. I also see *Viburnum dentatum* berries just beginning to turn on one side. Their turning or ripening looks like decay — a dark spot — and so does the rarely ripe side of the naked viburnum and the sweet; but we truly regard it as a ripening still, not falsely a decaying as when we describe the tints of the autumnal foliage. —Journal, August 7, 1853

How trivial and uninteresting and wearisome and unsatisfactory are all employments for which men will pay you money! The ways by which you may get money all lead downward. To have done anything by which you earned money merely is to have been truly idle. If the laborer gets no more than the wages his employer pays him, he is cheated, he cheats himself. Those services which the world will most readily pay for, it is most disagreeable to render. You are paid for being something less than a man. The state will pay a genius only for some service which it is offensive to him to render. Even the poet-laureate would rather not have to celebrate the accidents of royalty. —Journal, August 7, 1853

Is it not as language that all natural objects affect the poet? He sees a flower or other object, and it is beautiful or affecting to him because it is a symbol of his thought, and what he indistinctly feels or perceives is matured in some other organization. The objects I behold correspond to my mood. —Journal, August 7, 1853

Do you not feel the fruit of your spring and summer begin to ripen, to harden its seed within you? Do not your thoughts begin to acquire consistency as well as flavor and ripeness? How can we expect a harvest of thought who have not had a seed-time of character? Already some of my small thoughts — fruit of my spring life — are ripe, like the berries which feed the first broods of birds; and other some are prematurely ripe and bright, like the lower leaves of the herbs which have felt the summer's drought.
—Journal, August 7, 1854

With thinking we may be beside ourselves in a sane sense. By a conscious effort of the mind we can stand aloof from actions and their consequences; and all things, good and bad, go by us like a torrent. We are not wholly involved in Nature. I may be either the driftwood in the stream, or Indra in the sky looking down on it. I may be affected by a theatrical exhibition; on the other hand, I may not be affected by an actual event which appears to concern me much more. I only know myself as a human entity; the scene, so to speak, of thoughts and affections; and am sensible of a certain doubleness by which I can stand as remote from myself as from another. However intense my experience, I am conscious of the presence and criticism of a part of me, which, as it were, is not a part of me, but spectator, sharing no experience, but taking note of it, and that is no more I than it is you. When the play, it may be the tragedy, of life is over, the spectator goes his way. It was a kind of fiction, a work of the imagination only, so far as he was concerned. This doubleness may easily make us poor neighbors and friends sometimes.

I find it wholesome to be alone the greater part of the time. To be in company, even with the best, is soon wearisome and dissipating. I love to be alone. I never found the companion that was so companionable as solitude. We are for the most part more lonely when we go abroad among men than when we stay in our chambers. A man thinking or working is always alone, let him be where he will. Solitude is not measured by the miles of space that intervene between a man and his fellows. The really diligent student in one of the crowded hives of Cambridge College is as solitary as a dervish in the desert. The farmer can work alone in the field or the woods all day, hoeing or chopping, and not feel lonesome, because he is employed; but when he comes home at night he cannot sit down in a room alone, at the mercy of his thoughts, but must be where he can "see the folks," and recreate, and, as he thinks, remunerate himself for his day's solitude; and hence he wonders how the student can sit alone in the house all night and most of the day without ennui and "the blues"; but he does not realize that the student, though in the house, is still at work in his field, and chopping in his woods, as the farmer in his, and in turn seeks the same recreation and society that the latter does, though it may be a more condensed form of it. —Walden, "Solitude"

Men have, perchance, detected every kind of flower that grows in this township, have pursued it with children's eyes into the thickets and darkest woods and swamps, where the painter's color has betrayed it. Have they with proportionate thoroughness plucked every flower of thought which it is possible for a man to entertain, proved every sentiment which it is possible for a man to experience, here? Men have circumnavigated this globe of land and water, but how few have sailed out of sight of common sense over the ocean of knowledge! —Journal, August 8, 1852

Do the duty that lies nearest to thee. —Journal, August 8, 1856

Do what nobody can do for you. Omit to do everything else. —Journal, August 9, 1850

Cultivate the tree which you have found to bear fruit in your soil. —Journal, August 9, 1850

It is not easy to make our lives respectable to ourselves by any course of activity. We have repeatedly to withdraw ourselves into our shells of thought like the tortoise, somewhat helplessly; and yet there is even more than philosophy in that. —Journal, August 9, 1850

What is peculiar in the life of a man consists not in his obedience, but his opposition, to his instincts. In one direction or another he strives to live a supernatural life. —Journal, August 9, 1850

As for conforming outwardly, and living your own life inwardly, I do not think much of that. Let not your right hand know what your left hand does in that line of business. It will prove a failure. Just as successfully can you walk against a sharp steel edge which divides you cleanly right and left. —Letter to Harrison Blake, August 9, 1850

This is the season of small fruits. I trust, too, that I am maturing some small fruit as palatable in these months, which will communicate my flavor to my kind. —Journal, August 9, 1853

The tinkling notes of goldfinches and bobolinks which we hear nowadays are of one character and peculiar to the season. They are not voluminous flowers, but rather nuts, of sound — ripened seeds of sound. It is the tinkling of ripened grains in Nature's basket. —Journal, August 10, 1854

How meanly and miserably we live for the most part! We escape fate continually by the skin of our teeth, as the saying is. We are practically desperate. But as every man, in

respect to material wealth, aims to become independent or wealthy, so, in respect to our spirits and imagination, we should have some spare capital and superfluous vigor, have some margin and leeway in which to move. What kind of gift is life unless we have spirits to enjoy it and taste its true flavor? if, in respect to spirits, we are to be forever cramped and in debt? In our ordinary estate we have not, so to speak, quite enough air to breathe, and this poverty qualifies our piety; but we should have more than enough and breathe it carelessly. Poverty is the rule. We should first of all be full of vigor like a strong horse, and beside have the free and adventurous spirit of his driver; i.e., we should have such a reserve of elasticity and strength that we may at any time be able to put ourselves at the top of our speed and go beyond our ordinary limits.
—Journal, August 10, 1857

This was my curious labor all summer — to make this portion of the earth's surface, which had yielded only cinquefoil, blackberries, johnswort, and the like, before, sweet wild fruits and pleasant flowers, produce instead this pulse. What shall I learn of beans or beans of me? I cherish them, I hoe them, early and late I have an eye to them; and this is my day's work....

Removing the weeds, putting fresh soil about the bean stems, and encouraging this weed which I had sown, making the yellow soil express its summer thought in bean leaves and blossoms rather than in wormwood and piper and millet grass, making the earth say beans instead of grass — this was my daily work. As I had little aid from horses or cattle, or hired men or boys, or improved implements of husbandry, I was much slower, and became much more intimate with my beans than usual. But labor of the hands, even when pursued to the verge of drudgery, is perhaps never the worst form of idleness. It has a constant and imperishable moral, and to the scholar it yields a classic result. —Walden, "The Bean-Field"

It is not all books that are as dull as their readers. There are probably words addressed to our condition exactly, which, if we could really hear and understand, would be more salutary than the morning or the spring to our lives, and possibly put a new aspect on the face of things for us. How many a man has dated a new era in his life from the reading of a book! The book exists for us, perchance, which will explain our miracles and reveal new ones. The at present unutterable things we may find somewhere uttered. These same questions that disturb and puzzle and confound us have in their turn occurred to all the wise men; not one has been omitted; and each has answered them, according to his ability, by his words and his life. —Walden, "Reading "

I did not read books the first summer; I hoed beans. Nay, I often did better than this. There were times when I could not afford to sacrifice the bloom of the present moment to any work, whether of the head or hands. I love a broad margin to my life. Sometimes, in a summer morning, having taken my accustomed bath, I sat in my sunny doorway from sunrise till noon, rapt in a revery, amidst the pines and hickories and sumachs, in undisturbed solitude and stillness, while the birds sing around or flitted noiseless through the house, until by the sun falling in at my west window, or the noise of some traveller's wagon on the distant highway, I was reminded of the lapse of time. I grew in those seasons like corn in the night, and they were far better than any work of the hands would have been. They were not time subtracted from my life, but so much over and above my usual allowance. I realized what the Orientals mean by contemplation and the forsaking of works. For the most part, I minded not how the hours went. The day advanced as if to light some work of mine; it was morning, and lo, now it is evening, and nothing memorable is accomplished. Instead of singing like the birds, I silently smiled at my incessant good fortune. —Walden, "Sounds"

Early apples begin to be ripe about the first of August; but I think that none of them are so good to eat as some to smell. One is worth more to scent your handkerchief with than any perfume which they sell in the shops. The fragrance of some fruits is not to be forgotten, along with that of flowers. Some gnarly apple which I pick up in the road reminds me by its fragrance of all the wealth of Pomona, carrying me forward to those days when they will be collected in golden and ruddy heaps in the orchards and about the cider-mills.

A week or two later, as you are going by orchards or gardens, especially in the evenings, you pass through a little region possessed by the fragrance of ripe apples, and thus enjoy them without price, and without robbing anybody.

There is thus about all natural products a certain volatile and ethereal quality which represents their highest value, and which cannot be vulgarized, or bought and sold. No mortal has ever enjoyed the perfect flavor of any fruit, and only the godlike among men begin to taste its ambrosial qualities. For nectar and ambrosia are only those fine flavors of every earthly fruit which our coarse palates fail to perceive, just as we occupy the heaven of the gods without knowing it. When I see a particularly mean man carrying a load of fair and fragrant early apples to market, I seem to see a contest going on between him and his horse, on the one side, and the apples on the other, and, to my mind, the apples always gain it. Pliny says that apples are the heaviest of all things, and that the oxen begin to sweat at the mere sight of a load of them. Our driver begins to lose his load the moment he tries to transport them to where they do not belong, that is, to any but the most beautiful. Though he gets out from time to time, and feels of them, and thinks they are all there, I see the stream of their evanescent and celestial qualities going to heaven from his cart, while the pulp and skin and core only are going to market. They are not apples, but pomace. Are not these still Iduna's apples, the taste of which keeps the gods forever young? and think you that they will let Loki or Thjassi carry them off to Jotunheim, while they grow wrinkled and gray? No, for Ragnarok, or the destruction of the gods, is not yet. —"Wild Apples"

There are berries which men do not use, like choke-berries, which here in Hubbard's Swamp grow in great profusion and blacken the bushes. How much richer we feel fro this unused abundance and superfluity! Nature would not appear so rich, the profusion so rich, if we knew a use for everything. —Journal, August 11, 1853

Found ____ rather garrulous (his breath smelled of rum). Was complaining that his sons did not get married. He told me his age when he married (thirty-odd years ago), how his wife bore him eight children and then died, and in what respect she proved herself a true woman, etc., etc. I saw that it was as impossible to speak of marriage to such a man — to the mass of men — as of poetry. Its advantages and disadvantages are not such as they have dreamed of. Their marriage is prose or worse. To be married at least should be the one poetical act of a man's life. If you fail in this respect, in what respect will you succeed? The marriage which the mass of men comprehend is but little better than the marriage of the beasts. It would be just as fit for such a man to discourse to you on the love of flowers, thinking of them as hay for his oxen. —Journal, August 11, 1853

What shall we name this season? — this very late afternoon, or very early evening, this severe and placid season of the day, most favorable for reflection, after the insufferable heats and bustle of the day are over and before the dampness and twilight of evening! The serene hour, the Muses' hour, the season of reflection! It is commonly desecrated by being made tea-time. It begins perhaps with the earliest condensation of moisture in the air, when the shadows of hills are first observed, and the breeze begins to go down, and birds begin again to sing. The pensive season. It is earlier than the "chaste eve" of the poet. Bats have not come forth. It is not twilight. There is no dew yet on the grass, and still less any early star in the heavens. It is the turning-point between afternoon and evening. The few sounds now heard, far or near, are delicious. It is not more dusky and obscure, but clearer than before. The clearing of the air by condensation of mists more than balances the increase of shadows. Chaste eve is merely *preparing* with "dewy finger" to draw o'er all "the gradual dusky veil." Not yet "the ploughman homeward plods his weary way," nor owls nor beetles are abroad. It is a season somewhat earlier than is celebrated by the poets. There is not such a sense of lateness and approaching night as they describe. I mean when the first emissaries of Evening come to smooth the lakes and streams. The poet arouses himself and collects his thoughts. He postpones tea indefinitely. Thought has taken her siesta. Each sound has a broad and deep relief of silence. —Journal, August 11, 1853

I remember only with a pang the past spring and summer thus far. I have not been an early riser. Society seems to have invaded and overrun me. I have drank tea and coffee and made myself cheap and vulgar. My days have all been noontides, without sacred mornings and evenings. I desire to rise early henceforth, to associate with those whose influence is elevating, to have such dreams and waking

thoughts that my diet may not be indifferent to me.
—Journal, August 13, 1854

I have but just returned from a pedestrian excursion somewhat similar to that you propose, *parvis componere magna*, to the Catskill Mountains, over the principal mountains of this State, subsisting mainly on bread and berries, and slumbering on the mountain-tops. As usually happens, I now feel a slight sense of dissipation. Still, I am strongly tempted by your proposal, and experience a decided schism between my outward and inward tendencies. Your method of traveling, especially — to live along the road, citizens of the world, without haste or petty plans — I have often proposed this to my dreams, and still do. But the fact is, I cannot so decidedly postpone exploring the *Farther Indies*, which are to be reached, you know, by other routes and other methods of travel. I mean that I constantly return from every external enterprise with disgust, to fresh faith in a kind of Brahminical, Artesian, Inner Temple life. All my experience, as yours probably, proves only this reality. —Letter to Isaac Hecker, August 14, 1844

This is the result of my experience in raising beans: Plant the common small white bush bean about the first of June, in rows three feet by eighteen inches apart, being careful to select fresh round and unmixed seed. First look out for worms, and supply vacancies by planting anew. Then look out for woodchucks, if it is an exposed place, for they will nibble off the earliest tender leaves almost clean as they go; and again, when the young tendrils make their appearance, they have notice of it, and will shear them off with both buds and young pods, sitting erect like a squirrel. But above all harvest as early as possible, if you would escape frosts and have a fair and salable crop; you may save much loss by this means.

This further experience also I gained: I said to myself, I will not plant beans and corn with so much industry another summer, but such seeds, if the seed is not lost, as sincerity, truth, simplicity, faith, innocence, and the like, and see if they will not grow in this soil, even with less toil and manurance, and sustain me, for surely it has not been exhausted for these crops. Alas! I said this to myself; but now another summer is gone, and another, and another, and I am obliged to say to you, Reader, that the seeds which I planted, if indeed they were the seeds of those virtues, were wormeaten or had lost their vitality, and so did not come up. —Walden, "The Bean-Field"

I feel as if this coolness would do me good. If it only makes my life more pensive! Why should pensiveness be akin to sadness? There is a certain fertile sadness which I would not avoid, but rather earnestly seek. It is positively joyful to me. It saves my life from being trivial. My life flows with a deeper current, no longer as a shallow and brawling stream, parched and shrunken by the summer heats. This coolness comes to condense the dews and clear the atmosphere. The stillness seems more deep and significant. Each sound seems to come from out a greater thoughtfulness in nature, as if nature had acquired some character and mind. The cricket, the gurgling stream, the rushing wind amid the trees, all speak to me soberly yet encouragingly of the steady onward progress of the universe. My heart leaps in my mouth at the sound of the wind in the woods. I, whose life was but yesterday so desultory and shallow, suddenly recover my spirits, my spirituality, through my hearing. I see a goldfinch go twittering through the still, louring day, and am reminded of the peeping flocks which will soon herald the thoughtful season. Ah! if I could so live that there should be no desultory moment in all my life! that in the trivial season, when small fruits are ripe, my fruits might be ripe also! that I could match nature always with my moods! that in each season when some part of nature especially flourishes, then a corresponding part of me may not fail to flourish! Ah, I would walk, I would sit and sleep, with natural piety! What if I could pray aloud or to myself as I went along by the brooksides a cheerful prayer like the birds! For joy I could embrace the earth; I shall delight to be buried in it. —Journal, August 17, 1851

There is indeed something royal about the month of August. —Journal, August 18, 1852

Perceived today and some weeks since (August 3d) the strong invigorating aroma of green walnuts, astringent and bracing to the spirits, the fancy and the imagination, suggesting a tree that has its roots well in amid the bowels of nature. Their shells are, in fact and from association, exhilarating to smell, suggesting a strong, nutty native vigor. A fruit which I am glad that our zone produces, looking like the nutmeg of the East. I acquire some of the hardness and elasticity of the hickory when I smell them. —Journal, August 18, 1852

What means this sense of lateness that so comes over one now — as if the rest of the year were down-hill, and if we had not performed anything before, we should not now? The season of flowers or of promise may be said to be over, and now is the season of fruits; but where is our fruit? The night of the year is approaching. What have we done with our talent? All nature prompts and reproves us. How early in the year it begins to be late! The sound of the crickets, even in the spring, makes our hearts beat with its awful reproof, while it encourages with its seasonable warning. It matters not by how little we have fallen behind; it seems irretrievably late. The year is full of warnings of its shortness, as is life. The sound of so many insects and the sight of so many flowers affect us so — the creak of the cricket and the sight of the *prunella* and autumnal dandelion. They say, "For the night cometh in which no man may work." —Journal, August 18, 1853

As I go along the hillsides in sprout-lands, amid the *Solidago stricta*, looking for the blackberries left after the rain, the sun warm as ever, but the air cool nevertheless, I hear the *steady* (not intermittent) shrilling of apparently the alder cricket, clear, loud, and autumnal, a season sound. Hear it, but see it not. It reminds me of past autumns and the lapse of time, suggesting a pleasing, thoughtful melancholy, like the sound of a flail. Such preparation, such an outfit has our life, and so little brought to pass! —Journal, August 18, 1856

With regard to essentials, I have never had occasion to change my mind. The aspect of the world varies from year to year, as the landscape is differently clothed, but I find that the truth is still true, and I never regret any emphasis which it may have inspired. Ktaadn is there still, but much more surely my old conviction is there, resting with more than mountain breadth and weight on the world, the source still of fertilizing streams, and affording glorious views from its summit, if I can get up to it again. —Letter to Harrison Blake, August 18, 1857

What is religion? That which is never spoken. —Journal, August 18, 1858

The grass in the high pastures is almost as dry as hay. The seasons do not cease a moment to revolve, and therefore Nature rests no longer at her culminating point than at any other. If you are not out at the right instant, the summer may go by and you not see it. How much of the year is spring and fall! how little can be called summer! The grass is no sooner grown than it begins to wither. —Journal, August 19, 1851

The poet must be continually watching the moods of his mind as the astronomer watches the aspects of the heavens. What might we not expect from a long life faithfully spent in this wise? The humblest observer would see some stars shoot. A faithful description as by a disinterested person of the thoughts which visited a certain mind in threescore years and ten as when one reports the number and character of the vehicles which pass a particular point. As travellers go round the world and report natural objects and phenomena, so faithfully let another stay at home and report the phenomena of his own life — catalogue stars, those thoughts whose orbits are as rarely calculated as comets. It matters not whether they visit my mind or yours — whether the meteor falls in my field or in yours — only that it comes from heaven. (I am not concerned to express that kind of truth which Nature has expressed. Who knows but I may suggest some things to her? Time was when she was indebted to such suggestions from another quarter, as her present advancement shows. I deal with the truths that recommend themselves to me — please me — not those merely which any system has voted to accept.) A meteorological journal of the mind. You shall observe what occurs in your latitude, I in mine. —Journal, August 19, 1851

I was going to sit and write or mope all day in the house, but it seems wise to cultivate animal spirits, to embark in enterprises which employ and recreate the whole body. Let the divine spirits like the huntsman with his bugle accompany the animal spirit that would fain range forest and meadow. Even the gods and goddesses, Apollo and Diana, are found in the field, though they are superior to the dog and the deer. —Journal, August 19, 1853

It is a glorious and ever-memorable day. We observe attentively the first beautiful days in the spring, but not so much in the autumn. We might expect that the first fair days after so much rain would be remarkable. It is a day affecting the spirits of men, but there is nobody to enjoy it but ourselves. What does the laborer ox and the laborer man care for the beautiful days? Will the haymaker when he comes home tonight know that this has been such a beautiful day? This day itself has been the great phenomenon, but will it be reported in any journal, as the storm is, and the heat? It is like a great and beautiful flower unnamed. I see a man trimming willows on the Sudbury causeway and others raking hay out of the water in the midst of all this clarity and brightness, but are they aware of the splendor of this day? The mass of mankind, who live in houses or shops or are *bent* upon their labor out of doors, know nothing of the beautiful days which are passing above and around them. Is not such a day worthy of a hymn? It is such a day as mankind might spend in praising and glorifying nature. It might be spent as a natural sabbath, if only all men would accept the hint, devoted to unworldly thoughts. The first bright day of the fall, the earth reflector. The dog-day mists are gone; the washed earth shines; the cooler air braces man. No summer day is so beautiful as the fairest spring and fall days. —Journal, August 19, 1853

As toward the evening of the day the lakes and streams are smooth, so in the fall, the evening of the year, the waters are smoothed more perfectly than at any other season. The day is an epitome of the year. —Journal, August 19, 1853

Whether a man spends his day in an ecstasy or despondency, he must do some work to show for it, even as there are flesh and bones to show for him. We are superior to the joy we experience. —Letter to Harrison Blake, August 19, 1853

It is still cool weather with a northwest wind. This weather is a preface to autumn. There is more shadow in the landscape than a week ago, methinks, and the creak of the cricket sounds cool and steady.

The grass and foliage and landscape generally are of a more thought-inspiring color, suggest what some perchance would call a pleasing melancholy. —Journal, August 19, 1858

Moralists say of men, By their fruits ye shall know them, but botanists say of plants, By their flowers ye shall know them. This is very well generally, but they must make exceptions sometimes when the fruit is fairer than the flowers. They are to be compared at that stage in which they are most significant to man. —Journal, August 21, 1852

The coloring and reddening of the leaves toward fall is interesting; as if the sun had so prevailed that even the leaves, better late than never, were turning to flowers — so filled with mature juices, the whole plant turns at length to one flower, and all its leaves are petals around its fruit or dry seed. A second flowering to celebrate the maturity of the fruit. The first to celebrate the age of puberty, the marriageable age; the second, the maturity of the parent, the age of wisdom, the fullness of years. —Journal, August 21, 1852

When I used to pick the berries for dinner on the East Quarter hills I did not eat one till I had done, for going a-berrying implies more things than eating the berries. They at home got only the pudding: I got the forenoon out of doors, and the appetite for the pudding.

It is true, as is said, that we have as good a right to make berries private property as to make grass and trees and such; but what I chiefly regret is the, in effect, dog-in-the-manger result, for at the same time that we exclude mankind from gathering berries in our field, we exclude them from gathering health and happiness and inspiration and a hundred other far finer and nobler fruits than berries, which yet we shall not gather ourselves there, nor even carry to market. We strike only one more blow at a simple and wholesome relation to nature. —Journal, August 22, 1860

Most men have forgotten that it was ever morning; but a few serene memories, healthy and wakeful natures, there are who assure us that the sun rose clear, heralded by the singing of birds — this very day's sun, which rose before Memnon was ready to greet it. —Journal, August 23, 1845

Resolve to read no book, to take no walk, to undertake no enterprise, but such as you can endure to give an account of to yourself. Live thus deliberately for the most part. —Journal, August 23, 1851

Observing the blackness of the foliage, especially between me and the light, I am reminded that it begins in the spring, the dewy dawn of the year, with a silvery hoary downiness, changing to a yellowish or light green — the saffron-robed morn — then to a pure, spotless, glossy green with light under sides reflecting the light — the forenoon — and now the dark green or early afternoon, when shadows begin to increase, and next it will turn yellow or red — the sunset sky — and finally sere brown and black, when the night of the year sets in....

I am again struck by the perfect correspondence of a day — say an August day — and the year. I think that a perfect parallel may be drawn between the seasons of the day and of the year. Perhaps after middle age man ceases to be interested in the morning and in the spring. —Journal, August 23, 1853

Poke stems are now ripe. I walked through a beautiful grove of them, six or seven feet high, on the side of Lee's Cliff, where they have ripened early. Their stems are a deep, rich purple with a bloom, contrasting with the clear green leaves. Every part but the leaves is a brilliant purple (lake purple); or, more strictly speaking, the racemes without the berries are a brilliant lake-red with crimson flame-like reflections. Hence the *lacca*. Its cylindrical racemes of berries of varied hues from green to dark purple, six or seven inches long, are drooping on all sides, beautiful both with and without berries, all afire with ripeness. Its stalks, thus full of purple wine, are one of the fruits of autumn. It excites me to behold it. What a success is it! What maturity it arrives at, ripening from leaf to root! May I mature as perfectly, root and branch, as the poke. Its stems are more beautiful than most flowers. It is the emblem of a successful life, a not premature death — whose death is an ornament to nature. —Journal, August 23, 1853

Live in each season as it passes; breathe the air, drink the drink, taste the fruit, and resign yourself to the influences of each. Let them be your only diet drink and botanical medicines. In August live on berries, not dried meats and pemmican, as if you were on shipboard making your way through a waste ocean, or in a northern desert. Be blown on by all the winds. Open all your pores and bathe in all the tides of Nature, in all her streams and oceans, at all seasons. Miasma and infection are from within, not without. The invalid, brought to the brink of the grave by an unnatural life, instead of imbibing only the great influence that Nature is, drinks only the tea made of a particular herb, while he still continues his unnatural life — saves at the spile and wastes at the bung. He does not

love Nature or his life, and so sickens and dies, and no doctor can cure him. Grow green with spring, yellow and ripe with autumn. Drink of each season's influence as a vial, a true panacea of all remedies mixed for your especial use. The vials of summer never made a man sick, but those which he stored in his cellar. Drink the wines, not of your bottling, but Nature's bottling; not kept in goat-skins or pig-skins, but the skins of a myriad fair berries. Let Nature do your bottling and your pickling and preserving. For all Nature is doing her best each moment to make us well. She exists for no other end. Do not resist her. With the least inclination to be well, we should not be sick. Men have discovered — or think they have discovered — the salutariness of a few wild things only, and not of all nature. Why, "nature" is but another name for health, and the seasons are but different states of health. Some men think that they are not well in spring, or summer, or autumn, or winter; it is only because they are not *well in* them.
—Journal, August 23, 1853

Everywhere in woods and swamps I am already reminded of fall. I see the spotted sarsaparilla leaves and brakes, and, in swamps, the withering and blackened skunk-cabbage and hellebore, and, by the river, the already blackening pontederias and pipes. There is no plateau on which Nature rests at midsummer, but she instantly commences the descent to winter. —Journal, August 23, 1858

I only desire *sincere* relations with the worthiest of my acquaintances, that they may give me an opportunity once in a year to speak the truth.... The hospitable man will invite me to an atmosphere where truth can be spoken, where a man can live and breathe. —Journal, August 24, 1852

The year is but a succession of days, and I see that I could assign some office to each day which, summed up, would be the history of the year. Everything is done in season, and there is no time to spare. —Journal, August 24, 1852

It is the bravest thing we do for one moment to put so much confidence in our companion as to treat him for what he aspires to be. —Journal, August 24, 1852

The bright crimson-red under sides of the great white lily pads turned up by the wind in broad fields on the sides of the stream, are a great ornament to the stream.... It is a very wholesome color, and, after the calm summer, an exhilarating sight, with a strong wind heard and felt, cooling and condensing your thoughts. This has the effect of a ripening of the leaf on the river. —Journal, August 24, 1854

Two interesting tall purplish grasses appear to be the prevailing ones now in dry and sterile neglected fields and hillsides.... I have sympathy with them because they are despised by the farmer and occupy sterile and neglected soil. They also by their rich purple reflections or tinges seem to express the ripeness of the year. It is high-colored like ripe grapes, and expresses a maturity which the spring did not suggest. —Journal, August 26, 1858

What is often called poverty, but which is a simpler and truer relation to nature, gives a peculiar relish to life, just as to be kept short gives us an appetite for food. —Journal, August 27, 1859

In the Hindoo scripture the idea of man is quite illimitable and sublime. There is nowhere a loftier conception of his destiny. He is at length lost in Brahma himself, "the divine male." Indeed, the distinction of races in this life is only the commencement of a series of degrees which ends in Brahma.

The veneration in which the Vedas are held is itself a remarkable fact. Their code embraced the whole moral life of the Hindoo, and in such a case there is no other truth than sincerity. Truth is such by reference to the heart of man within, not to any standard without. —Journal, August 28, 1841

June, July, and August, the tortoise eggs are hatching a few inches beneath the surface in sandy fields. You tell of active labors, of works of art, and wars the past summer; meanwhile the tortoise eggs underlie this turmoil. What events have transpired on the lit and airy surface three inches above them! Sumner knocked down; Kansas living an age of suspense. Think what is a summer to them! How many worthy men have died and had their funeral sermons preached since I saw the mother turtle bury her eggs here! They contained an undeveloped liquid then, they are now turtles. July, July, and August — the livelong summer — what are they with their heats and fevers but sufficient to hatch a tortoise in. Be not in haste; mind your private affairs. Consider the turtle. A whole summer — June, July, and August — is not too good nor too much to hatch a turtle in. Perchance you have worried yourself, despaired of the world, meditated the end of life, and all things seemed rushed to destruction; but nature has steadily and serenely advanced with a turtle's pace. s—Journal, August 28, 1856

We are wont to forget that the sun looks on our cultivated fields and on the prairies and forests without distinction. They all reflect and absorb his rays alike, and the former make but a small part of the glorious picture which he beholds in his daily course. In his view the earth is all equally cultivated like a garden. Therefore we should receive the benefit of his light and heat with a corresponding trust and magnanimity. What though I value the seed of these beans, and harvest that in the fall of the year? This broad field which I have looked at so long looks not to me as the principal cultivator, but away from me to influences more genial to it, which water and make it green. These beans have results which are not harvested by me. Do they not grow for woodchucks partly? The ear of wheat (in Latin spica, obsoletely speca, from spe, hope) should not be the only hope of the husbandman; its kernel or grain (granum from gerendo, bearing) is not all that it bears. How, then, can our harvest fail? Shall I not rejoice also at the abundance of the weeds whose seeds are the granary of the birds? It matters little comparatively whether the fields fill the farmer's barns. The true husbandman will cease from anxiety, as the squirrels manifest no concern whether the woods will bear chestnuts this year or not, and finish his labor with every day, relinquishing all claim to the produce of his fields, and sacrificing in his mind not only his first but his last fruits also. —Walden, "The Bean-Field"

Early for several mornings I have heard the sound of a flail. It leads me to ask if I have spent as industrious a spring and summer as the farmer, and gathered as rich a crop of experience. If so, the sound of my flail will be heard by those who have ears to hear, separating the kernel from the chaff all the fall and winter, and a sound no less cheering it will be. If the drought has destroyed the corn, let not all harvests fail. Have you commenced to thresh your grain? —Journal, August 29, 1854

Coolness and clarity go together. —Journal, August 29, 1854

The ghost-horse (*Spectrum*) is seen nowadays — several of them. All these high colors in the stems and leaves and other portions of plants answer to some maturity in us. I presume if I am the wiser for having lived this season through, such plants will emblazon the truth of my experience over the face of nature, and I shall be aware of a beauty and sweetness there.

Has not the mind, too, its harvest? Do not some scarlet leaves of thought come scatteringly down, though it may be prematurely, some which, perchance, the summer's drought has ripened, and the rain loosened? Are there no purple reflections from the culms of thought in my mind?
—Journal, August 29, 1858

It is so cool a morning that for the first time I move into the entry to sit in the sun. But in this cooler weather I feel as if the fruit of my summer were hardening and maturing a little, acquiring color and flavor like the corn and other fruits in the field. When the very earliest ripe grapes begin to be scented in the cool nights, then, too, the first cooler airs of autumn begin to waft my sweetness on the desert airs of summer. Now, too, poets nib their pens afresh. I scent their first-fruits in the cool evening air of the year. By the coolness the experience of the summer is condensed and matured, whether our fruits be pumpkins or grapes. Man, too, ripens with the grapes and apples. —Journal, August 29, 1859

To our nearsightedness this mere outward life seems a constituent part of us, and we do not realize that as our soul expands it will cast off the shell of routine and convention, which afterward will only be an object for the cabinets of the curious. But of this people the temples are now crumbled away, and we are introduced to the very hearth of Hindoo life and to the primeval conventicle where how to eat and to drink and to sleep were the questions to be decided.

The simple life herein described confers on us a degree of freedom even in the perusal. We throw down our packs and go on our way unencumbered. Wants so easily and gracefully satisfied that they seem like a more refined pleasure and repleteness. —Journal, August 30, 1841

Sometimes, having had a surfeit of human society and gossip, and worn out all my village friends, I rambled still farther westward than I habitually dwell, into yet more unfrequented parts of the town, "to fresh woods and pastures new," or, while the sun was setting, made my supper of huckleberries and blueberries on Fair Haven Hill, and laid up a store for several days. The fruits do not yield their true flavor to the purchaser of them, nor to him who raises them for the market. There is but one way to obtain it, yet few take that way. If you would know the flavor of huckleberries, ask the cowboy or the partridge. It is a vulgar error to suppose that you have tasted huckleberries who never plucked them. A huckleberry never reaches Boston; they have not been known there since they grew on her three hills. The ambrosial and essential part of the fruit is lost with the bloom which is rubbed off in the market cart, and they become mere provender. As long as Eternal Justice reigns, not one innocent huckleberry can be transported thither from the country's hills. —Walden, "The Ponds"

I have come out this afternoon a-cranberrying, chiefly to gather some of the small cranberry, *Vaccinium Oxycoccus*, which Emerson says is the common cranberry of the north of Europe. This was a small object, yet not to be postponed, on account of imminent frosts, i.e., if I would know this year the flavor of the European cranberry as compared with our larger kind. I thought I should like to have a dish of this sauce on the table at Thanksgiving of my own gathering. I could hardly make up my mind to come this way, it seemed so poor an object to spend the afternoon on. I kept foreseeing a lame conclusion — how should I cross the Great Fields, look into Beck Stow's, and then retrace my steps no richer than before. In fact, I expected little of this walk, yet it did pass through the side of my mind that somehow, on this very account (my small expectation), it would turn out well, as also the advantage of having some purpose, however small, to be accomplished — of letting your deliberate wisdom and foresight in the house to some extent direct and control your steps. If you would really take a position outside the street and daily life of men, you must have deliberately planned your course, you must have business which is not your neighbors' business, which they cannot understand. For only absorbing employment prevails, succeeds, takes up space, occupies territory, determines the future of individuals and states, drives Kansas out of your head, and actually and permanently occupies the only desirable and free Kansas against all border ruffians. The attitude of resistance is one of weakness, inasmuch as it only faces an enemy; it has its back to all that is truly attractive. You shall have your affairs, I will have mine. You will spend this afternoon in setting up your neighbor's stove, and be paid for it; I will spend it in gathering the few berries of the *Vaccinium Oxycoccus* which Nature produces here, before it is too late, and be paid for it also after another fashion. I have always reaped unexpected and incalculable advantages from carrying out at last however tardily, any little enterprise which my genius suggested to me long ago as a thing to be done — some step to be taken, however slight, out of the usual course.

How many schools I have thought of which I might go to but did not go to! expecting foolishly that some greater advantage or schooling would come to me! It is these comparatively cheap and private expeditions that substantiate our existence and batten our lives as where a vine touches the earth in its undulating course, it puts forth roots and thickens its stock. Our employment generally is tinkering, mending the old worn-out teapot of society. Our stock in trade is solder. Better for me, says my genius, to go cranberrying this afternoon for the *Vaccinium Oxycoccus* in Gowing's Swamp, to get but a pocketful and learn its peculiar flavor, aye, and the flavor of Gowing's Swamp and of *life* in New England, than to go consul to Liverpool and get I don't know how many thousand dollars for it, with no such flavor. Many of our days should be spent, not in vain expectations and lying on our oars, but in carrying out deliberately and faithfully the hundred little purposes which every man's genius must have suggested to him. Let not your life be wholly without an object, though it be only to ascertain the flavor of a cranberry, for it will not be only the quality of an insignificant berry that you will have tasted, but the flavor of your life to that extent, and it will be such a sauce as no wealth can buy.

Both a conscious and an unconscious life are good. Neither is good exclusively, for both have the same source. The wisely conscious life springs out of an unconscious suggestion. I have found my account in travelling in having prepared beforehand a list of questions which I would get answered, not trusting to my interest at the moment, and can then travel with the most profit. Indeed, it is by obeying the suggestions of a higher light within you that you escape from yourself and, in the transit, as it were see with the unworn sides of your eye, travel totally new paths. What is that pretended life that does not take up a claim, that does not occupy ground, that cannot build a causeway to its objects, that sits on a bank looking over a bog, singing its desires? —Journal, August 30, 1856

I see that men do not make or choose their own paths, whether they are railroads or trackless through the wilds, but what the powers permit each one enjoys. My solitary course has the same sanction that the Fitchburg Railroad has. If they have a charter from Massachusetts and — what is of much more importance — from Heaven, to

travel the course and in the fashion they do, I have a charter, though it be from Heaven alone, to travel the course I do — to take the necessary lands and pay the damages. It is by the grace of God in both cases.
—Journal, August 31, 1850

The trivialness of the day is past. The greater stillness, the *serenity* of the air, its coolness and transparency, the mistiness being condensed, are favorable to thought. (The pensive eve.) The coolness of evening comes to condense the haze of noon and make the air transparent and the outline of objects firm and distinct, and chaste (chaste eve); even as I am made more vigorous by my bath, am more *continent* of thought. After bathing, even at noonday, a man realizes a morning or evening life. The evening air is such a bath for both mind and body. When I have walked all day in vain under the torrid sun, and the world has been all trivial — as well field and wood as highway — then at eve the sun goes down westward, and the wind goes down with it, and the dews begin to purify the air and make it transparent, and the lakes and rivers acquire a glassy stillness, reflecting the skies, the reflex of the day. I too am at the top of my condition for perceiving beauty. Thus, long after feeding, the diviner faculties begin to be fed, to feel their oats, their nutriment, and are not oppressed by the belly's load. It is abstinence from loading the belly anew until the brain and divine faculties have felt their vigor. —Journal, August 31, 1851

In the fall, after so much sun, all leaves turn to petals and blossoms. The evening of the year is colored like the sunset. —Journal, August 31, 1852

This is the most glorious part of this day, the serenest, warmest, brightest part, and the most suggestive. Evening is fairer than morning. It is chaste eve, for it has sustained the trials of the day, but to the morning such praise was inapplicable. It is incense-breathing. Morning is full of promise and vigor. Evening is pensive. —Journal, August 31, 1852

AUTUMN

SEASONS OF THOREAU

September

Gardening is civil and social, but it wants the vigor and freedom of the forest and the outlaw. There may be an excess of cultivation as well as of anything else, until civilization becomes pathetic. A highly cultivated man — all whose bones can be bent! whose heaven-born virtues are but good manners! The young pines springing up in the cornfields from year to year are to me a refreshing fact. We talk of civilizing the Indian, but that is not the name for his improvement. By the wary independence and aloofness of his dim forest life he preserves his intercourse with his native gods, and is admitted from time to time to a rare and peculiar society with Nature. He has glances of starry recognition to which our saloons are strangers. The steady illumination of his genius, dim only because distant, is like the faint but satisfying light of the stars compared with the dazzling but ineffectual and short-lived blaze of candles. The Society-Islanders had their day-born gods, but they were not supposed to be "of equal antiquity with the *atua fauau po*, or night-born gods." It is true, there are the innocent pleasures of country life, and it is sometimes pleasant to make the earth yield her increase, and gather the fruits in their season, but the heroic spirit will not fail to dream of remoter retirements and more rugged paths. It will have its garden-plots and its *parterres* elsewhere than on the earth, and gather nuts and berries by the way for its subsistence, or orchard fruits with such heedlessness as berries. We would not always be soothing and taming nature, breaking the horse and the ox, but sometimes ride the horse wild and chase the buffalo. The Indian's intercourse with Nature is at least such as admits of the greatest independence of each. If he is somewhat of a stranger in her midst, the gardener is too much of a familiar. There is something vulgar and foul in the latter's closeness to his mistress, something noble and cleanly in the former's distance. —A Week on the Concord and Merrimack Rivers, "Sunday" (September 1, 1839)

Most people with whom I talk, men and women even of some originality and genius, have their scheme of the universe all cut and dried — very *dry*, I assure you, to hear, dry enough to burn, dry-rotted and powder-post, methinks — which they set up between you and them in the shortest intercourse; an ancient and tottering frame with all its boards blown off. They do not walk without their bed. Some, to me, seemingly very unimportant and unsubstantial things and relations, are for them everlastingly settled — as Father, Son, and Holy Ghost, and the like. These are like the everlasting hills to them. But in all my wanderings I never came across the least vestige of authority for these things. They have not left so distinct a trace as the delicate flower of a remote geological period on the coal in my grate. The wisest man preaches no doctrines; he has no scheme; he sees no rafter, not even a cobweb, against the heavens. It is clear sky. —A Week on the Concord and Merrimack Rivers, "Sunday"

Christ was a sublime actor on the stage of the world. He knew what he was thinking of when he said, "Heaven and earth shall pass away, but my words shall not pass away." I draw near to him at such a time. Yet he taught mankind but imperfectly how to live; his thoughts were all directed toward another world. There is another kind of success than his. Even here we have a sort of living to get, and must buffet it somewhat longer. There are various tough problems yet to solve, and we must make shift to live, betwixt spirit and matter, such a human life as we can. —A Week on the Concord and Merrimack Rivers, "Sunday"

Yet, after all, the truly efficient laborer will not crowd his day with work, but will saunter to his task surrounded by a wide halo of ease and leisure, and then do but what he loves best. He is anxious only about the fruitful kernels of time. Though the hen should sit all day, she could lay only one egg, and, besides, would not have picked up materials for another. Let a man take time enough for the most trivial deed, though it be but the paring of his nails. The buds swell imperceptibly, without hurry or confusion, as if the short spring days were an eternity.

> Then spend an age in whetting thy desire,
> Thou needs't not *hasten* if thou dost *stand fast*.

Some hours seem not to be occasion for any deed, but for resolves to draw breath in. We do not directly go about the execution of the purpose that thrills us, but shut our doors behind us and ramble with prepared mind, as if the half were already done. Our resolution is taking root or hold on the earth then, as seeds first send a shoot downward which is fed by their own albumen, ere they send one upward to the light. —A Week on the Concord and Merrimack Rivers, "Sunday"

Let us know and conform only to the fashions of eternity.
—Journal, September 1, 1841

The very austerity of these Hindoos is tempting to the devotional as a more refined and nobler luxury. They seem to have indulged themselves with a certain moderation and temperance in the severities which their code requires, as divine exercises not to be excessively used as yet. One may discover the root of a Hindoo religion in his own private history, when, in the silent intervals of the day or the night, he does sometimes inflict on himself like austerities with a stern satisfaction.

The "Laws of Menu" are a manual of private devotion, so private and domestic and yet to public and universal a word as is not spoken in the parlor or pulpit in these days. It is so impersonal that it exercises our sincerity more than any other. —Journal, September 1, 1841

This is a very warm and serene evening, and the surface of the pond is perfectly smooth except where the skaters dimple it, for at equal intervals they are scattered over its whole extent, and, looking west, they make a fine sparkle in the sun. Here and there is a thistle-down floating on its surface, which the fishes dart at, and dimple the water — delicate hint of approaching autumn, when the first thistle-down descends on some smooth lake's surface, full of reflections, in the woods, sign to the fishes of the ripening year. These white faery vessels are annually wafted over the cope of their sky. Bethink thyself, O man, when the first thistle-down is in the air. Buoyantly it floated high in the air over hills and fields all day, and now, weighed down with evening dews, perchance, it sinks gently to the surface of the lake. Nothing can stay the thistle-down, but with September winds it unfailingly sets sail. The irresistible revolution of time. It but comes down upon the sea in its ship, and is still perchance wafted to the shore with its delicate sails. The thistle-down is in the air. Tell me, is thy fruit also there? Dost thou approach maturity? Do gales shake windfalls from thy tree? —Journal, September 1, 1852

Pickering says that "the missionaries [at the Hawaiian Islands] regarded as one main obstacle to improvement the extremely limited views of the natives in respect to style of living; 'a little fish and a little poi, and they were content.'" But this is putting the cart before the horse, the real obstacle being their limited views in respect to the object of living. A philosopher has equally limited views in their sense, but then he is not content with material comforts, nor is it, perhaps, quite necessary that he first be glutted with them in order to become wise. "A native, I was assured, 'could be supported for less than two cents a day.'" (They had adopted the use of coin.)

The savage lives simply through ignorance and idleness or laziness, but the philosopher lives simply through wisdom. In the case of the savage, the accompaniment of simplicity is idleness with its attendant vices, but in the case of the philosopher, it is the highest employment and development. The fact for the savage, and for the mass of mankind, is that it is better to plant, weave, and build than do nothing or worse; but the fact for the philosopher, or a nation loving wisdom, is that it is most important to cultivate the highest faculties and spend as little time as possible in planting, weaving, building, etc. It depends upon the height of your standard, and no doubt through manual labor as a police men are educated up to a certain level. The simple style is bad for the savage because he does worse than to obtain the luxuries of life; it is good for the philosopher because he does better than to work for them. The question is whether you can bear freedom. At present the vast majority of men, whether black or white, require the discipline of labor which enslaves them for their good. If the Irishman did not shovel all day, he would get drunk and quarrel. But the philosopher does not require the same discipline; if he shovelled all day, we should receive no elevating suggestions from him....

There are two kinds of simplicity — one that is akin to foolishness, the other to wisdom. The philosopher's style of living is only outwardly simple, but inwardly complex. The savage's style is both outwardly and inwardly simple. A simpleton can perform many mechanical labors, but is not capable of profound thought. It was their limited view, not in respect to *style*, but to the *object* of living. A man who has equally limited views with respect to the end of living will not be helped by the most complex and refined style of living. It is not the tub that makes Diogenes, the Jove-born, but Diogenes the tub. —Journal, September 1, 1853

We occasionally rested in the shade of a maple or a willow, and drew forth a melon for our refreshment, while we contemplated at our leisure the lapse of the river and of human life; and as that current, with its floating twigs and leaves, so did all things pass in review before us, while far away in cities and marts on this very stream, the old routine was proceeding still. There is, indeed, a tide in the affairs of men, as the poet says, and yet as things flow they circulate, and the ebb always balances the flow. All streams are but tributary to the ocean, which itself does not stream, and the shores are unchanged, but in longer periods than man can measure. Go where we will, we discover infinite change in particulars only, not in generals. When I go into a museum and see the mummies wrapped in their linen bandages, I see that the lives of men began to need reform as long ago as when they walked the earth. I come out into the streets, and meet men who declare that the time is near at hand for the redemption of the race. But as men lived in Thebes, so do they live in Dunstable today. "Time drinketh up the essence of every great and noble action which ought to be performed, and is delayed in the execution." So says Veeshnoo Sarma; and we perceive that the schemers return again and again to common sense and labor. Such is the evidence of history.

"Yet I doubt not through the ages one increasing purpose runs,
And the thoughts of men are widened with the process of the Suns."

There are secret articles in our treaties with the gods, of more importance than all the rest, which the historian can never know.

There are many skillful apprentices, but few master workmen. On every hand we observe a truly wise practice, in education, in morals, and in the arts of life, the embodied wisdom of many an ancient philosopher. Who does not see that heresies have some time prevailed, that reforms have already taken place? All this worldly wisdom might be regarded as the once unamiable heresy of some wise man. Some interests have got a footing on the earth which we have not made sufficient allowance for. Even they who first built these barns and cleared the land thus, had some valor. The abrupt epochs and chasms are smoothed down in history as the inequalities of the plain are concealed by distance. But unless we do more than simply learn the trade of our time, we are but apprentices, and not yet masters of the art of life.

Now that we are casting away these melon seeds, how can we help feeling reproach? He who eats the fruit, should at least plant the seed; aye, if possible, a better seed than that whose fruit he has enjoyed. Seeds! there are seeds enough which need only to be stirred in with the soil where they lie, by an inspired voice or pen, to bear fruit of a divine flavor. O thou spendthrift! Defray thy debt to the world; eat not the seed of institutions, as the luxurious do, but plant it rather, while thou devourest the pulp and tuber for thy subsistence; that so, perchance, one variety may at last be found worthy of preservation. —A Week on the Concord and Merrimack Rivers, "Monday" (September 2, 1839)

Men do not fail commonly for want of knowledge, but for want of prudence to give wisdom the preference. What we need to know in any case is very simple. It is but too easy to establish another durable and harmonious routine. Immediately all parts of nature consent to it. Only make something to take the place of something, and men will behave as if it was the very thing they wanted. They *must* behave, at any rate, and will work up any material. There is always a present and extant life, be it better or worse, which all combine to uphold. We should be slow to mend, my friends, as slow to require mending, "Not hurling, according to the oracle, a transcendent foot towards piety." The language of excitement is at best picturesque merely. You must be calm before you can utter oracles. What was the excitement of the Delphic priestess compared with the calm wisdom of Socrates?—or whoever it was that was wise. —Enthusiasm is a supernatural serenity.

"Men find that action is another thing
Than what they in discoursing papers read;
The world's affairs require in managing
More arts than those wherein you clerks proceed."

As in geology, so in social institutions, we may discover the causes of all past change in the present invariable order of society. The greatest appreciable physical revolutions are the work of the light-footed air, the stealthy-paced water, and the subterranean fire. Aristotle said, "As time never fails, and the universe is eternal, neither the Tanais nor the Nile can have flowed forever." We are independent of the change we detect. The longer the lever the less perceptible its motion. It is the slowest pulsation which is the most vital. The hero then will know how to wait, as well as to make haste. All good abides with him who waiteth *wisely*; we shall sooner overtake the dawn by remaining here than by hurrying over the hills of the west. Be assured that every man's success is in proportion to his *average* ability. The meadow flowers spring and bloom where the waters annually deposit their slime, not where they reach in some freshet only. A man is not his hope, nor his despair, nor yet his past deed. We know not yet what we have done, still less what we are doing. Wait till evening, and other parts of our day's work will shine than we had thought at noon, and we shall discover the real purport of our toil. As when the farmer has reached the end of the furrow and looks back, he can tell best where the pressed earth shines most. —A Week on the Concord and Merrimack Rivers, "Monday"

As our domestic fowls are said to have their original in the wild pheasant of India, so our domestic thoughts have their prototypes in the thoughts of her philosophers. We are dabbling in the very elements of our present conventional and actual life; as if it were the primeval conventicle where how to eat, and to drink, and to sleep, and maintain life with adequate dignity and sincerity, were the questions to be decided. It is later and more intimate with us even than the advice of our nearest friends. And yet it is true for the widest horizon, and read out of doors has relation to the dim mountain line, and is native and aboriginal there. Most books belong to the house and street only, and in the fields their leaves feel very thin. They are bare and obvious, and have no halo nor haze about them. Nature lies far and fair behind them all. But this, as it proceeds from, so it addresses, what is deepest and most abiding in man. It belongs to the noontide of the day, the midsummer of the year, and after the snows have melted, and the waters evaporated in the spring, still its truth speaks freshly to our experience. It helps the sun to shine, and his rays fall on its page to illustrate it. It spends the mornings and the evenings, and makes such an impression on us overnight as to awaken us before dawn, and its influence lingers around us like a fragrance late into the day. It conveys a new gloss to the meadows and the depths of the wood, and its spirit, like a more subtile ether, sweeps along with the prevailing winds of a country. The very locusts and crickets of a summer day are but later or earlier glosses on the Dherma Sastra of the Hindoos, a continuation of the sacred code. —A Week on the Concord and Merrimack Rivers, "Monday"

If I am not I, who will be? —A Week on the Concord and Merrimack Rivers, "Monday"

What are ears? what is Time? that this particular series of sounds called a strain of music, an invisible and fairy troop which never brushed the dew from any mead, can be wafted down through the centuries from Homer to me, and he have been conversant with that same aerial and mysterious charm which now so tingles my ears? What a fine communication from age to age, of the fairest and noblest thoughts, the aspirations of ancient men, even such as were never communicated by speech, is music! It is the flower of language, thought colored and curved, fluent and flexible, its crystal fountain tinged with the sun's rays, and its purling ripples reflecting the grass and the clouds. A strain of music reminds me of a passage of the Vedas, and I associate with it the idea of infinite remoteness, as well as of beauty and serenity, for to the senses that is farthest from us which addresses the greatest depth within us. It teaches us again and again to trust the remotest and finest as the divinest instinct, and makes a dream our only real experience. We feel a sad cheer when we hear it, perchance because we that hear are not one with that which is heard. —A Week on the Concord and Merrimack Rivers, "Monday"

There is but one obligation, and that is the obligation to obey the highest dictate. None can lay me under another which will supersede this. The gods have given me these years without any incumbrance; society has no mortgage on them. —Journal, September 2, 1841

The sublime sentences of Menu carry us back to a time when purification and sacrifice and self-devotion had a place in the faith of men, and were not as now a superstition. They contain a subtle and refined philosophy also, such as in these times is not accompanied with so lofty and pure a devotion. —Journal, September 2, 1841

Not till after several months does an infant find its hands, and it may be seen looking at them with astonishment, holding them up to the light; and so also it finds its toes. How many faculties there are which we have never found! —Journal, September 2, 1851

It is always essential that we love to do what we are doing, do it with a heart. The maturity of the mind, however, may perchance consist with a certain dryness. —Journal, September 2, 1851

While the farmer is concerned about the crops which his fields bear, I will be concerned about the fertility of my human farm. I will watch the winds and the rains as they affect the crop of thought — the crop of crops, ripe thoughts, which glow and rustle and fill the air with fragrance for centuries. —Journal, September 2, 1851

We rowed for some hours between glistening banks before the sun had dried the grass and leaves, or the day had established its character. Its serenity at last seemed the more profound and secure for the denseness of the morning's fog. The river became swifter, and the scenery more pleasing than before. The banks were steep and clayey for the most part, and trickling with water, and where a spring oozed out a few feet above the river the boatmen had cut a trough out of a slab with their axes, and placed it so as to receive the water and fill their jugs conveniently. Sometimes this purer and cooler water, bursting out from under a pine or a rock, was collected into a basin close to the edge of and level with the river, a fountain-head of the Merrimack. So near along life's stream are the fountains of innocence and youth making fertile its sandy margin; and the voyageur will do well to replenish his vessels often at these uncontaminated sources. Some youthful spring, perchance, still empties with tinkling music into the oldest river, even when it is falling into the sea, and we imagine that its music is distinguished by the river-gods from the general lapse of the stream, and falls sweeter on their ears in proportion as it is nearer to the ocean. As the evaporations of the river feed thus these unsuspected springs which filter through its banks, so, perchance, our aspirations fall back again in springs on the margin of life's stream to refresh and purify it. The yellow and tepid river may float his scow, and cheer his eye with its reflections and its ripples, but the boatman quenches his thirst at this small rill alone. It is this purer and cooler element that chiefly sustains his life. —A Week on the Concord and Merrimack Rivers, "Tuesday" (September 3, 1839)

In such a day, in September or October, Walden is a perfect forest mirror, set round with stones as precious to my eye as if fewer or rarer. Nothing so fair, so pure, and at the same time so large, as a lake, perchance, lies on the surface of the earth. Sky water. It needs no fence. Nations come and go without defiling it. It is a mirror which no stone can crack, whose quicksilver will never wear off, whose gilding Nature continually repairs; no storms, no dust, can dim its surface ever fresh; — a mirror in which all impurity presented to it sinks, swept and dusted by the sun's hazy brush — this the light dust-cloth — which retains no breath that is breathed on it, but sends its own to float as clouds high above its surface, and be reflected in its bosom still. —Walden, "The Ponds"

White Pond and Walden are great crystals on the surface of the earth, Lakes of Light. If they were permanently congealed, and small enough to be clutched, they would, perchance, be carried off by slaves, like precious stones, to adorn the heads of emperors; but being liquid, and ample,

and secured to us and our successors forever, we disregard them, and run after the diamond of Kohinoor. They are too pure to have a market value; they contain no muck. How much more beautiful than our lives, how much more transparent than our characters, are they! We never learned meanness of them. How much fairer than the pool before the farmer's door, in which his ducks swim! Hither the clean wild ducks come. Nature has no human inhabitant who appreciates her. The birds with their plumage and their notes are in harmony with the flowers, but what youth or maiden conspires with the wild luxuriant beauty of Nature? She flourishes most alone, far from the towns where they reside. Talk of heaven! ye disgrace earth.
—Walden, "The Ponds"

I see yonder some men in a boat, which floats buoyantly amid the reflections of the trees, like a feather poised in mid-air, or a leaf wafted gently from its twig to the water without turning over. They seem very delicately to have availed themselves of the natural laws, and their floating there looks like a beautiful and successful experiment in philosophy. It reminds me how much more refined and noble the life of man might be made, how its whole economy might be as beautiful as a Tuscan villa — a new and more catholic art, the art of life, which should have its impassioned devotees and make the schools of Greece and Rome to be deserted. —Journal, September 4, 1841

To have a hut here, and a footpath to the brook! For roads, I think that a poet cannot tolerate more than a footpath through the fields; that is wide enough, and for purposes of winged poesy suffices. It is not for the muse to speak of cart-paths. I would fain travel by a footpath round the world. I do not ask the railroads of commerce, not even the cart-paths of the farmer. Pray, what other path would you have than a footpath? What else should wear a path? This is the track of man alone. What is more suggestive to the pensive walker? One walks in a wheel-track with less emotion; he is at a greater distance from man; but this footpath was, perchance, worn by the bare feet of human beings, and he cannot but think with interest of them....

And now, methinks, this wider wood-path is not bad, for it admits of society more conveniently. Two can walk side by side in it in the ruts, aye, and one more in the horse-track. The Indian walked in a single file, more solitary — not side by side, chatting as he went. The woodman's cart and sled make just the path two walkers want through the wood.
—Journal, September 4, 1851

We do not avoid evil by fleeing before it, but by rising above or diving below its plane; as the worm escapes drought and frost by boring a few inches deeper. The frontiers are not east or west, north or south, but wherever a man *fronts* a fact, though that fact be his neighbor, there is an unsettled wilderness between him and Canada, between him and the setting sun, or, farther still, between him and *it*. Let him build himself a log-house with the bark on where he is, *fronting* it, and wage there an Old French war for seven or seventy years, with Indians and Rangers, or whatever else may come between him and the reality, and save his scalp if he can. —A Week on the Concord and Merrimack Rivers, "Thursday" (September 5, 1839)

All the world reposes in beauty to him who preserves equipoise in his life, and moves serenely on his path without secret violence; as he who sails down a stream, he has only to steer, keeping his bark in the middle, and carry it round the falls. —A Week on the Concord and Merrimack Rivers, "Thursday"

No doubt, like plants, we are fed through the atmosphere, and the varying atmospheres of various seasons of the year feed us variously. How often we are sensible of being thus fed and invigorated! And all nature contributes to this aerial diet its food of finest quality. Methinks that in the fragrance of the fruits I get a finer flavor, and in beauty (which is appreciated by sight — the taste and smell of the eye) a finer still. —Journal, September 5, 1851

As we grow old we live more coarsely, we relax a little in our disciplines, and, to some extent, cease to obey our finest instincts. We are more careless about our diet and our chastity. But we should be fastidious to the extreme of sanity. All wisdom is the reward of a discipline, conscious or unconscious. —Journal, September 5, 1851

When a shadow flits across the landscape of the soul, where is the substance? Probably, if we were wise enough, we should see to what virtue we are indebted for any happier moment we enjoy. No doubt we have earned it at some time; for the gifts of Heaven are never quite gratuitous. The constant abrasion and decay of our lives makes the soil of our future growth. The wood which we now mature, when it becomes virgin mould, determines the character of our second growth, whether that be oaks or pines. Every man casts a shadow; not his body only, but his imperfectly mingled spirit. This is his grief. Let him turn which way he will, it falls opposite to the sun; short at noon, long at eve. Did you never see it?—But, referred to the sun, it is widest at its base, which is no greater than his own opacity. The divine light is diffused almost entirely around us, and by means of the refraction of light, or else by a certain self-luminousness, or, as some will have it, transparency, if we preserve ourselves untarnished, we are able to enlighten our shaded side. At any rate, our darkest grief has that bronze color of the moon eclipsed. There is no ill which may not be dissipated, like the dark, if you let in a stronger light upon it. —A Week on the Concord and Merrimack Rivers, "Friday" (September 6, 1839)

The true poem is not that which the public read. There is always a poem not printed on paper, coincident with the production of this, stereotyped in the poet's life. It is *what he has become through his work*. Not how is the idea expressed in stone, or on canvas or paper, is the question, but how far it has obtained form and expression in the life of the artist. His true work will not stand in any prince's gallery.

My life has been the poem I would have writ,
But I could not both live and utter it. —A Week on the Concord and Merrimack Rivers, "Friday"

Behind every man's busy-ness there should be a level of undisturbed serenity and industry, as within the reef encircling a coral isle there is always an expanse of still water, where the depositions are going on which will finally raise it above the surface. —A Week on the Concord and Merrimack Rivers, "Friday"

In summer we live out of doors, and have only impulses and feelings, which are all for action, and must wait commonly for the stillness and longer nights of autumn and winter before any thought will subside; we are sensible that behind the rustling leaves, and the stacks of grain, and the bare clusters of the grape, there is the field of a wholly new life, which no man has lived; that even this earth was made for more mysterious and nobler inhabitants than men and women. In the hues of October sunsets, we see the portals to other mansions than those which we occupy, not far off geographically —

There is a place beyond that flaming hill,
From whence the stars their thin appearance shed,
A place beyond all place, where never ill,
Nor impure thought was ever harbored."

Sometimes a mortal feels in himself Nature, not his Father but his Mother stirs within him, and he becomes immortal with her immortality. From time to time she claims kindredship with us, and some globule from her veins steals up into our own.

I am the autumnal sun,
With autumn gales my race is run;
When will the hazel put forth its flowers,
Or the grape ripen under my bowers?
When will the harvest or the hunter's moon,
Turn my midnight into mid-noon?
I am all sere and yellow,
And to my core mellow.
The mast is dropping within my woods,
The winter is lurking within my moods,
And the rustling of the withered leaf
Is the constant music of my grief.

To an unskilful rhymer the Muse thus spoke in prose:

The moon no longer reflects the day, but rises to her absolute rule, and the husbandman and hunter acknowledge her for their mistress. Asters and golden-rods reign along the way, and the life-everlasting withers not. The fields are reaped and shorn of their pride, but an inward verdure still crowns them. The thistle scatters its down on the pool, and yellow leaves clothe the vine, and naught disturbs the serious life of men. But behind the sheaves, and under the sod, there lurks a ripe fruit, which the reapers have not gathered, the true harvest of the year, which it bears forever, annually watering and maturing it, and man never severs the stalk which bears this palatable fruit. —A Week on the Concord and Merrimack Rivers, "Friday"

Men nowhere, east or west, live yet a *natural* life, round which the vine clings, and which the elm willingly shadows. Man would desecrate it by his touch, and so the beauty of the world remains veiled to him. He needs not only to be spiritualized, but *naturalized*, on the soil of earth. Who shall conceive what kind of roof the heavens might extend over him, what seasons minister to him, and what employment dignify his life! Only the convalescent raises the veil of nature. An immortality in his life would confer immortality on his abode. The winds should be his breath, the seasons his moods, and he should impart of his serenity to Nature herself. But such as we know him he is ephemeral like the scenery which surrounds him, and does not aspire to an enduring existence. When we come down into the distant village, visible from the mountain-top, the nobler inhabitants with whom we peopled it have departed, and left only vermin in its desolate streets. It is the imagination of poets which puts those brave speeches into the mouths of their heroes. They may feign that Cato's last words were

"The earth, the air, and seas I know, and all
The joys and horrors of their peace and wars;
And now will view the Gods' state and the stars,"

but such are not the thoughts nor the destiny of common men. What is this heaven which they expect, if it is no better than they expect? Are they prepared for a better than they can now imagine? Where is the heaven of him who dies on a stage, in a theatre? Here or nowhere is our heaven. —A Week on the Concord and Merrimack Rivers, "Friday"

Nothing is so much to be feared as fear. Atheism may comparatively be popular with God himself. —Journal, September 7, 1851

Our ecstatic states, which appear to yield so little fruit, have this value at least: though in the seasons when our genius reigns we may be powerless for expression, yet, in calmer seasons, when our talent is active, the memory of those rarer moods comes to color our picture and the permanent paint-pot, as it were, into which we dip our brush. Thus no life or experience goes unreported at last; but if it be not solid gold it is gold-leaf, which gilds the furniture of the mind....

We are receiving our portion of the infinite. The art of life! Was there ever anything memorable written upon it? By what discipline to secure the most life, with what care to watch our thoughts. To observe what transpires, not in the street, but in the mind and heart of me! I do not remember any page which will tell me how to spend this afternoon. I do not so much wish to know how to economize time as how to spend it, by what means to grow rich, that the day may not have been in vain....

The scenery, when it is truly seen, reacts on the life of the seer. How to live. How to get the most life. As if you were to teach the young hunter how to entrap his game. How to extract honey from the flower of the world. That is my every-day business. I am as busy as a bee about it.
—Journal, September 7, 1851

I am convinced that men are not well employed, that this is not the way to spend a day. If by patience, if by watching, I can secure one new ray of light, can feel myself elevated for an instant upon Pisgah, the world which was dead prose to me become living and divine, shall I not watch ever? shall I not be a watchman henceforth? If by watching a whole year on the city's walls I may obtain a communication from heaven, shall I not do well to shut up my shop and turn a watchman? Can a youth, a man, do more wisely than to go where his life is to be found? As if

I had suffered that to be rumor which may be verified. We are surrounded by a rich and fertile mystery. May we not probe it, pry into it, employ ourselves about it, a little? To devote your life to the discovery of the divinity in nature or to the eating of oysters, would they not be attended with very different results? —Journal, September 7, 1851

The discoveries which we make abroad are special and particular; those which we make at home are general and significant. The further off, the nearer the surface. The nearer home, the deeper. Go in search of the springs of life, and you will get exercise enough. —Journal, September 7, 1851

To watch for, describe, all the divine features which I detect in Nature.

My profession is to be always on the alert to find God in nature, to know his lurking-places, to attend all the oratorios, the operas, in nature. —Journal, September 7, 1851

I see one of those peculiarly green locusts with long and slender legs on a grass stem, which are often concealed by their color. What green, herbaceous, graminivorous ideas he must have! I wish that my thoughts were as *seasonable* as his! —Journal, September 7, 1857

I am as unfit for any practical purpose — I mean for the furtherance of the world's ends — as gossamer for ship-timber; and I, who am going to be a pencil-maker tomorrow, can sympathize with God Apollo, who served King Admetus for a while on earth. But I believe he found it for his advantage at last — as I am sure I shall, though I shall hold the nobler part at least out of the service. — Letter to Lucy Brown, September 8, 1841

Do not the song of birds and the fireflies go with the grass? While the grass is fresh, the earth is in its vigor. The greenness of the grass is the best symptom or evidence of the earth's youth or health. Perhaps it will be found that when the grass ceases to be fresh and green, or after June, the birds have ceased to sing, and that the fireflies, too, no longer in *myriads* sparkle in the meadows. Perhaps a history of the year would be a history of the grass, or of a leaf, regarding the grass-blades as leaves, for it is equally true that the leaves soon lose their freshness and soundness, and become the prey of insects and of drought. Plants commonly soon cease to grow for the year, unless they may have a fall growth, which is a kind of second spring. In the feelings of the man, too, the year is already past, and he looks forward to the coming winter. His occasional rejuvenescence and faith in the current time is like the aftermath, a scanty crop. The enterprise which he has not already undertaken cannot be undertaken this year. The period of youth is past. The year may be in its summer, its manhood, but it is no longer in the flower of its age. It is a season of withering, of dust and heat, a season of small fruits and trivial experiences. Summer thus answers to manhood. But there is an aftermath in early autumn, and some spring flowers bloom again, followed by an Indian summer of finer atmosphere and pensive beauty. May my life be not destitute of its Indian summer, a season of fine and clear, mild weather in which I may prolong my hunting before the winter comes, when I may once more lie on the ground with faith, as in spring, and even with more serene confidence. And then I will wrap the drapery of summer about me and lie down to pleasant dreams. As one year passes into another through the medium of winter, so does this our life pass into another through the medium of death. —Journal, September 8, 1851

It is good policy to be stirring about your affairs, for the reward of activity and energy is that if you do not accomplish the object that you had professed to yourself, you do accomplish something else. So, in my botanizing or natural history walks, it commonly turns out that, going for one thing, I get another thing. "Though man proposeth, God dispotheth all." —Journal, September 8, 1858

Simple sincerity and truth are rare indeed. —Journal, September 9, 1852

I go to Flint's Pond for the sake of the mountain view from the hill beyond, looking over Concord. I have thought it the best, especially in the winter, which I can get in this neighborhood. It is worth the while to see the mountains in the horizon once a day. I have thus seen some earth which corresponds to my least earthly and trivial, to my most heavenward-looking, thoughts. The earth seen through an azure, an ethereal, veil. They are the natural *temples*, elevated brows, of the earth, looking at which, the thoughts of the beholder are naturally elevated and sublimed — etherealized. I wish to see the earth through the medium of much air or heaven, for there is no paint like the air. Mountains thus seen are worthy of worship. I go to Flint's Pond also to see a rippling lake and a reedy island in its midst — Reed Island. A man should feed his senses with the best that the land affords.

At the entrance to the Deep Cut, I heard the telegraph-wire vibrating like an aeolian harp. It reminded me suddenly — reservedly, with a beautiful paucity of communication, even silently, such was its effect on my thoughts — it reminded me, I say, with a certain pathetic moderation, of what finer and deeper stirrings I was susceptible, which grandly set all argument and dispute aside, a triumphant though transient exhibition of the truth. It told me by the faintest imaginable strain, it told me by the finest strain that a human ear can hear, yet conclusively and past all refutation, that there were higher, infinitely higher, planes of life which it behooved me never to forget. As I was entering the Deep Cut, the wind, which was conveying a message to me from heaven, dropped it on the wire of the telegraph which it vibrated as it passed. I instantly sat down on a stone at the foot of the telegraph-pole, and attended to the communication. It merely said: "Bear in mind, Child, and never for an instant forget, that there are higher planes, infinitely higher planes, of life than this thou art travelling on. Know that the goal is distant, and is upward, and is worthy of all your life's efforts to attain to." And then it ceased, and though I sat some minutes longer I heard nothing more. —Journal, September 12, 1851

The cinnamon fern has begun to yellow and wither. How rich in its decay! *Sic transit gloria mundi!* Die like the leaves, which are most beautiful in their decay. Thus gradually and successively each plant lends its richest color to the general effect, and in the fittest place, and passes away. —Journal, September 12, 1858

How earnestly and rapidly each creature, each flower, is fulfilling its part while its day lasts! Nature never lost a day, nor a moment. As the planet in its orbit and around its axis, so do the seasons, so does time, revolve, with a rapidity inconceivable. In the moment, in the eon, well employed, time ever advances with this rapidity. To an idler the man employed is terribly rapid. He that is not behind his time is swift. The immortals are swift. Clear the track! The plant that waited a whole year, and then blossomed the instant it was ready and the earth was ready for it, without the conception of delay, was rapid. To the conscience of the idle man, the stillness of a placid September day sounds like the din and whirl of a factory. Only employment can still this din in the air. —Journal, September 13, 1852

I must walk more with free senses. It is as bad to study stars and clouds as flowers and stones. I must let my senses wander as my thoughts, my eyes see without looking. Carlyle said that how to observe was to look, but I say that it is rather to see, and the more you look the less you will observe. I have the habit of attention to such excess that my senses get no rest, but suffer from a constant strain. Be not preoccupied with looking. Go not to the object; let it come to you. When I have found myself ever looking down and confining my gaze to the flowers, I have thought it might be well to get into the habit of observing the clouds as a corrective; but no! that study would be just as bad. What I need is not to look at all, but a true sauntering of the eye. —Journal, September 13, 1852

I see in the swamp under the Cliffs the dark, decaying leaves of the skunk-cabbage, four or five spreading every way and so flat and decated as to look like a fungus or mildew, making it doubtful at first what plant it is; but there is the sharp green bud already revealed in the centre between the leaf-stalks, ready to expand in the spring. —Journal, September 14, 1859

Like the fruits, when cooler weather and frosts arrive, we too are braced and ripened. When we shift from the shady to the sunny side of the house, and sit there in an extra coat for warmth, our green and leafy and pulpy thoughts acquire color and flavor, and perchance a sweet nuttiness at last, worth your cracking. —Journal, September 14, 1859

All transcendent goodness is one, though appreciated in different ways, or by different senses. In beauty we see it, in music we hear it, in fragrance we scent it, in the palatable the pure palate tastes it, and in rare health the whole body feels it. The variety is in the surface or manifestation; but the radical identity we fail to express. The lover sees in the glance of his beloved the same beauty that in the sunset paints the western skies. It is the same daimon, here lurking under a human eyelid, and there under the closing eyelids of the day. Here, in small compass, is the ancient and natural beauty of evening and morning. What loving astronomer has ever fathomed the ethereal depths of the eye? —"Love" (an essay included with a letter to Harrison Blake, September, 1852)

It is not enough that we are truthful; we must cherish and carry out high purposes to be truthful about. —"Love"

As I was leaving the Irishman's roof after the rain, bending my steps again to the pond, my haste to catch pickerel, wading in retired meadows, in sloughs and bog-holes, in forlorn and savage places, appeared for an instant trivial to me who had been sent to school and college; but as I ran down the hill toward the reddening west, with the rainbow over my shoulder, and some faint tinkling sounds borne to my ear through the cleansed air, from I know not what quarter, my Good Genius seemed to say — Go fish and hunt far and wide day by day — farther and wider — and rest thee by many brooks and hearth-sides without misgiving. Remember thy Creator in the days of thy youth. Rise free from care before the dawn, and seek adventures. Let the noon find thee by other lakes, and the night overtake thee everywhere at home. There are no larger fields than these, no worthier games than may here be played. Grow wild according to thy nature, like these sedges and brakes, which will never become English bay. Let the thunder rumble; what if it threaten ruin to farmers' crops? That is not its errand to thee. Take shelter under the cloud, while they flee to carts and sheds. Let not to get a living be thy trade, but thy sport. Enjoy the land, but own it not. Through want of enterprise and faith men are where they are, buying and selling, and spending their lives like serfs.

Men come tamely home at night only from the next field or street, where their household echoes haunt, and their life pines because it breathes its own breath over again; their shadows, morning and evening, reach farther than their daily steps. We should come home from far, from adventures, and perils, and discoveries every day, with new experience and character. —Walden, "Baker Farm"

If one listens to the faintest but constant suggestions of his genius, which are certainly true, he sees not to what extremes, or even insanity, it may lead him; and yet that way, as he grows more resolute and faithful, his road lies. The faintest assured objection which one healthy man feels will at length prevail over the arguments and customs of mankind. No man ever followed his genius till it misled him. Though the result were bodily weakness, yet perhaps no one can say that the consequences were to be regretted, for these were a life in conformity to higher principles. If the day and the night are such that you greet them with joy, and life emits a fragrance like flowers and sweet-scented herbs, is more elastic, more starry, more immortal — that is your success. All nature is your congratulation, and you have cause momentarily to bless yourself. The greatest gains and values are farthest from being appreciated. We easily come to doubt if they exist. We soon forget them. They are the highest reality. Perhaps the facts most astounding and most real are never communicated by man to man. The true harvest of my daily life is somewhat as intangible and indescribable as the tints of morning or evening. It is a little star-dust caught, a segment of the rainbow which I have clutched. —Walden, "Higher Laws"

Every man is the builder of a temple, called his body, to the god he worships, after a style purely his own, nor can he get off by hammering marble instead. We are all sculptors and painters, and our material is our own flesh and blood and bones. Any nobleness begins at once to refine a man's features, any meanness or sensuality to imbrute them. —Walden, "Higher Laws"

I think that I could spend a year in the woods, fishing and hunting just enough to sustain myself, with satisfaction. This would be next to living like a philosopher on the fruits of the earth which you had raised, which also attracts me. —"Chesuncook" (September 18, 1853)

As we paddle westward, toward College Meadow, I perceive that a new season has come. The air is incredibly clear. The surface of both land and water is bright, as if washed by the recent rain and then seen through a much finer, clearer, and cooler air. The surface of the river sparkles. I am struck by the soft yellow-brown or brown-yellow of the black willows, stretching in cloud-shaped wreaths far away along the edges of the stream, of a so much mellower and maturer tint than the elms and oaks and most other trees seen above and beyond them....

The sunset was uncommonly fair. Some long amber clouds in the horizon, all on fire with gold, were more glittering than any jewelry. An Orient city to adorn the plates of an annual could not be contrived or imagined more gorgeous. And when you looked with head inverted the effect was increased tenfold, till it seemed a world of enchantment. We only regretted that it had not a due moral effect on us scapegraces.

Nevertheless, when turning my head, I looked at the willowy edge of a Cyanean Meadow and onward to the sober-colored but fine-grained Clamshell Hills, about which there was no glitter, I was inclined to think that the truest beauty was that which surrounded us but which we failed to discern, that the forms and colors which adorn our daily life, not seen afar in the horizon, are our fairest jewelry. —Journal, September 18, 1858

This is a beautiful day, warm but not too warm, a harvest day (I am going down the railroad causeway), the first unquestionable and conspicuous autumnal day, when the willows and button-bushes are a yellowed bower in parallel lines along the swollen and shining stream. The first autumnal tints (of red maples) are now generally noticed. The shrilling of the alder locust fills the air. A brightness as of spring is reflected from the green shorn fields. Both sky and earth are bright. The first clear blue and shining white (of clouds). Cornstalk-tops are stacked about the fields; potatoes are being dug; smokes are seen in the horizon. It is the season or agricultural fairs. If you are not happy today you will hardly be so tomorrow. —Journal, September 18, 1860

Let me see; where was I? Methinks I was nearly in this frame of mind; the world lay about at this angle. Shall I go to heaven or a-fishing? If I should soon bring this meditation to an end, would another so sweet occasion be likely to offer? I was as near being resolved into the essence of things as ever I was in my life. I fear my thoughts will not come back to me. If it would do any good, I would whistle for them. When they make us an offer, is it wise to say, We will think of it? My thoughts have left no track, and I cannot find the path again. What was it that I was thinking of? It was a very hazy day. I will just try these three sentences of Confutsee; they may fetch that state about again. I know not whether it was the dumps or a budding ecstasy. Mem. There never is but one opportunity of a kind. —Walden, "Brute Neighbors"

Thinking this afternoon of the prospect of my writing lectures and going abroad to read them the next winter, I realized how incomparably great the advantages of obscurity and poverty which I have enjoyed so long (and may still perhaps enjoy). I thought with what more than princely, with what poetical, leisure I had spent my years hitherto, without care or engagement, fancy-free. I have given myself up to nature; I have lived so many springs and summers and autumns and winters as if I had nothing else to do but *live* them, and imbibe whatever nutriment they had for me; I have spent a couple of years, for instance, with the flowers chiefly, having none other so binding engagement as to observe when they opened; I could have afforded to spend a whole fall observing the changing tints of the foliage. Ah, how I have thriven on solitude and poverty! I cannot overstate this advantage. I do not see how I could have enjoyed it, if the public had been expecting as much of me as there is danger now that they will. If I go abroad lecturing, how shall I ever recover the lost winter? —Journal, September 19, 1854

As I go through the fields, endeavoring to recover my tone and sanity and to perceive things truly and simply again, after having been perambulating the bounds of the town all the week, and dealing with the most commonplace and worldly-minded men, and emphatically *trivial* things, I feel as if I had committed suicide in a sense. I am again forcibly struck with the truth of the fable of Apollo serving King Admetus, its universal applicability. A fatal coarseness is the result of mixing in the trivial affairs of men. Though I have been associating even with the *select* men of this and the surrounding towns, I feel inexpressibly begrimed. My Pegasus has lost his wings; he has turned a reptile and gone on his belly. Such things are compatible only with a cheap and superficial life. —Journal, September 20, 1851

Already, by the first of September, I had seen two or three small maples turned scarlet across the pond, beneath where the white stems of three aspens diverged, at the point of a promontory, next the water. Ah, many a tale their color told! And gradually from week to week the character of each tree came out, and it admired itself reflected in the smooth mirror of the lake. Each morning the manager of this gallery substituted some new picture, distinguished by more brilliant or harmonious coloring, for the old upon the walls. —Walden, "House Warming"

The maples begin to be ripe. How beautiful when a whole maple on the edge of a swamp is like one great scarlet fruit, full of ripe juices! A sign of the ripening. Every leaf, from lowest limb to topmost spire, is aglow. —Journal, September 21, 1852

In love we impart, each to each, in subtlest immaterial form of thought or atmosphere, the best of ourselves, such as commonly vanishes or evaporates in aspirations, and mutually enrich each other. The lover alone perceives and dwells in a certain human fragrance. To him humanity is not only a flower, but an aroma and a flavor also.
—Journal, September 21, 1852

I sometimes seem to myself to owe all my little success, all for which men commend me, to my vices. I am perhaps more willful than others and make enormous sacrifices, even of others' happiness, it may be, to gain my ends. It would seem even as if nothing good could be accomplished without some vice to aid it. —Journal, September 21, 1854

I do not mean to prescribe rules to strong and valiant natures, who will mind their own affairs whether in heaven or hell, and perchance build more magnificently and spend more lavishly than the richest, without ever impoverishing themselves, not knowing how they live — if, indeed, there are any such, as has been dreamed; nor to those who find their encouragement and inspiration in precisely the present condition of things, and cherish it with the fondness and enthusiasm of lovers — and, to some extent, I reckon myself in this number; I do not speak to those who are well employed, in whatever circumstances, and they know whether they are well employed or not; — but mainly to the mass of men who are discontented, and idly complaining of the hardness of their lot or of the times, when they might improve them. There are some who complain most energetically and inconsolably of any, because they are, as they say, doing their duty. I also have in my mind that seemingly wealthy, but most terribly impoverished class of all, who have accumulated dross, but know not how to use it, or get rid of it, and thus have forged their own golden or silver fetters. —Walden, "Economy"

What an army of non-producers society *produces* — ladies generally (old and young) and gentlemen of *leisure*, so called! Many think themselves well employed as charitable dispensers of wealth which somebody else earned, and these produce nothing, being of the most luxurious habits, are precisely they who want the most, and complain the loudest when they do not get what they want. —Journal, September 23, 1859

It is important, then, that we should air our lives from time to time by removals, and excursions into the fields and woods — starve our vices. Do not sit so long over any cellar-hole as to tempt your neighbor to bid for the privilege of digging saltpetre there.

So live that only the most beautiful wild-flowers will spring up where you have dwelt — harebells, violets, and blue-eyed grass. —Journal, September 23, 1859

I have many affairs to attend to, and feel hurried these days. Great works of art have endless leisure for a background, as the universe has space. Time stands still while they are created. The artist cannot be in a hurry. The earth moves round the sun with inconceivable rapidity, and yet the surface of the lake is not ruffled by it. It is not by compromise, it is not by a timid and feeble repentence, that a man will save his soul and *live*, at last. He has got to *conquer* a clear field, letting Repentence & Co. go. That's a well-meaing but weak firm that has assumed the debts of an old and worthless one. You are to fight in a field where no allowances will be made, no courteous bowing to one-handed knights. You are expected to do your duty, not in spite of every thing but *one*, but in spite of *everything*.
—Journal, September 24, 1859

The red maple has fairly begun to blush in some places by the river. I see one, by the canal behind Barrett's mill, all aglow against the sun. These first trees that change are the most interesting, since they are seen against others still freshly green — such brilliant red on green. I go half a mile out of my way to examine such a red banner. A single tree becomes the crowning beauty of some meadowy vale and attracts the attention of the traveller from afar. At the eleventh hour of the year, some tree which has stood mute and inglorious in some distant vale thus proclaims its character as effectually as if it stood by the highway-side, and it leads our thoughts away from the dusty road into those brave solitudes which it inhabits. The whole tree, thus ripening in advance of its fellows, attains a singular preeminence. I am thrilled at the sight of it, bearing aloft its scarlet standard for its regiment of green-clad foresters around. The forest is the more spirited. —Journal, September 25, 1857

Why will not I, having common sense, write in plain English always; *teach* men in detail how to live a simpler life, etc.; not go off into ——? But I say that I have no scheme about it — no designs on men at all; and, if I had, my mode would be to tempt them with the fruit, and not with the manure. To what end do I lead a simple life at all, pray? That I may teach others to simplify their lives?—and so all our lives be *simplified* merely, like an algebraic formula? Or not, rather, that I may make use of the ground I have cleared, to live more worthily and profitably? I would fain lay the most stress forever on that which is the most important — imports the most to me — though it were only (what it is likely to be) a vibration in the air. As a preacher, I should be prompted to tell men, not so much how to get their wheat bread cheaper, as of the bread of life compared with which *that* is bran. Let a man only taste these loaves, and he becomes a skillful economist at once. He'll not waste much time in earning those. Don't spend your time in drilling soldiers, who may turn out hirelings after all, but give to undrilled peasantry a *country* to fight for. —Letter to Harrison Blake, September 26, 1855

A small red maple has grown, perchance, far away on some moist hillside, a mile from any road, unobserved. It has faithfully discharged the duties of a maple there, all winter and summer, neglected none of its economies, added to its stature in the virtue which belongs to a maple, by a steady growth all summer, and is nearer heaven than it was in the spring, never having gone gadding abroad; and now, in this month of September, when men are turned travellers, hastening to the seaside, or the mountains, or the lakes — in this month of travelling — this modest maple, having ripened its seeds, still without budging an inch, travels on its reputation, runs up its scarlet flag on that hillside, to show that it has finished its summer's work before all other trees, and withdraws from the contest. Thus that modest worth which no scrutiny could have detected when it was most industrious, is, by the very tint of its maturity, by its very blushes, revealed at last to the careless and distant observer. It rejoices in its existence; its reflections are unalloyed. It is the day of thanksgiving with it. At last, its labors for the year being fully consummated and every leaf ripened to its full, it flashes out conspicuous to the eye of the most casual observer, with all the virtue and beauty of a maple — *Acer rubrum*. In its hue is no regret nor pining. Its leaves have been asking their parent from time to time in a whisper, "When shall we redden?" It has faithfully husbanded its sap, and builded without babbling nearer and nearer to heaven. Long since it committed its seeds to the winds and has the satisfaction of knowing perhaps that a thousand little well-behaved maples are already established in business somewhere. It deserves well of Mapledom. It has afforded a shelter to the wandering bird. Its autumnal tint shows how it has spent its summer; it is the hue of its virtue. —Journal, September 27, 1857

It is with leaves as with fruits and woods, animals and men; when they are mature their different characters appear. —Journal, September 30, 1851

The rambler in the most remote woods and pastures little thinks that the bees which are humming so industriously on the rare wild flowers he is plucking for his herbarium, in some out-of-the-way nook, are, like himself, ramblers from the village, perhaps from his own yard, come to get their honey for his hives. All the honey-bees we saw were on the blue-stemmed goldenrod (*Solidago caesia*), which is late, lasts long, which emitted a sweet agreeable fragrance, not on the asters. I felt the richer for this experience. It taught me that even the insects in my path are not loafers, but have their special errands. Not merely and vaguely in this world, but in this hour, each is about its businesss....

It is not in vain that the flowers bloom, and bloom late too, in favored spots. To us they are a culture and a luxury, but to bees meat and drink. The tiny bee which we thought lived far away there in a flower-bell in that remote vale, he is a great voyager, and anon he rises over the top of the wood and sets sail with his sweet cargo straight for his distant haven. How well they know the woods and fields and haunt of every flower! The flowers, perchance, are widely dispersed, because the sweet which they collect from the atmosphere is rare but also widely dispersed, and the bees are enabled to travel far to find it. A precious burthen, like their color and fragrance, a crop which the heavens bear and deposit on the earth. —Journal, September 30, 1852

October

Now too, the first of October, or later, the elms are at the height of their autumnal beauty — great brownish-yellow masses, warm from their September oven, hanging over the highway. Their leaves are perfectly ripe. I wonder if there is any answering ripeness in the lives of the men who live beneath them. —"Autumnal Tints"

The leaves of some trees merely wither, turn brown, and drop off at this season, without any conspicuous flush of beauty, while others now first attain to the climax of their beauty. —Journal, October 2, 1857

Minott is, perhaps, the most poetical farmer — who most realizes to me the poetry of the farmer's life — that I know. He does nothing with haste and drudgery, but as if he loved it. He makes the most of his labor, and takes infinite satisfaction in every part of it. He is not looking forward to the sale of his crops or any pecuniary profit, but he is paid by the constant satisfaction which his labor yields him. He has not too much land to trouble him — too much work to do — no hired man nor boy — but simply to amuse himself and live. He cares not so much to raise a large crop as to do his work well. He knows every pin and nail in his barn. If another linter is to be floored, he lets no hired man rob him of that amusement, but he goes slowly to the woods and, at his leisure, selects a pitch pine tree, cuts it, and hauls it or gets it hauled to the mill; and so he knows the history of his barn floor.

Farming is an amusement which has lasted him longer than gunning or fishing. He is never in a hurry to get his garden planted and yet it is always planted soon enough, and none in the town is kept so beautifully clean.

He always prophesies a failure of the crops, and yet is satisfied with what he gets. His barn floor is fastened down with oak pins, and he prefers them to iron spikes, which he says will rust and give way. He handles and amuses himself with every ear of his corn crop as much as a child with its playthings, and so his small crop goes a great way. He might well cry if it were carried to market. The seed of weeds is no longer in his soil. —Journal, October 4, 1851

See B— a-fishing notwithstanding the wind. A man runs down, fails, loses self-respect, and goes a-fishing, though he were never seen on the river before. Yet methinks his "misfortune" is good for him, and he is the more mellow and humane. Perhaps he begins to perceive more clearly that the object of life is something other than acquiring property, and he really stands in a truer relation to his fellow-men than when he commanded a false respect of them. There he stands at length, perchance better employed than ever, holding communion with nature and himself and coming to understand his real position and relation to men in this world. It is better than a poor debtors' prison, better than most successful money-getting. —Journal, October 4, 1858

It is well to find your employment and amusement in simple and homely things. These wear best and yield most. I think I would rather watch the motions of these cows in their pasture for a day, which I now see all headed one way and slowly advancing — watch them and project their course carefully on a chart, and report all their behavior faithfully — than wander to Europe or Asia and watch other motions there; for it is only ourselves that we report in either case, and perchance we shall report a more restless and worthless self in the latter case than in the first. —Journal, October 5, 1856

The earth shines now as much as, or more than, ever in spring, especially the bare and somewhat faded fields, pastures, stubble, etc. The light is reflected as from a ripe surface, no longer absorbed to secure maturity. —Journal, October 5, 1857

Everything — all fruits and leaves, the reddish-silvery feather grass in clumps, even the surfaces of stone and stubble — are all ripe in this air. Yes, the hue of maturity has come even to that fine silver-topped feathery grass, two or three feet high, in clumps on dry places. I am riper for thought, too. —Journal, October 6, 1857

There is a great difference between this season and a month ago — warm as this happens to be — as between one period of your life and another. A little frost is at the bottom of it. —Journal, October 7, 1851

Look into that hollow all aglow, where the trees are clothed in their vestures of most dazzling tints. Does it not suggest a thousand gypsies beneath, rows of booths, and that man's spirits should rise as high, that the routine of his life should be interrupted by an analogous festivity and rejoicing? —Journal, October 7, 1857

I hear the tolling of a distant funeral bell, and they are conveying a corpse to the churchyard from one of the houses that I see, and its serious sound is more in harmony with this scenery than any ordinary bustle could be. It suggests that a man must die to his present life before he can appreciate his opportunities and the beauty of the abode that is appointed him. —Journal, October 7, 1857

Many people have a foolish way of talking about small things, and apologize for themselves or another having attended to a small thing, having neglected their ordinary business and amused or instructed themselves by attending to a small thing; when, if the truth were known, their ordinary business was the small thing, and almost their whole lives were misspent, but they were such fools as not to know it. —Journal, October 7, 1860

The witch-hazel here is in full blossom on this magical hillside, while its broad yellow leaves are falling. Some bushes are completely bare of leaves, and leather-colored they strew the ground. It is an extremely interesting plant — October and November's child, and yet reminds me of the very earliest spring. Its blossoms smell like the spring, like the willow catkins; by their color as well as fragrance they belong to the saffron dawn of the year, suggesting amid all these signs of autumn, falling leaves and frost, that the life of Nature, by which she eternally flourishes, is untouched. It stands here in the shadow of the side of the hill, while the sunlight from over the top of the hill lights up its top-most sprays and yellow blossoms. Its spray, so joined and angular, is not to be mistaken for any other. I lie on my back with joy under its boughs. While its leaves fall, its blossoms spring. The autumn, then, is indeed a spring. All the year is a spring. I see two blackbirds high overhead, going south, but I am going north in my thought with these hazel blossoms. It is a faery place. This is a part of the immortality of the soul. When I was thinking that it bloomed too late for bees or other insects to extract honey from its flowers — that perchance they yielded no honey — I saw a bee upon it. How important, then, to the bees this late-blossoming plant! —Journal, October 8, 1851

It is the individual and private that demands our sympathy. —Cape Cod (October 9, 1849)

The elms are now at the height of their change. As I look down our street, which is lined with them, now clothed in their very rich brownish-yellow dress, they remind me of the yellowing sheaves of grain, as if the harvest had come to the village itself, and we might expect to find some maturity and *flavor* in the thoughts of the villagers at last. Under those light-rustling piles, just ready to fall on the heads of the walker, how can any crudity or greenness of thought or act prevail? —Journal, October 9, 1857

This is the most serene autumn weather. The chirp of crickets may be heard at noon over all the land. As in summer they are heard only at nightfall, so now by their incessant chirp they usher in the evening of the year. The lively decay of autumn promises as infinite duration and freshness as the green leaves of spring. —Journal, 1839 (undated)

This is the end of the sixth day of glorious weather, which I am tempted to call the finest of the year, so bright and serene the air and such a sheen from the earth, so brilliant the foliage, so pleasantly warm (except, perhaps, this day, which is cooler), too warm for a thick coat — yet not sultry nor oppressive — so ripe the season and our thoughts. Certainly these are the most brilliant days in the year, ushered in, perhaps, by a frosty morning, as this. As a dewy morning in the summer compared with a parched and sultry, languid one, so a frosty morning at this season compared with a merely dry or foggy one. These days you may say that the year is ripened like a fruit by frost, and puts on brilliant tints of maturity but not yet of decay.
—Journal, October 10, 1857

The simplest and most lumpish fungus has a peculiar interest to us, compared with a mere mass of earth, because it is so obviously organic and related to ourselves, however mute. It is the expression of an idea; growth according to a law; matter not dormant, not raw, but inspired, appropriated by spirit. If I take up a handful of earth, however separately interesting the particles may be, their relation to one another appears to be that of mere juxtaposition generally. I might have thrown them together thus. But the humblest fungus betrays a life akin to my own. It is a successful poem in its kind. There is suggested something superior to any particle of matter, in the idea or mind which uses and arranges the particles. —Journal, October 10, 1858

Now it is true autumn; all things are crisp and ripe. —Journal, October 11, 1852

I love very well this cloudy afternoon, so sober and favorable to reflection after so many bright ones. What if the clouds shut out the heavens, provided they concentrate my thoughts and make a more celestial heaven below! I hear crickets plainer; I wander less in my thoughts, am less dissipated; am aware how shallow was the current of my thoughts before. Deep streams are dark, as if there were a cloud in the sky; shallow ones are bright and sparkling, reflecting the sun from their bottoms. The very wind on my cheek seems more fraught with meaning. —Journal, October 12, 1857

The leaves of the azaleas are falling, mostly fallen, and revealing the large blossom-buds, so prepared are they for another year. With man all is uncertainty. He does not confidently look forward to another spring. But examine the root of the savory-leaved aster, and you will find the new shoots, fair purple shoots, which are to curve upward and bear the next year's flowers, already grown half an inch or more in length. Nature is confident. —Journal, October 12, 1858

The alert and energetic man leads a more intellectual life in winter than in summer. In summer the animal and vegetable in him are perfected as in a torrid zone; he lives in his senses mainly. In winter cold reason and not warm passion has her sway; he lives in thought and reflection; he lives a more spiritual, a less sensual, life. If he has passed a merely sensual summer, he passes his winter in a torpid state like some reptiles and other animals.

The mind of man in the two seasons is like the atmosphere of summer compared with the atmosphere of winter. He depends more on himself in winter — on his own resources — less on outward aid. Insects, it is true, disappear for the most part, and those animals which depend on them; but the nobler animals abide with man the severity of winter. He migrates into his mind, to perpetual summer. And to the healthy man the winter of discontent never comes. —Journal, October 13, 1851

The swamp amelanchier is leafing again, as usual. What a pleasing phenomenon, perhaps an Indian-summer growth, an anticipation of the spring, like the notes of birds and frogs, etc., an evidence of warmth and genialness. Its buds are annually awakened by the October sun as if it were spring. The shad-bush is leafing again by the sunny swamp-side. It is like a youthful or poetic thought in old age. Several times I have been cheered by this sight when surveying in former years. The chickadee seems to lisp a sweeter note at the sight of it. I would not fear the winter more than the shad-bush which puts forth fresh and tender leaves on its approach. In the fall I will take this for my coat-of-arms. It seems to detain the sun that expands it. These twigs are so full of life that they can hardly contain themselves. They ignore winter. They anticipate spring. What faith! Away in some warm and sheltered recess in the swamp you find where these leaves have expanded. It is a foretaste of spring. In my latter years, let me have some *shad-bush* thoughts. —Journal, October 13, 1859

In the psychological world there are phenomena analogous to what zoologists call *alternate reproduction*, in which it requires several generations unlike each other to evolve to the perfect animal. Some men's lives are but an aspiration, a yearning toward a higher state, and they are wholly misapprehended, until they are referred to, or traced through, all their metamorphoses. We cannot pronouce upon a man's intellectual and moral state until we foresee what metamorphosis it is preparing him for. —Journal, October 14, 1851

Another, the tenth of these memorable days. We have had some fog the last two or three nights, and this forenoon it was slow to disperse, dog-day-like, but this afternoon it is warmer even than yesterday. I should like it better if it were not so warm. I am glad to reach the coolness of Hubbard's Grove; the coolness is refreshing. It is indeed a golden autumn. These ten days are enough to make the reputation of any climate. A tradition of these might be handed down to posterity. They deserve a notice in history, in the history of Concord. All kinds of crudities have a chance to get ripe this year. Was there ever such an autumn? And yet there was never such a panic and hard times in the commercial world. The merchants and banks are suspending and failing all the country over, but not the sand-banks, solid and warm, and streaked with bloody blackberry vines. You may run upon them as much as you please — even as the crickets do, and find their account in it. They are the stockholders in these banks, and I hear them creaking their content. You may see them on chance any warmer hour. In these banks, too, and such as these, are my funds deposited, a fund of health and enjoyment. Their (the crickets) prosperity and happiness and, I trust, mine do not depend on whether the New York banks suspend or no. We do not rely on such slender security as the thin paper of the Suffolk Bank. To put your trust in such a bank is to be swallowed up and undergo suffocation. Invest, I say, in these country banks. Let your capital be simplicity and contentment. —Journal, October 14, 1857

Sat in the old pasture beyond the Corner Spring Woods to look at that pine wood now at the height of its change, pitch and white. Their change produces a very singular and pleasing effect. They are regularly parti-colored. The last year's leaves, about a foot beneath the extremities of the twigs on all sides, now changed and ready to fall, have their period of brightness as well as broader leaves. They are a clear yellow, contrasting with the fresh and liquid green of the terminal plumes, or this year's leaves. These two quite distinct colors are thus regularly and equally distributed over the whole tree. You have the warmth of the yellow and the coolness of the green. So it should be with our own maturity, not yellow to the very extremity of our shoots, but youthful and untried green ever putting forth afresh at the extremities, foretelling a maturity as yet unknown. The ripe leaves fall to the ground and become nutriment for the green ones, which still aspire to heaven. —Journal, October 14, 1857

If you examine a wood-lot after numerous fires and cuttings, you will be surprised to find how extremely vivacious are the roots of oaks, chestnuts, hickories, birches, cherries, etc. The little trees which look like seedlings of the year will be found commonly to spring from an older root or horizontal shoot or a stump. Those layers which you may have selected to transplant will be found to have too much of old stump and root underground to be removed. They have commonly met with accidents and seen a good deal of the world already. They have learned to endure and bide their time. When you see an oak fully grown and of fair proportions, you little suspect what difficulties it may have encountered in its early youth, what sores it has overgrown, how for years it was a feeble layer lurking under the leaves and scarcely daring to show its head above them, burnt and cut, and browsed by rabbits. Driven back to earth again twenty times — as often as it aspires to the heavens. —Journal, October 14, 1860

It is pleasant to walk over the beds of these fresh, crisp, and rustling leaves. How beautifully they go to their graves! how gently lay themselves down and turn to mould! — painted of a thousand hues, and fit to make the beds of us living. So they troop to their last resting-place, light and frisky. They put on no weeds, but merrily they go scampering over the earth, selecting the spot, choosing a lot, ordering no iron fence, whispering all through the woods about it — some choosing the spot where the bodies of men are mouldering beneath, and meeting them half-way. How many flutterings before they rest quietly in their graves! They that soared so loftily, how contentedly they return to dust again, and are laid low, resigned to lie and decay at the foot of the tree, and afford nourishment to new generations of their kind, as well as to flutter on high! They teach us how to die. One wonders if the time will ever come when men, with their boasted faith in immortality, will lie down as gracefully and as ripe — with such an Indian-summer serenity will shed their bodies, as they do their hair and nails. —"Autumnal Tints"

Be sure your fate
Both keep apart its state,
Not linked with any band,
Even the nobles of the land;
In tended fields with cloth of gold
No place doth hold,
But is more chivalrous than they are,
And sigheth for a nobler war;
A finer strain its trumpet sings,
A brighter gleam its armor flings.

The life that I aspire to live
No man proposeth me,
Only the promise of my heart
Wears its emblazonry.
—The Black Knight, published in *The Dial*, October 1842

There is a vale which none hath seen,
Where foot of man has never been,
Such as here lives with toil and strife,
An anxious and a sinful life.

There every virtue has its birth,
Ere it descends upon the earth,
And thither every deed returns,
Which in the generous bosom burns.

There love is warm, and youth is young,
And poetry is yet unsung.
For Virtue still adventures there,
And freely breathes her native air.

And ever, if you hearken well,
You still may hear its vesper bell,
And tread of high-souled men go by,
Their thoughts conversing with the sky.
—Rumors from an Aeolian Harp, published in *The Dial*,
October 1842

The chickadees sing as if at home. They are not travelling singers hired by any Barnum. Theirs is an honest, homely, heartfelt melody. Shall not the voice of man express as much content as the note of a bird? —Journal, October 15, 1859

To tell the truth, I am planning to get seriously to work after these long months of inefficiency and idleness. I do not know whether you are haunted by any such demon which puts you on the alert to pluck the fruit of each day as it passes, and store it safely in your bin. —Letter to Daniel Ricketson, October 16, 1855

A great part of the pine-needles have just fallen. See the carpet of pale-brown needles under this pine. How light it lies up on the grass, and that great rock, and the wall, resting thick on its top and its shelves, and on the bushes and underwood, hanging lightly! They are not yet flat and reddish, but a more delicate pale brown, and lie up light as joggle-sticks just dropped. The ground is nearly concealed by them. How beautifully they die, making cheerfully their annual contribution to the soil! They fall to rise again; as if they knew that it was not one annual deposit alone that made this rich mould in which pine trees grow. They live in the soil whose fertility and bulk they increase, and in the forests that spring from it. —Journal, October 16, 1857

They go on publishing the "chronological cycles" and "movable festivals of the Church" and the like from mere habit, but how insignificant are these compared with the annual phenomena of your life, which fall within your experience! —Journal, October 16, 1859

The weeds are dressed in their frost jackets, naked down to their close-fitting downy or flannel shirts. Like athletes they challenge the winter, these bare twigs. This cold refines and condenses us. Our spirits are strong, like that pint of cider in the middle of a frozen barrel. —Journal, October 16, 1859

Just as a biennial plant devotes its energies the first year to producing a stock on which it can feed the next, so these little oaks in their earliest years are forming the great fusiform vigorous roots on which they can draw when they are suddenly left to seek their fortunes in a sprout-land. —Journal, October 16, 1860

Methinks the reflections are never purer and more distinct than now at the season of the fall of the leaf, just before the cool twilight has come, when the air has a finer grain. Just as our mental reflections are more distinct at this season of the year, when the evenings grow cool and lengthen and our winter evenings with their brighter fires may be said to begin. And painted ducks, too, often come and sail or float amid the painted leaves. —Journal, October 17, 1858

Why should we not stay at home? This is the land and we are the inhabitants so many travellers come to see. Why should we suffer ourselves to drift outside and lose all our advantages? They were bold navigators once who merely sighted these shores. We were born and bred further in the land than Captain John Smith got. —Journal, October 17, 1858

When La Mountain and Haddock dropped down in the Canada wilderness the other day, they came near starving, or dying of cold and wet and fatigue, not knowing where to look for food or how to shelter themselves. Thus far we have wandered from a simple and independent life. I think that a wise and independent, self-reliant man will have a complete list of the edibles to be found in a primitive country or wilderness, a bill of fare, in his waistcoat pocket at least, to say nothing of matches and warm clothing, so that he can commence a systematic search for them without loss of time. —Journal, October 17, 1858

Last night I was reading Howitt's account of the Australian gold-diggings, and had in my mind's eye the numerous valleys with their streams all cut up with foul pits, ten to a hundred feet deep and half a dozen feet across, as close as

they can be dug, and half full of water, where men
furiously rushed to probe for their fortunes, uncertain
where they shall break ground, not knowing but the gold is
under their camp itself; sometimes digging a hundred and
sixty feet before they strike the vein, or then missing it by a
foot; turned into demons and regardless of each other's
rights in their thirst after riches; whole valleys for thirty
miles suddenly honeycombed by the pits of the miners, so
that hundreds are drowned in them. Standing in water and
covered with mud and clay, they work night and day, dying
of exposure and disease. Having read this and partly
forgotten it, I was thinking of my own unsatisfactory life,
doing as others do without any fixed star habitually in my
eye, my foot not planted on any blessed isle. Then, with
that vision of the diggings before me, I asked myself why I
might not be washing some gold daily, though it were only
the finest particles, or might not sink a shaft down to the
gold within me and work that mine. There is a Ballarat or
Bendigo for you. What though it were a "Sulky Gully"?
Pursue some path, however narrow and crooked, in which
you can walk with love and reverence. Wherever a man
separates from the multitude and goes his own way, there
is a fork in the road, though travellers along the highway
see only a gap in the paling....

Men rush to California and Australia as if the true gold
were to be found in that direction; but that is to go in the
very opposite extreme to where it lies. They go
prospecting further and further away from the true lead,
and are most unfortunate when most successful. Is not our
native soil auriferous? Does not a stream from the golden
mountains flow through our native valley? and has it not
for more than geologic ages been bringing down the
shining particles and the nuggets? Yet, strange to tell, if a
digger steal away prospecting for this true gold into the
unexplored solitudes, there is no danger, alas, that any will
dog his steps and endeavor to supplant him. He may claim

and undermine the whole valley, even the cultivated and uninhabited portions, his whole life long in peace, and no one will ever dispute his claim. —Journal, October 18, 1855

The sugar maples on the Common are now at the height of their beauty. One, the earliest to change, is partly bare. This turned so early and so deep a scarlet that some thought that it was surely going to die. Also that one at the head of the Turnpike reveals its character now as far as you can see it. —Journal, October 18, 1858

A man of rare common sense and directness of speech, as of action; a transcendentalist above all, a man of ideas and principles — that was what distinguished him. Not yielding to a whim or transient impulse, but carrying out the purpose of a life. —"A Plea for Captain John Brown" (based on a lecture first delivered October 18, 1859)

Such do not know that like the seed is the fruit, and that, in the moral world, when good seed is planted, good fruit is inevitable, and does not depend on our watering and cultivating; that when you plant, or bury, a hero in his field, a crop of heroes is sure to spring up. This is a seed of such force and vitality, that it does not ask our leave to germinate. —"A Plea for Captain John Brown"

Though you may not approve of his method or his principles, recognize his magnanimity. —"A Plea for Captain John Brown"

Do your work, and finish it. If you know how to begin, you will know when to end. —"A Plea for Captain John Brown"

Why can we not oftener refresh one another with original thoughts? If the fragrance of the dicksonia fern is so grateful and suggestive to us, how much more refreshing and encouraging — re-creating — would be fresh and fragrant thoughts communicated to us fresh from a man's experience and life! I want none of his pity, nor sympathy, in the common sense, but that he should emit and communicate to me his essential fragrance, that he should not be forever repenting and going to church (when not otherwise sinning), but, as it were, going a-huckleberrying in the fields of thought, and enrich all the world with his visions and his joys. —Journal, October 18, 1859

For aught I know, I would much rather have a young oak wood which has succeeded to pines than one that has succeeded to oaks, for they will make better trees, not only because the soil is new to them, but because they are all seedlings, while in the other case far the greater part are sprouts; just as I would prefer apple trees five or six years from the seed for my orchard to suckers from those which have come to maturity or decayed. Otherwise your young oaks will soon, when half grown, have the diseases of old trees — warts and decay. —Journal, October 18, 1860

Agreeable to me is the scent of the withered and decaying leaves and pads, pontederias, on each side as I paddle up the river this still cloudy day, with the faint twittering or chirping of a sparrow still amid the bare button-bushes. It is the scent of the year, passing away like a decaying fungus, but leaving a rich mould, I trust. —Journal, October 20, 1855

It is always a recommendation to me to know that a man has ever been poor, has been regularly born into this world, knows the language. I require to be assured of certain philosophers that they have once been barefooted, footsore, have eaten a crust because they had nothing better, and know what sweetness resides in it. —Journal, October 20, 1855

I had gone but little way on the old Carlisle road when I saw Brooks Clark, who is now about eighty and bent like a bow, hastening along the road, barefooted, as usual, with an axe in his hand; was in haste perhaps on account of the cold wind on his bare feet. It is he who took the *Centinel* so long. When he got up to me, I saw that beside the axe in one hand, he had his shoes in the other, filled with knurly apples and a dead robin. He stopped and talked with me a few moments; said that we had a noble autumn and might now expect some cold weather. I asked if he had found the robin dead. No, he said, he found it with its wing broken and killed it. He also added that he had found some apples in the woods, and as he hadn't anything to carry them in, he put 'em in his shoes. They were queer looking trays to carry fruit in. How many he got in along toward the toes, I don't know. I noticed, too, that his pockets were stuffed with them. His old tattered frock coat was hanging in strips about the skirts, as were his pantaloons about his naked feet. He appeared to have been out on a scout this gusty afternoon, to see what he could find, as the youngest boy might. It pleased me to see this cheery old man, with such a feeble hold on life, bent almost double, thus enjoying the evening of his days. Far be it from me to call it avarice or penury, this childlike delight in finding something in the woods or fields and carrying it home in the October evening, as a trophy to be added to his winter's store. Oh, no; he was happy to be Nature's pensioner still, and bird-like to pick up his living. Better his robin than your turkey, his shoes full of apples than your barrels full; they will be sweeter and suggest a better tale. He can afford to tell how he got them, and we to listen. There is an old wife too, at home, to share them and hear how they were obtained. Like an old squirrel shuffling to his hole with his nut. Far less pleasing to me the loaded wain, more suggestive of avarice and of spiritual penury.

This old man's cheeriness was worth a thousand of the church's sacraments and memento mori's. It was better than a prayerful mood. It proves to me old age as tolerable, as happy, as infancy. I was glad of an occasion to suspect that this afternoon he had not been at "work" but living somewhat after my own fashion (though he did not explain the axe) — had been out to see what nature had for him, and now was hastening home to a burrow he knew, where he could warm his old feet. If he had been a young man, he would probably have thrown away his apples and put on his shoes when he saw me coming, for shame. But old age is manlier; it has learned to live, makes fewer apologies, like infancy. —Journal, October 20, 1857

Ebby Hubbard's oaks, now turned a sober and warm red and yellow, have a very rich crisp and curled look, especially against the green pines. This is when the ripe high-colored leaves have begun to curl and wither. Then they have a warm and harmonious tint. First they are ripened by the progress of the year, and the character of each appears in distinct colors. Then come the severe frosts and, dulling the brilliancy of most, produce a harmony of warm brown or red and yellow tinges throughout the forest, something like marbling and painting over it, making one shade run into another.
—Journal, October 22, 1852

Yesterday, toward night, gave Sophia and mother a sail as far as the Battle-Ground. One-eyed John Goodwin, the fisherman, was loading into a hand-cart and conveying home the piles of driftwood which of late he had collected with his boat. It was a beautiful evening, and a clear amber sunset lit up all the eastern shores; and that man's employment, so simple and direct — though he is regarded by most as a vicious character — whose whole motive was so easy to fathom — thus to obtain his winter's wood — charmed me unspeakably. So much do we love actions that are simple. They are all poetic. We, too, would fain be so employed. So unlike the pursuits of most men, so artificial or complicated. Consider how the broker collects his winter's wood, what sport he makes of it, what is his boat and hand-cart! Postponing instant life, he makes haste to Boston in the cars, and there deals in stocks, not quite relishing his employment — and so earns the money with which he buys his fuel. And when, by chance, I meet him about this indirect and complicated business, I am not struck with the beauty of his employment. It does not harmonize with the sunset. How much more the former consults his genius, some genius at any rate! Now I should love to get my fuel so — I have got some so — but though I may be glad to have it, I do not love to get it in any other way less simple and direct. For if I buy one necessary of life, I cheat myself to some extent, I deprive myself of the pleasure, the inexpressible joy, which is the unfailing reward of satisfying any want of our nature simply and truly.

No *trade* is simple, but artificial and complex. It postpones life and substitutes death. It goes against the grain. If the first generation does not die of it, the third or fourth does. —Journal, October 22, 1853

How welcome this still, cloudy day! An inward sunniness more than makes up for the want of an external one. —Journal, October 22, 1855

There are two seasons when the leaves are in their glory, their green and perfect youth in June and this their ripe old age. —Journal, October 22, 1855

The oaks stand browned and crisped (amid the pines), their bright colors for the most part burnt out, like a loaf that is baked, and suggest an equal wholesomeness. The whole tree is now not only ripe but, as it were, a fruit perfectly cooked by the sun. That same sun which called forth its leaves in the spring has now, aided by the frost, sealed up their fountains for the year and withered them. The order has gone forth for them to rest. As each tree casts its leaves it stands careless and free, like a horse freed from his harness, or like one who has done his year's work and now stands unnoticed, but with concentrated strength and contentment, ready to brave the blasts of winter without a murmur. —Journal, October 22, 1858

Now is the time for chestnuts. A stone cast against the trees shakes them down in showers upon one's head and shoulders. But I can cannot excuse myself for using the stone. It is not innocent, it is not just, so to maltreat the tree that feeds us. I am not disturbed by considering that if I thus shorten its life I shall not enjoy its fruit so long, but am prompted to a more innocent course by motives purely of humanity. I sympathize with the tree, yet I heaved a big stone against the trunks like a robber — not too good to commit murder. I trust I shall never do it again. These gifts should be accepted, not merely with gentleness, but with a certain humble gratitude. The tree whose fruit we would obtain should not be too rudely shaken even. It is not a time of distress, when a little haste and violence even might be pardoned. It is worse than boorish, it is criminal, to inflict an unnecessary injury on the tree that feeds or shadows us. Old trees are our parents, and our parents' parents, perchance. If you would learn the secrets of Nature, you must practice more humanity than others. The thought that I was robbing myself by injuring the tree did not ocur to me, but I was affected as if I had cast a rock at a sentient being — with a duller sense than my own, it is true, but yet a distant relation. Behold a man cutting down a tree to come at the fruit! What is the moral of such an act? —Journal, October 23, 1855

Every part of nature teaches that the passing away of one life is the making room for another. The oak dies down to the ground, leaving within its rind a rich virgin mould, which will impart a vigorous life to an infant forest. The pine leaves a sandy and sterile soil, the harder woods a strong and fruitful mould.

So this constant abrasion and decay makes the soil of my future growth. As I live now so shall I reap. If I grow pines and birches, my virgin mould will not sustain the oak; but pines and birches, or, perchance, weeds and brambles, will constitute my second growth. —Journal, October 24, 1837

I think you may have a grand time this winter pursuing some study — keeping a journal, or the like — while the snow lies deep without. Winter is the time for study, you know, and the colder it is the more studious we are.
—Letter to Sophia Thoreau, October 24, 1847

I find my account in this long-continued monotonous labor of picking chestnuts all the afternoon, brushing the leaves aside without looking up, absorbed in that, and forgetting better things awhile. My eye is educated to discover anything on the ground, as chestnuts, etc. It is probably wholesomer to look at the ground much than at the heavens. As I go stooping and brushing the leaves aside by the hour, I am not thinking of chestnuts merely, but I find myself humming a thought of more significance. This occupation affords a certain broad pause and opportunity to start again afterward — turn over a new leaf. —Journal, October 24, 1857

A northeast storm, though not much rain falls today, but a fine driving mizzle or "drisk." This, as usual, brings the geese, and at 2:30 P.M. I see two flocks go over. I hear that some were seen two or three weeks ago (??), faintly honking. A great many must go over today and also alight in this neighborhood. This weather warns them of the approach of winter, and this wind speeds them on their way. Surely, then, while geese fly overhead we can live here as contentedly as they do at York Factory on Hudson's Bay. We shall perchance be as well provisioned and have as good society as they. Let us be of good cheer, then, and expect the annual vessel which brings the spring to us without fail. —Journal, October 24, 1858

The brilliant autumnal colors are red and yellow and the various tints, hues, and shades of these. Blue is reserved to be the color of the sky, but yellow and red are the colors of the earth flower. Every fruit, on ripening, and just before its fall, acquires a bright tint. So do the leaves; so the sky before the end of the day, and the year near its setting. October is the red sunset sky, November the later twilight. Color stands for all ripeness and success. We have dreamed that the hero should carry his color aloft, as a symbol of the ripeness of his virtue. The noblest feature, the eye, is the fairest-colored, the jewel of the body. The warrior's flag is the flower which precedes his fruit. He unfurls his flag to the breeze with such confidence and brag as the flower its petals. Now we shall see what kind of fruit will succeed. —Journal, October 24, 1858

The autumnal change of our woods has not made a deep impression on our own literature yet. October has hardly tinged our poetry.

A great many, who have spent their lives in cities, and have never chanced to come into the country at this season, have never seen this, the flower, or rather the ripe fruit, of the year. I remember riding with one such citizen, who, though a fortnight too late for the most brilliant tints, was taken by surprise, and would not believe that there had been any brighter. He had never heard of this phenomenon before. Not only many in our towns have never witnessed it, but it is scarcely remembered by the majority from year to year.

Most appear to confound changed leaves with withered ones, as if they were to confound ripe apples with rotten ones. I think that the change to some higher color in a leaf is an evidence that it has arrived at a late and perfect maturity, answering to the maturity of fruits. It is generally the lowest and oldest leaves which change first. But as the perfect-winged and usually bright-colored insect is short-lived, so the leaves ripen but to fall.

Generally, every fruit, on ripening, and just before it falls, when it commences a more independent and individual existence, requiring less nourishment from any source, and that not so much from the earth through its stem as from the sun and air, acquires a bright tint. So do leaves. The physiologist says it is "due to an increased absorption of oxygen." That is the scientific account of the matter — only a reassertion of the fact. But I am more interested in the rosy cheek than I am to know what particular diet the maiden fed on. The very forest and herbage, the pellicle of the earth, must acquire a bright color, an evidence of its ripeness — as if the globe itself were a fruit on its stem, with ever a cheek toward the sun.

Flowers are but colored leaves, fruits but ripe ones. The edible part of most fruits is, as the physiologist says, "the parenchyma or fleshy tissue of the leaf," of which they are formed.

Our appetites have commonly confined our views of ripeness and its phenomena, color, mellowness, and perfectness, to the fruits which we eat, and we are wont to

forget that an immense harvest which we do not eat, hardly use at all, is annually ripened by Nature. At our annual cattle-shows and horticultural exhibitions, we make, as we think, a great show of fair fruits, destined, however, to a rather ignoble end, fruits not valued for their beauty chiefly. But round about and within our towns there is annually another show of fruits, on an infinitely grander scale, fruits which address our taste for beauty alone.
—"Autumnal Tints"

Now that the leaves are fallen (for a few days), the long yellow buds (often red-pointed) which sleep along the twigs of the *S. discolor* are very conspicuous and quite interesting, already even carrying our thoughts forward to spring. I noticed them first on the 22nd. They may be put with the azalea buds already noticed. Even bleak and barren November wears these gems on her breast in sign of the coming year. How many thoughts lie undeveloped, as it were dormant, like these buds, in the minds of men!

This is the coolest day thus far, reminded me that I have only a half-thick coat on. The easterly wind comes cold into my ear, as yet unused to it. Yet this first decided coolness — not to say wintriness — is not only bracing but exhilirating and concentrating our forces. So much the more I have a hearth and heart *within* me. We step more briskly, and brace ourselves against the winter. —Journal, October 25, 1858

How watchful we must be to keep the crystal well that we were made, clear! that it be not made turbid by our contact with the world, so that it will not reflect objects. What other liberty is there worth having, if we have not freedom and peace in our minds — if our inmost and most private man is but a sour and turbid pool? Often we are so jarred by chagrins in dealing with the world, that we cannot reflect. Everything beautiful impresses us as sufficient to itself. Many men who have had much intercourse with the world and not borne the trial well affect me as all resistance, all bur and rind, without any gentleman, or tender and innocent core left. They have become hedgehogs.

Ah! the world is too much with us, and our whole soul is stained by what it works in, like the dyer's hand. A man had better starve at once than lose his innocence in the process of getting his bread. This is the pool of Bethsaida which must be stilled and become smooth before we can enter to be healed. If within the old man there is not a young man — within the sophisticated, one unsophisticated — then he is but one of the devil's angels.

It is surprising how any reminiscence of a different season of the year affects us. When I meet with any such in my Journal, it affects me as poetry, and I appreciate that other season and that particular phenomenon more than at any time. The world so seen is all one spring, full of beauty. You only need to make a faithful record of an average summer's day experience and summer mood, and read it in the winter, and it will carry you back to more than that summer day alone could show. Only the rarest flower, the purest melody, of the season thus comes down to us.
—Journal, October 26, 1853

When, after feeling dissatisfied with my life, I aspire to something better, am more scrupulous, more reserved and continent, as if expecting somewhat, suddenly I find myself full of life as a nut of meat — am overflowing with a quiet, genial mirthfulness. I think to myself, I must attend to my diet; I must get up earlier and take a morning walk; I must have done with luxuries and devote myself to the muse. So I dam up my stream, and my waters gather to a head. I am freighted with thought. —Journal, October 26, 1853

I sometimes think that I must go off to some wilderness where I can have a better opportunity to play life — can find more suitable materials to build my house with, and enjoy the pleasure of collecting my fuel in the forest. I have more taste for the wild sports of hunting, fishing, wigwam-building, making garments of skins, and collecting wood wherever you find it, than for butchering, farming, carpentry, working in a factory, or going to a wood market.
—Journal, October 26, 1855

A driving east or northeast storm. I can see through the drisk only a mile. The river is getting partly over the meadows at last, and my spirits rise with it. Methinks this rise of the waters must affect every thought and deed in the town. It qualifies my sentence and life....

These regular phenomena of the seasons get at last to be — they were *at first*, of course — simply and plainly phenomena or phases of my life. The seasons and all their changes are in me. I see not a dead eel or a floating snake, or a gull, but it rounds my life and is like a line or accent in its poem. Almost I believe the Concord would not rise and overflow its banks again, were I not here. After a while I learn what my moods and seasons are. I would have nothing subtracted. I can imagine nothing added. My moods are thus periodical, not two days in my year alike. The perfect correspondence of Nature to man, so that he is at home in her! —Journal, October 26, 1857

My loftiest thought is somewhat like an eagle that suddenly comes into the field of view, suggesting great things and thrilling the beholder, as if it were bound hitherward with a message for me; but it comes no nearer, but circles and soars away, growing dimmer, disappointing me, till it is lost behind a cliff or a cloud. —Journal, October 26, 1857

Winter, with its *inwardness*, is upon us. A man is constrained to sit down, and to think. —Journal, October 27, 1851

I try one of the wild apples in my desk. It is remarkable that the wild apples which I praise as so spirited and racy when eaten in the fields and woods, when brought into the house have a harsh and crabbed taste. As shells and pebbles must be beheld on the seashore, so these October fruits must be tasted in a bracing walk amid the somewhat bracing airs of late October. To appreciate their wild and sharp flavors, it seems necessary that you be breathing the sharp October or November air. The outdoor air and exercise which the walker gets give a different tone to his palate, and he craves a fruit which the sedentary would call harsh and crabbed even. The palate rejects a wild apple eaten in the house — so of haws and acorns — and demands a tamed one, for here you miss that October air which is the wine it is eaten with. I frequently pluck wild apples of so rich and spicy a flavor that I wonder all orchardists do not get a scion from them, but when I have brought home my pockets full, and taste them in the house, they are unexpectedly harsh, crude things. They must be eaten in the fields, when your system is all aglow with exercise, the frosty weather nips your fingers (in November), the wind rattles the bare boughs and rustles the leaves, and the jay is heard screaming around.

So there is one thought for the field, another for the house. I would have my thoughts, like wild apples, to be food for walkers, and will not warrant them to be palatable if tasted in the house. —Journal, October 27, 1855

The fall (strictly speaking) is approaching an end in this probably annual northeast storm. Thus the summer winds up its accounts. The Indians, it is said, did not look for winter till the springs were full. Long-continued rain and wind come to settle the accounts of the year, filling the springs for winter. The ducks and other fowl, reminded of the lateness thus, go by. The few remaining leaves come fluttering down. The snow-flea (as today) is washed out of the bark of meadow trees and covers the surface of the flood. The winter's wood is bargained for and being hauled. This storm reminds men to put things on a winter footing. There is not much more for the farmer to do in the fields. —Journal, October 27, 1857

It was a serene, elysian light, in which the deeds I have dreamed of but not realized might have been performed. At the eleventh hour, late in the year, we have visions of the life we might have lived. No perfectly fair weather ever offered such an arena for noble acts. It was such a light as we behold but dwell not in! —Journal, October 28, 1857

Suppose I see a single green apple, brought to perfection on some thorny shrub, far in a wild pasture where no cow has plucked it. It is an agreeable surprise. What chemistry has been work there? It affects me somewhat like a work of art. I see some shrubs which cattle have browsed for twenty years, keeping them down and compelling them to spread, until at last they are so broad they become their own fence and some interior shoot darts upward and bears its fruit! What a lesson to man! So are human beings, referred to the highest standard, the celestial fruit which they suggest and aspire to bear, browsed on by fate, and only the most persistent and strongest genius prevails, defends itself, sends a tender scion upward at last, and drops its perfect fruit on the ungrateful earth; and that fruit, though somewhat smaller, perchance, is essentially the same in flavor as if it had grown in a garden. That fruit seems all the sweeter and more palatable even for the very difficulties it has contended with.
—Journal, October 28, 1857

How munificent is Nature to create this profusion of wild fruit, as it were merely to gratify our eyes! Though inedible they are more wholesome to my immortal part, and stand by me longer, than the fruits which I eat. If they had been plums or chestnuts I should have eaten them on the spot and probably forgotten them. They would have afforded only a momentary gratification, but being acorns, I remember, as it were *feed* on, them still. They are untasted fruits forever in store for me. I know not of their flavor as yet. That is postponed to some still unimagined winter evening. Those which we admire but do not eat are nuts of the gods. When time is no more we shall crack them.
—Journal, October 28, 1858

When the leaves fall, the whole earth is a cemetery pleasant to walk in. I love to wander and muse over them in their graves, returning to dust again. Here are no lying or vain epitaphs. The scent of their decay is pleasant to me. I buy no lot in the cemetery which my townsmen have just *consecrated* with a poem and an auction, paying so much for a choice. *Here* is room enough for me. —Journal, October 29, 1855

Forever in my dream and in my morning thought
Eastward a mount ascends —
But when in the sunbeam its hard outline is sought—
It all dissolves and ends.

The woods that way are gates — the pastures too slope up
To an unearthly ground—
But when I ask my mates, to take the staff and cup
It can no more be found—

Perchance I have no shoes fit for the lofty soil
Where my thoughts graze—
No properly spun clues — nor well strained midday oil!
Or — must I mend my ways?

It is a promised land which I have not yet earned,
I have not made beginning.
With consecrated hand — I have not even learned
To lay the underpinning.

The mountain sinks by day — as do my lofty thoughts,
Because I'm not high-minded.
If I could think alway above these hills and warts
I should see it, though blinded.

It is a spiral path within the pilgrim's soul
Leads to this mountain's brow
Commencing at his hearth he reaches to this goal
He knows not when nor how.
—Journal, October 29, 1857

I think that men generally are mistaken with regard to amusements. Every one who deserves to be regarded as higher than the brute may be supposed to have an earnest purpose, to accomplish which is the object of his existence, and this is at once his work and his supremest pleasure; and for diversion and relaxation, for suggestion and education and strength, there is offered the never-failing amusement of getting a living — never-failing, I mean, when temperately indulged in. I know of no such amusement — so wholesome and in every sense profitable — for instance, as to spend an hour or two in a day picking some berries or other fruits which will be food for the winter, or collecting driftwood from the river for fuel, or cultivating the few beans and potatoes which I want. Theatres and operas, which intoxicate for a season, are as nothing compared to these pursuits. And so it is with all the true arts of life. Farming and building and manufacturing and sailing are the greatest and wholesomest amusements that were ever invented (for God invented them), and I suppose that the farmers and mechanics know it, only I think they indulge to excess generally, and so what was meant for a joy becomes the sweat of the brow. Gambling, horse-racing, loafing, and rowdyism generally, after all tempt but few. The mass are tempted by those other amusements, of farming, etc. It is a great amusement, and more profitable than I could have invented, to go and spend an afternoon hour picking cranberries. By these various pursuits your experience becomes singularly complete and rounded. The novelty and significance of such pursuits are remarkable. Such is the path by which we climb to the heights of our being; and compare the poetry which such simple pursuits have inspired with the unreadable volumes which have been written about art.

Who is the most profitable companion? He who has been picking cranberries and chopping wood, or he has been attending the opera all his days? I find when I have been building a fence or surveying a farm, or even collecting simples, that these were the true paths to perception and enjoyment. My being seems to have put forth new roots and to be more strongly planted. This is the true way to crack the nut of happiness. If, as a poet or naturalist, you wish to explore a given neighborhood, go and live in it, i.e., get your living in it. Fish in its streams, hunt in its forests, gather fuel from its water, its woods, cultivate the ground, and pluck the wild fruits, etc., etc. This will be the surest and speediest way to those perceptions you covet. No amusement has worn better than farming. It tempts men just as strongly today as in the day of Cincinnatus. Healthily and properly pursued, it is not a whit more grave than huckleberrying, and if it takes any airs on itself as superior then there's something wrong about it.

I have aspired to practice in succession all the honest arts of life, that I may gather all their fruits. But then, if you are intemperate, if you toil to raise an unnecessary amount of corn, even the large crop of wheat becomes as a small crop of chaff.

If our living were once honestly got, then it would be time to invent other amusements. —Journal, October 29, 1857

I suspect that spouts, like the chestnut, for example, may grow very rapidly, and make large trees in comparatively few years, but they will be decaying as fast at the core as they are growing at the circumference. The stumps of chestnuts, especially sprouts, are very shaky. It is with men as with trees; you must grow slowly to last long. —Journal, October 29, 1860

If you are afflicted with melancholy at this season, go to the swamp and see the brave spears of skunk-cabbage buds already advanced toward a new year. Their gravestones are not bespoken yet. Who shall be sexton to them? Is it the winter of their discontent? Do they seem to have lain down to die, despairing of skunk-cabbagedom? "Up and at 'em," "Give it to 'em,", "Excelsior," "Put it through," — these are their mottoes. Mortal human creatures must take a little respite in this fall of the year; their spirits do flag a little. There is a little questioning of destiny, and thinking to go like cowards to where the "weary shall be at rest." But not so with the skunk-cabbage. Its withered leaves are transfixed by a rising bud. Winter and death are ignored; the circle of life is complete. Are these false prophets? Is it a lie or a vain boast underneath the skunk-cabbage bud, pushing it upward and lifting the dead leaves with it? They rest with spears advanced; they rest to shoot! —Journal, October 31, 1857

Going up the side of a cliff about the first of November, I saw a vigorous young apple-tree, which, planted by birds or cows, had shot up amid the rocks and open woods there, and had now much fruit on it, uninjured by the frosts, when all cultivated apples were gathered. It was a rank wild growth, with many green leaves on it still, and made an impression of thorniness. The fruit was hard and green, but looked as if it would be palatable in the winter. Some was dangling on the twigs, but more half-buried in the wet leaves under the tree, or rolled far down the hill amid the rocks. The owner knows nothing of it. The day was not observed when it first blossomed, nor when it first bore fruit, unless by the chickadee. There was no dancing on the green beneath it in its honor, and now there is no hand to pluck its fruit, which is only gnawed by squirrels, as I perceive. It has done double duty, not only borne this crop, but each twig has grown a foot into the air. And this is such fruit! bigger than many berries, we must admit, and carried home will be sound and palatable next spring. What care I for Iduna's apples so long as I can get these?

When I go by this shrub thus late and hardy, and see its dangling fruit, I respect the tree, and I am grateful for Nature's bounty, even though I cannot eat it. Here on this rugged and woody hillside has grown an apple-tree, not planted by man, no relic of a former orchard, but a natural growth, like the pines and oaks. Most fruits which we prize and use depend entirely on our care. Corn and grain, potatoes, peaches, melons, etc., depend altogether on our planting; but the apple emulates man's independence and enterprise. —"Wild Apples"

But though these [crab apples] are indigenous, like the Indians, I doubt whether they are any hardier than those back-woodsmen among the apple-trees, which, though descended from cultivated stocks, plant themselves in distant fields and forests, where the soil is favorable to them. I know of no trees which have more difficulties to contend with, and which more sturdily resist their foes. These are the ones whose story we have to tell. It oftentimes reads thus:

Near the beginning of May, we notice little thickets of apple-trees just springing up in the pastures where cattle have been, as the rocky ones of our Easter-brooks Country, or the top of Nobscot Hill in Sudbury. One or two of these perhaps survive the drought and other accidents, their very birthplace defending them against the encroaching grass and some other dangers, at first.

In two years' time 't had thus
    Reached the level of the rocks,
Admired the stretching world,
    Nor feared the wandering flocks.
But at this tender age
    Its sufferings began:
There came a browsing ox
    And cut it down a span.

This time, perhaps, the ox does not notice it amid the grass; but the next year, when it has grown more stout, he recognizes it for a fellow-emigrant from the old country, the flavor of whose leaves and twigs he well knows; and though at first he pauses to welcome it, and express his surprise, and gets for answer, "The same cause that brought you here brought me," he nevertheless browses it again, reflecting, it may be, that he has some title to it.

Thus cut down annually, it does not despair; but, putting forth two short twigs for every one cut off, it spreads out low along the ground in the hollows or between the rocks, growing more stout and scrubby, until it forms, not a tree as yet, but a little pyramidal, stiff, twiggy mass, almost as solid and impenetrable as a rock. Some of the densest and most impenetrable clumps of bushes that I have ever seen, as well, on account of the closeness and stubbornness of their branches as of their thorns, have been these wild-apple scrubs. They are more like the scrubby fir and black spruce on which you stand, and sometimes walk, on the tops of mountains, where cold is the demon they contend with, than anything else. No wonder they are prompted to grow thorns at last, to defend themselves against such foes. In their thorniness, however, there is no malice, only some malic acid.

The rocky pastures of the tract I have referred to for they maintain their ground best in a rocky field are thickly sprinkled with these little tufts, reminding you often of some rigid gray mosses or lichens, and you see thousands of little trees just springing up between them, with the seed still attached to them.

Being regularly clipped all around each year by the cows, as a hedge with shears, they are often of a perfect conical or pyramidal form, from one to four feet high, and more or less sharp, as if trimmed by the gardener's art. In the pastures on Nobscot Hill and its spurs they make fine dark shadows when the sun is low. They are also an excellent covert from hawks for many small birds that roost and build in them. Whole flocks perch in them at night, and I have seen three robins' nests in one which was six feet in diameter.

No doubt many of these are already old trees, if you reckon from the day they were planted, but infants still when you consider their development and the long life before them. I counted the annual rings of some which were just one foot high, and as wide as high, and found that they were about twelve years old, but quite sound and thrifty! They were so low that they were unnoticed by the walker, while many of their contemporaries from the nurseries were already bearing considerable crops. But what you gain in time is perhaps in this case, too, lost in power, that is, in the vigor of the tree. This is their pyramidal state.

The cows continue to browse them thus for twenty years or more, keeping them down and compelling them to spread, until at last they are so broad that they become their own fence, when some interior shoot, which their foes cannot reach, darts upward with joy: for it has not forgotten its high calling, and bears its own peculiar fruit in triumph.

Such are the tactics by which it finally defeats its bovine foes. Now, if you have watched the progress of a particular shrub, you will see that it is no longer a simple pyramid or cone, but out of its apex there rises a sprig or two, growing more lustily perchance than an orchard-tree, since the plant now devotes the whole of its repressed energy to these upright parts. In a short time these become a small tree, an inverted pyramid resting on the apex of the other, so that the whole has now the form of a vast hour-glass. The spreading bottom, having served its purpose, finally disappears, and the generous tree permits the now harmless cows to come in and stand in its shade, and rub against and redden its trunk, which has grown in spite of them, and even to taste a part of its fruit, and so disperse the seed.

Thus the cows create their own shade and food; and the tree, its hour-glass being inverted, lives a second life, as it were.

It is an important question with some nowadays, whether you should trim young apple-trees as high as your nose or as high as your eyes. The ox trims them up as high as he can reach, and that is about the right height, I think.

In spite of wandering kine and other adverse circumstance, that despised shrub, valued only by small birds as a covert and shelter from hawks, has its blossom-week at last, and in course of time its harvest, sincere, though small.

By the end of some October, when its leaves have fallen, I frequently see such a central sprig, whose progress I have watched, when I thought it had forgotten its destiny, as I had, bearing its first crop of small green or yellow or rosy fruit, which the cows cannot get at over the bushy and thorny hedge which surrounds it; and I make haste to taste the new and undescribed variety. We have all heard of the numerous varieties of fruit invented by Van Mons and Knight. This is the system of Van Cow, and she has invented far more and more memorable varieties than both of them.

Through what hardships it may attain to bear a sweet fruit! Though somewhat small, it may prove equal, if not superior, in flavor to that which has grown in a garden, will perchance be all the sweeter and more palatable for the very difficulties it has had to contend with. Who knows but this chance wild fruit, planted by a cow or a bird on some remote and rocky hillside, where it is as yet unobserved by man, may be the choicest of all its kind, and foreign potentates shall hear of it, and royal societies seek to propagate it, though the virtues of the perhaps truly crabbed owner of the soil may never be heard of, at least, beyond the limits of his village? It was thus the Porter and the Baldwin grew.

Every wild-apple shrub excites our expectation thus, somewhat as every wild child. It is, perhaps, a prince in disguise. What a lesson to man! So are human beings, referred to the highest standard, the celestial fruit which they suggest and aspire to bear, browsed on by fate; and only the most persistent and strongest genius defends itself and prevails, sends a tender scion upward at last, and drops its perfect fruit on the ungrateful earth. Poets and philosophers and statesmen thus spring up in the country pastures, and outlast the hosts of unoriginal men.

Such is always the pursuit of knowledge. The celestial fruits, the golden apples of the Hesperides, are ever guarded by a hundred-headed dragon which never sleeps, so that it is an herculean labor to pluck them. —"Wild Apples"

What a healthy out-of-door appetite it takes to relish the apple of life, the apple of the world, then!

"Nor is it every apple I desire,
    Nor that which pleases every palate best;
'T is not the lasting Deuxan I require,
    Nor yet the red-cheeked Greening I request,
Nor that which first beshrewed the name of wife,
Nor that whose beauty caused the golden strife:
No, no! bring me an apple from the tree of life."

So there is one thought for the field, another for the house. I would have my thoughts, like wild apples, to be food for walkers, and will not warrant them to be palatable, if tasted in the house. —"Wild Apples"

November

First of all a man must see, before he can say. Statements are made but partially. Things are said with reference to certain conventions or existing institutions, not absolutely. A fact truly and absolutely stated is taken out of the region of common sense and acquires a mythologic or universal significance. Say it and have done with it. Express it without expressing yourself. See not with the eye of science, which is barren, nor of youthful poetry, which is impotent. But taste the world and digest it. It would seem as if things got said but rarely and by chance. As you see, so at length will you say. When facts are seen superficially, they are seen as they lie in relation to certain institutions, perchance. But I would have them expressed as more deeply seen, with deeper references; so that the hearer or reader cannot recognize them or apprehend their significance from the platform of common life, but it will be necessary that he be in a sense translated in order to understand them; when the truth respecting his things shall naturally exhale from a man like the odor of the muskrat from the coat of the trapper. At first blush a man is not capable of reporting truth; he must be drenched and saturated with it first. What was *enthusiasm* in the young man must become *temperament* in the mature man. Without excitement, heat, or passion, he will survey the world which excited the youth and threw him off his balance.
—Journal, November 1, 1851

After a rain-threatening morning it is a beautiful Indian-summer day, the most remarkable hitherto and equal to any of the kind. Yet we kept fires in the forenoon, the warmth not having got into the house. It is akin to sin to spend such a day in the house. The air is still and warm. This, too, is the *recovery* of the year — as if the year, having nearly or quite accomplished its work, and abandoned all design, were in a more favorable and poetic mood, and thought rushed in to fill the vacuum. —Journal, November 1, 1855

A higher truth, though only dimly hinted at, thrills us more than a lower expressed. —Journal, November 1, 1857

As the afternoons grow shorter, and the early evening drives us home to complete our chores, we are reminded of the shortness of life, and become more pensive, at least in this twilight of the year. We are prompted to make haste and finish our work before the night comes. —Journal, November 1, 1858

It was as if I was promised the greatest novelty the world has ever seen or shall see, though the utmost possible novelty would be the difference between me and myself a year ago. This alone encouraged me, and was my fuel for the approaching winter. That we may behold the panorama with this slight improvement or change, this is what we sustain life for with so much effort from year to year.

And yet there is no more tempting novelty than this new November. No going to Europe or another world is to be named with it. Give me the old familiar walk, post-office and all, with this ever new self, with this infinite expectation and faith, which does not know when it is beaten. We'll go nutting once more. We'll pluck the nut of the world and crack it in the winter evenings. Theatres and all other sightseeing are puppet-shows in comparison. I will take another walk to the Cliff, another row on the river, another skate on the meadow, be out in the first snow, and associate with the winter birds. Here I am at home. In the bare and bleached crust of the earth I recognize my friend. —Journal, November 1, 1858

What is Nature unless there is an eventful human life passing within her? Many joys and many sorrows are the lights and shadows in which she shows most beautiful. —Journal, November 2, 1853

I think that most men, as farmers, hunters, fishers, etc., walk along a river's bank, or paddle along its stream, without seeing the reflections. Their minds are not abstracted from the surface, from surfaces generally. It is only a reflecting mind that sees reflections. I am aware often that I have been occupied with shallow and commonplace thoughts, looking for something superficial, when I did not see the most glorious reflections, though exactly in the line of my vision. —Journal, November 2, 1857

By fall I mean literally the falling of the leaves, though some mean by it the changing or the acquisition of a brighter color. This I call the autumnal tint, the ripening to the fall. —Journal, November 3, 1858

Must be out-of-doors enough to get experience of wholesome reality, as a ballast to thought and sentiment. Health requires this relaxation, this aimless life. This life in the present. Let a man have thought what he will of Nature in the house, she will still be novel outdoors. I keep out of doors for the sake of the mineral, vegetable, and animal in me. —Journal, November 4, 1852

My thought is a part of the meaning of the world, and hence I use a part of the world as a symbol to express my thought. —Journal, November 4, 1852

Now that the sun is actually setting, the mountains are dark-blue from top to bottom. As usual, a small cloud attends the sun to the portals of the day and reflects this brightness to us, now that he is gone. But those grand and

glorious mountains, how impossible to remember daily
that they are there, and to live accordingly! They are meant
to be a perpetual reminder to us, pointing out the way.
—Journal, November 4, 1857

How wholesome winter is, seen far or near; how good,
above all mere sentimental, warm-blooded, short-lived,
soft-hearted, *moral* goodness, commonly so called. Give me
the goodness which has forgotten its own deeds — which
God has seen to be good, and let be. None of your *just
made perfect* — pickled eels! All that will save them will be
their picturesqueness, as with blasted trees. Whatever is,
and is not ashamed to be, is good. I value no moral
goodness or greatness unless it is good or great, even as
that snowy peak is. Pray, how could thirty feet of bowels
improve it? Nature is goodness crystallized. You looked
into the land of promise. Whatever beauty we behold, the
more it is distant, serene, and cold, the purer and more
durable it is. It is better to warm ourselves with ice than
with fire. —Letter to Daniel Ricketson, November 4, 1860

I hate the present modes of living and getting a living.
Farming and shopkeeping and working at a trade or
profession are all odious to me. I should relish getting my
living in a simple, primitive fashion. The life which society
proposes to me to live is so artificial and complex —
bolstered up on many weak supports, and sure to topple
down at last — that no man surely can ever be inspired to
live it, and only "old fogies" ever praise it. At best some
think it their duty to live it. I believe in the infinite joy and
satisfaction of helping myself to the extent of my ability.
But what is the use in trying to live simply, raising what
you eat, burning what you cut or dig, when those to whom
you are allied insanely want and will have a thousand other
things which neither you nor they can raise and nobody
else, perchance, will pay for? The fellow-man to whom you

are yoked is a steer that is ever bolting right the other way. —Journal, November 5, 1855

I am struck by the fact that the more slowly trees grow at first, the sounder they are at the core, and I think the same is true of human beings. We do not wish to see children precocious, making great strides in their early years like sprouts, producing a soft and perishable timber, but better if they expand slowly at first, as if contending with difficulties, and so are solidified and perfected. Such trees continue to expand with nearly equal rapidity to an extreme old age. —Journal, November 5, 1860

How can we expect to understand Nature unless we accept like children these her smallest gifts, valuing them more as her gifts than for their intrinsic value? I love to get my basket full, however small and comparatively worthless the nut. —Journal, November 7, 1853

I find it good to be out this still, dark, mizzling afternoon; my walk or voyage is more suggestive and profitable than in bright weather. The view is contracted by the misty rain, the water is perfectly smooth, and the stillness is favorable to reflection. I am more open to impressions, more sensitive (not calloused or indurated by sun and wind), as if in a chamber still. My thoughts are concentrated; I am all compact. The solitude is real, too, for the weather keeps other men at home. This mist is like a roof and walls over and around, and I walk with a domestic feeling. The sound of a wagon going over an unseen bridge is louder than ever, and so of other sounds. I am *compelled* to look at near objects. All things have a soothing effect; the very clouds and mists brood over me. My power of observation and contemplation is much increased. My attention does not wander. The world and my life are simplified. What now of Europe and Asia? —Journal, November 7, 1855

The stillness of the woods and fields is remarkable at this season of the year. There is not even the creak of a cricket to be heard. Of myriads of dry shrub oak leaves, not one rustles. Your own breath can rustle them, yet the breath of heaven does not suffice to. The trees have the aspect of waiting for winter. The autumnal leaves have lost their color; they are now truly sere, dead, and the woods wear a sombre color. Summer and harvest are over. The hickories, birches, chestnuts, no less than the maples, have lost their leaves. The sprouts, which had shot up so vigorously to repair the damage which the choppers had done, have stopped short for the winter. Everything stands silent and expectant. If I listen, I hear only the note of a chickadee — our most common and I may say native bird, most identified with our forests — or perchance the scream of a jay, or perchance from the solemn depths of these woods I hear tolling far away the knell of one departed. Thought rushes in to fill the vacuum. —Journal, November 8, 1850

When I saw the bare sand at Cochituate I felt my relation to the soil. These are *my* sands not yet run out. Not yet will the fates turn the glass. This air have I title to taint with my decay. In this clean sand my bones will gladly lie. Like *Viola pedata*, I shall be ready to bloom again here in my Indian summer days. Here ever springing, never dying, with perennial root I stand; for the winter of the land is warm to me. While the flowers bloom again as in the spring, shall I pine? When I see her sands exposed, thrown up from beneath the surface, it touches me inwardly, it reminds me of my origin; for I am such a plant, so native to New England, methinks, as springs from the sand cast up from below. —Journal, November 8, 1851

I too have my spring thoughts even in November.
—Journal, November 8, 1857

Each phase of nature, while not invisible, is yet not too
distinct and obtrusive. It is there to be found when we
look for it, but not demanding our attention. It is like a
silent but sympathizing companion in whose company we
retain most of the advantages of solitude, with whom we
can walk and talk, or be silent, naturally, without the
necessity of talking in a strain foreign to the place.
—Journal, November 8, 1858

I wandered over bare fields where the cattle, lately turned
out, roamed restless and unsatisfied with the feed; I dived
into a rustling young oak wood where not a green leaf was
to be seen; I climbed to the geological axis of elevation and
clambered over curly-pated rocks whose strata are on their
edges amid the rising woods; and again I thought, They are
all gone surely and left me alone. Not a man Friday
remains. What nutriment can I extract from these bare
twigs? Starvation stares me in the face. "Nay, Nay!" said a
nuthatch, making its way, head downward, about a bare
hickory close by. "The nearer the bone, the sweeter the
meat. Only the superfluous has been swept away. Now we
behold the naked truth. If at any time the weather is too
cold and bleak for you, keep the sunny side of the trunk,
for there is a wholesome and spring warmth such as the
summer never afforded. There are the winter mornings
with the sun on the oak wood tops. While buds sleep,
thoughts wake." ("Hear! Hear!" screamed the jay from a
neighboring copse, where I heard a twittering for some
time.) "Winter has a concentrated and nutty kernel, if you
know where to look for it." —Journal, November 8, 1858

I deal so much with my fuel — what with finding it,
loading it, conveying it home, sawing and splitting it — get
so many values out of it, am warmed in so many ways by
it, that the heat it will yield when in the stove is of a lower
temperature and a lesser value in my eyes — though when
I feel it I am reminded of all my adventures.... Yes, I lose

sight of the ultimate uses of this wood and work, the immediate ones are so great, and yet most of mankind, those called most successful in obtaining the necessaries of life — getting their living — obtain none of this except a mere vulgar and perhaps stupefying warmth. —Journal, November 9, 1855

It is of no use to plow deeper than the soil is, unless you mean to follow up that mode of cultivation persistently, manuring highly and carting on muck at each plowing — making a soil, in short. Yet many a man likes to tackle mighty themes, like immortality, but in his discourse he turns up nothing but yellow sand, under which what little fertile and available surface soil he may have is quite buried and lost. He should teach frugality rather — how to postpone the fatal hour — should plant a crop of beans. He might have raised enough of these to make a deacon of him, though never a preacher. Many a man runs his plow so deep in heavy or stony soil that it sticks fast in the furrow. It is a great art in the writer to improve from day to day just that soil and fertility which he has, to harvest that crop which his life yields, whatever it may be, not be straining as if to reach apples or oranges when he yields only ground-nuts. He should be digging, not soaring. Just as earnest as your life, so deep is your soil. If strong and deep, you will sow wheat and raise bread of life in it.
—Journal, November 9, 1858

Living much out-of-doors in the air, in the sun and wind, will, no doubt, produce a certain roughness of character, will cause a thicker cuticle to grow over some of the finer sensibilities of a man's nature, as on his face and hands, or those parts of his body which are exposed to the weather; as staying in the house, on the other hand, may produce a softness and smoothness, not to say thinness, of skin, accompanied by an increased sensibility to certain impressions. And no doubt it is a nice matter to proportion rightly the thick and thin skin. Perhaps we should be more susceptible to some influences important to our intellectual growth, if the sun had shone and the wind blown on us a little less. As too much manual labor callouses the hand and deprives it of the exquisiteness of the touch. But then methinks that is a scurf that will fall off fast enough — that the natural remedy is to be found in the proportion which the night bears to the day, winter to the summer, etc., thought to experience. —Journal, November 11, 1851

This is the month of nuts and nutty thoughts — that November whose name sounds so bleak and cheerless. Perhaps its harvest of thought is worth more than all the other crops of the year. —Journal, November 11, 1858

I yet lack discernment to distinguish the whole lesson of today; but it is not lost — it will come to me at last. My desire is to know *what* I have lived, that I may know *how* to live henceforth. —Journal, November 12, 1837

I cannot but regard it as a kindness in those who have the steering of me that, by the want of pecuniary wealth, I have been nailed down to this my native region so long and steadily, and made to study and love this spot of earth more and more. What would signify in comparison a thin and diffused love and knowledge of the whole earth instead, got by wandering? The traveller's is but a barren and comfortless condition. Wealth will not buy a man a home in nature — house nor farm there. The man of business does not by his business earn a residence in nature, but is denaturalized rather. What is a farm, house and land, office or shop, but a settlement in nature under the most favorable conditions? It is insignificant, and a merely negative good fortune, to be provided with thick garments against cold and wet, an unprofitable, weak, and defensive condition, compared with being able to extract some exhilaration, some warmth even, out of cold and wet themselves, and to clothe them with our sympathy. The rich man buys woolens and furs, and sits naked and shivering still in sprit, besieged by cold and wet. But the poor Lord of Creation, cold and wet he makes to warm him, and be his garments. —Journal, November 12, 1853

I hear one cricket singing still, faintly deep in the bank, now after one whitening of snow. His theme is life immortal. The last cricket, full of cheer and faith, piping to himself, as the last man might. —Journal, November 12, 1853

I think that the change to some higher color in a leaf is an evidence that it has arrived at a perfect and final maturity, answering to the maturity of fruits, and not to that of green leaves, etc., etc., which merely serve a purpose. The word "ripe" is thought by some to be derived from the verb "to reap," according to which that is ripe which is ready to be reaped. The fall of the leaf is preceded by a ripe old age. —Journal, November 12, 1858

A cold and dark afternoon, the sun being behind clouds in the west. The landscape is barren of objects, the trees being leafless, and so little light in the sky for variety. Such a day as will almost oblige a man to eat his own heart. A day in which you must hold on to life by your teeth. You can hardly ruck up any skin on Nature's bones. The sap is down; she won't peel. Now is the time to cut timber for yokes and ox-bows, leaving the tough bark on — yokes for your own neck. Finding yourself yoked to Matter and to Time. Not a mosquito left. Not an insect to hum. Crickets gone into winter quarters. Friends long since gone there, and you left to walk on frozen ground, with your hands in your pockets. Ah, but is not this a time for deep inward fires? —Journal, November 13, 1851

There is nowhere any apology for despondency. Always there is ilfe which, rightly lived, implies a divine satisfaction. —Journal, November 14, 1839

October is the month of painted leaves, of ripe leaves, when all the earth, not merely flowers, but fruits and leaves, are ripe. With respect to its colors and its season, it is the sunset month of the year, when the earth is painted like a sunset sky. This rich glow now flashes round the world. This light fades into the clear, white, leafless twilight of November, and whatever more glowing sunset or Indian summer we have then is the afterglow of the year. In October the man is ripe even to his stalk and leaves; he is pervaded by his genius, when all the forest is a universal harvest, whether he possesses the enduring color of the pines, which it takes two years to ripe and wither, or the brilliant color of the deciduous trees, which fade the first fall....

October answers to that period in the life of man when he is no longer dependent on his transient moods, when all his experience ripens into wisdom, but every root, branch, leaf of him glows with maturity. What he has been and done in his spring and summer appears. He bears his fruit. —Journal, November 14, 1853

It is remarkable that the highest intellectual mood which the world tolerates is the perception of the truth of the most ancient revelations, now in some respects out of date; but any direct revelation, any original thoughts, it hates like virtue.... We check and repress the divinity that stirs within us, to fall down and worship the divinity that is dead without us. —Journal, November 16, 1851

It would be a relief to breathe one's self occasionally among men. If there were any magnanimity in us, any grandeur of soul, anything but sects and parties undertaking to patronize God and keep the mind within bounds, how often we might encourage and provoke one another by a free expression! —Journal, November 16, 1858

Now the king of day plays at bo-peep round the world's corner, and every cottage window smiles a golden smile — a very picture of glee. I see the water glistening in the eye. The smothered breathings of awakening day strike the ear with an undulating motion; over hill and dale, pasture and woodland, come they to me, and I am at home in the world. —Journal, November 17, 1837

Some of our richest days are those in which no sun shines outwardly, but so much the more a sun shines inwardly. I love nature, I love the landscape, because it is so sincere. It never cheats me. It never jests. It is cheerfully, musically earnest. I lie and relie on the earth. —Journal, November 17, 1850

My Journal should be the record of my love. I would write in it only of the things I love, my affection for any aspect of the world, what I love to think of. I have no more distinctness or pointedness in my yearnings than an expanding bud, which does indeed point to flower and fruit, to summer and autumn, but is aware of the warm sun and spring influence only. I feel ripe for something, yet do nothing, can't discover what that thing is. I feel fertile merely. It is seedtime with me. I have lain fallow long enough. —Journal, November 17, 1850

I notice that many plants about this season of the year or earlier, after they have died down at top, put forth fresh and conspicuous radical leaves against another spring. So some human beings in the November of their days exhibit some fresh radical greenness, which, though the frosts may soon nip it, indicates and confirms their essential vitality.

When their summer leaves have faded and fallen, they put forth fresh radical leaves which sustain the life in their root still, against a new spring. The dry fields have for a long time been spotted with the small radical leaves of the fragrant life-everlasting not to mention the large primrose, johnswort, etc., etc. And almost every plant, although it may show no greenness above ground, if you dig about it, will be found to have fresh shoots already pointing upward and ready to burst forth in the spring. —Journal, November 17, 1853

It is interesting to me to talk with Rice, he lives so thoroughly and satisfactorily to himself. He has learned that rare art of living, the very elements of which most professors do not know. His life has not been a failure but a success. Seeing me going to sharpen some plane-irons, and hearing me complain of the want of tools he said that I ought to have a chest of tools. But I said it was not worth the while. I should not use them enough to pay for them. "You would use them more, if you had them," said he. "When I came to do a piece of work I used to find commonly that I wanted a certain tool, and I made it a rule first always to make that tool. I have spent as much as $3000 thus on my tools." Comparatively speaking, his life is a success; not such a failure as most men's. He gets more out of any enterprise than his neighbors, for he helps himself more and hires less. Whatever pleasure there is in it he enjoys. By good sense and calculation he has become rich and has invested his property well, yet practices a fair and neat economy, dwells not in untidy luxury. It costs him less to live, and he gets more out of life, than others. To get his living, or keep it, is not a hasty or disagreeable toil. He works slowly but surely, enjoying the sweet of it. He buys a piece of meadow at a profitable rate, works at it in pleasant weather, he and his son, when they are inclined, goes a-fishing or a-bee-hunting or a-rifle-shooting quite as often, and thus the meadow gets redeemed, and potatoes get planted, perchance, and he is very sure to have a good crop stored in his cellar in the fall, and some to sell. He always has the best of potatoes there. In the same spirit in which he and his son tackle up their Dobbin (he never keeps a fast horse) and go a-spearing or a-fishing through the ice, they also tackle up and go to their Sudbury farm to hoe or harvest a little, and when they return they bring home a load of stumps in their hay-rigging, which impeded their labors, but, perchance, supply them with their winter wood. All the woodchucks they shoot or trap in the bean-field are brought home also. And thus their life is a long sport and they know not what hard times are. —Journal, November 17, 1855

The pleasure, the warmth, is not so much in *having* as in a true and simple manner *getting* these necessaries.

Men prefer foolishly the gold to that of which it is the symbol — simple, honest, independent labor. Can gold be said to buy food, if it does not buy an appetite for food? It is fouler and uglier to have too much than not to have enough. —Journal, November 18, 1855

Flannery is the hardest-working man I know. Before sunrise and long after sunset he is taxing his unweariable muscles. The result is a singular cheerfulness. He is always in good spirits. He often overflows with his joy when you perceive no occasion for it. If only the gate sticks, some of it bubbles up and overflows in his passing comment on the accident. How much mere industry proves! —Journal, November 18, 1857

The fruitless enterprise of some persons who rush helter-skelter, carrying out their crazy scheme — merely "putting it through," as they phrase it — reminds me of those thistle-downs which, not being detained nor steadied by any seed at the base, are blown away at the first impulse and go rolling over all obstacles. They may indeed go fastest and farthest, but where they rest at last not even a thistle springs. I meet these useless barren thistle-downs driving over the fields. They remind me of busy merchants and brokers on 'change doing business on credit, gambling with fancy stocks, that have failed over and over again, assisted to get a-going again to no purpose — a great ado about nothing — all in my eye — with nothing to deposit, not of the slightest use to the great thistle tribe, not even tempting a jackass. When you right or extricate one of these fellows and set him before the wind again, it is worth the while to look and see if he has any seed of success under him. Such a one you may know afar — he floats more slowly and steadily — and of his enterprise expect results. —Journal, November 18, 1858

They who sit farthest off from the noisy and bustling world are not at pains to distinguish what is sweet and musical, for that alone can reach them; that chiefly comes down to posterity. —Journal, November 20, 1851

You walk fast and far, and every apple left out is grateful to your invigorated taste. You enjoy not only the bracing coolness, but all the heat and sunlight that there is, reflected back to you from the earth. The sandy road itself, lit by the November sun, is beautiful. Shrub oaks and young oaks generally, and hazel bushes and other hardy shrubs, now more or less bare, are your companions, as if it were an iron age, yet in simplicity, innocence, and strength a golden one. —Journal, November 22, 1860

It is glorious to consider how independent man is of all enervating luxuries; and the poorer he is in respect to them, the richer he is. Summer is gone with all its infinite wealth, and still nature is genial to man. Though he no longer bathes in the stream, or reclines on the bank, or plucks berries on the hills, still he beholds the same inaccessible beauty around him. —Journal, November 22, 1860

I find it to be the height of wisdom not to endeavor to oversee myself and live a life of prudence and common sense, but to see over and above myself, entertain sublime conjectures, to make myself the thoroughfare of thrilling thoughts, live all that can be lived. The man who is dissatisfied with himself, what can he not do? —Journal, November 23, 1850

If I would preserve my relation to nature, I must make my life more moral, more pure and innocent. The problem is as precise and simple as a mathematical one. I must not live loosely, but more and more continently. —Journal, November 23, 1853

The Indian summer itself, said to be more remarkable in this country than elsewhere, no less than the reblossoming of certain flowers, the peep of the hylodes, and sometimes the faint warble of some birds, is the reminiscence, or rather the return, of spring — the year renewing its youth. —Journal, November 23, 1853

Some poets have said that writing poetry was for youths only, but not so. In that fervid and excitable season we only get the impulse which is to carry us onward in our future career. Ideals are then exhibited to us distinctly which all our lives after we may aim at but not attain. The mere vision is little compared with the steady corresponding endeavor thitherward. It would be vain for us to be looking ever into promised lands toward which in the meanwhile we were not steadily and earnestly travelling, whether the way led over a mountain-top or through a dusky valley. In youth, when we are most elastic and there is a spring to us, we merely receive an impulse in the proper direction. To suppose that this is equivalent to having travelled the road, or obeyed the impulse faithfully throughout a lifetime, is absurd. We are shown fair scenes in order that we may be tempted to inhabit them, and not simply tell what we have seen. —Journal, November 24, 1857

The bitter-sweet of a white oak acorn which you nibble in a bleak November walk over the tawny earth is more to me than a slice of imported pineapple. We do not think much of table-fruits. They are especially for aldermen and epicures. They do not feed the imagination. That would starve on them. These wild fruits, whether eaten or not, are a dessert for the imagination. The south may keep her pineapples, and we will be content with our strawberries. —Journal, November 24, 1860

This afternoon the air was indescribably clear and exhilirating, and though the thermometer would have shown it to be cold, I thought that there was a finer and purer warmth than in summer; a wholesome, intellectual warmth, in which the body was warmed by the mind's contentment. The warmth was hardly sensuous, but rather the satisfaction of existence. —Journal, November 25, 1850

How often you make a man richer in spirit in proportion as you rob him of earthly luxuries and comforts! —Journal, November 25, 1860

The value of these wild fruits is not in the mere possession or eating of them, but in the sight or enjoyment of them. The very derivation of the word "fruit" would suggest this. It is from the Latin *fructus*, meaning that which is *used* or *enjoyed*. If it were not so, then going a-berrying and going to market would be nearly synonymous expressions. Of course it is the spirit in which you do a thing which makes it interesting, whether it is sweeping a room or pulling turnips. Peaches are unquestionably a very beautiful and palatable fruit, but the gathering of them for the market is not nearly so interesting as the gathering of huckleberries for your own use.

A man fits out a ship at a great expense and sends it to the West Indies with a crew of men and boys, and after six months or a year it comes back with a load of pineapples. Now, if no more gets accomplished than the speculator commonly aims at — if it simply turns out what is called a successful venture — I am less interested in this expedition than in some child's first excursion a-huckleberrying, in which it is introduced into a new world, experiences a new development, though it brings home only a gill of huckleberries in its basket. I know that the newspapers and the politicians declare otherwise, but they do not alter the fact. Then, I think that the fruit of the latter expedition was finer than that of the former. It was a more fruitful expedition. The value of any experience is measured, of course, not by the amount of money, but the amount of development we get out of it. If a New England boy's dealings with oranges and pineapples have had more to do with his development than picking huckleberries or pulling turnips have, then he rightly and naturally thinks more of the former; otherwise not. —Journal, November 26, 1860

The less you get, the happier and the richer you are. The rich man's son gets cocoanuts, and the poor man's, pignuts; but the worst of it is that the former never goes a-cocoanutting, and so he never gets the cream of the cocoanut as the latter does the cream of the pignut.

That on which commerce seizes is always the very coarsest part of a fruit — the mere husk and rind, in fact — for her hands are very clumsy. This is what fills the holds of ships, is exported and imported, pays duties, and is finally sold at the shops.

It is a grand fact that you cannot make the finer fruits or parts of fruits matter of commerce. You may buy a servant or slave, in short, but you cannot buy a friend. You can't buy the finer part of any fruit — i.e. the highest use and enjoyment of it. You cannot buy the pleasure which it yields to him who truly picks it; you can't buy a good appetite even. —Journal, November 28, 1860

If a man has spent all his days about some business, by which he has merely got to be rich, as it is called, i.e., has got much money, many houses and barns and woodlots, then his life has been a failure, I think; but if he has been trying to better his condition in a higher sense than this, has been trying to invent something, to be somebody — i.e., to invent and get a patent for himself — so that all may see his originality, though he should never get above board — and great inventors, you know, commonly die poor — I shall think him comparatively successful.
—Journal, November 29, 1860

This world and our life have practically a similar value only to most. The value of life is what anybody will give you for living. A man has his price at the South, is worth so many dollars, and so he has at the North. Many a man here sets out by saying, I will make so many dollars by such a time, or before I die, and that is his price, as much as if he were knocked off for it by a Southern auctioneer.

We hear a good deal about moonshine by so-called practical people, and the next day, perchance, we hear of their value, they having been dealing in fancy stocks; but there really never is any moonshine of this kind in the practice of poets and philosophers; there never are any hard times or failures with them, for they deal with permanent values. —Journal, November 29, 1860

Nothing is so attractive and unceasingly curious as character. There is no plant that needs such tender treatment, there is none that will endure so rough. It is the violet and the oak. It is the thing we mean, let us say what we will. We mean our own character, or we mean yours. It is divine and related to the heavens, as the earth is by the flashes of the Aurora. It has no acquaintance nor companion. It goes silent and unobserved longer than any planet in space, but when at length it does show itself, it seems like the flowering of all the world, and its before unseen orbit is lit up like the trail of a meteor. I hear no good news ever but some trait of a noble character. It reproaches me plaintively. I am mean in contrast, but again am thrilled and elevated that I can see my own meanness, and again still, that my own aspiration is realized in that other. —Journal, November 30, 1841

WINTER

SEASONS OF THOREAU

December

I see the old pale-faced farmer out again on his sled now for the five-thousandth time — Cyrus Hubbard, a man of a certain New England probity and worth, immortal and natural, like a natural product, like the sweetness of a nut, like the toughness of hickory. He, too, is a redeemer for me. How superior actually to the faith he professes! He is not an office-seeker. What an institution, what a revelation is a man! We are wont foolishly to think that the creed which a man professes is more significant than the fact he is. It matters not how hard the conditions seemed, how mean the world, for a man is a prevalent force and a new law himself. He is a system whose law is to be observed. The old farmer condescends to countenance still this nature and order of things. It is a great encouragement that an honest man makes this world his abode. He rides on the sled drawn by oxen, world-wise, yet comparatively so young, as if they had seen scores of winters. The farmer spoke to me, I can swear, clean, cold, moderate as the snow. He does not melt the snow where he treads. Yet what a faint impression that encounter may make on me after all! Moderate, natural, true, as if he were made of earth, stone, wood, snow. I thus meet in this universe kindred of mine, composed of these elements. —Journal, December 1, 1856

Look at the trees, bare or rustling with sere brown leaves, except the evergreens, their buds dormant at the foot of the leaf-stalks. Look at the fields, russet and withered, and the various sedges and weeds with dry bleached culms. Such is our relation to nature at present; such plants are we. We have no more sap nor verdure nor color now....

But even in winter we maintain a temperate cheer and a serene inward life, not destitute of warmth and melody.
—Journal, December 3, 1853

My themes shall not be far-fetched. I will tell of homely every-day phenomena and adventures. Friends! Society! It seems to me that I have an abundance of it, there is so much that I rejoice and sympathize with, and men, too, that I never speak to but only know and think of. What you call bareness and poverty is to me simplicity. God could not be unkind to me if he should try. I love the winter with its imprisonment and its cold, for it compels the prisoner to try new fields and resources. I love to have the river closed up for a season and a pause put to my boating, to be obliged to get my boat in. I shall launch it again in the spring with so much more pleasure. This is an advantage in point of abstinence and moderation compared with the seaside boating, where the boat ever lies on the shore. I love best to have each thing in its season only, and enjoy doing without it at all other times. It is the greatest of all advantages to enjoy no advantage at all. I find it invariably true, the poorer I am, the richer I am. What you consider my disadvantage, I consider my advantage. While you are pleased to get knowledge and culture in many ways, I am delighted to think that I am getting rid of them. I have never got over my surprise that I should have been born into the most estimable place in all the world, and in the very nick of time, too. —Journal, December 5, 1856

It is remarkable that there is little or nothing to be remembered written on the subject of getting a living; how to make getting a living not merely holiest and honorable, but altogether inviting and glorious; for if *getting* a living is not so, then living is not. —"Life Without Principle" (based on a lecture first delivered December 6, 1854)

The title wise is, for the most part, falsely applied. How can one be a wise man, if he does not know any better how to live than other men? — if he is only more cunning and intellectually subtle? Does Wisdom work in a treadmill? or does she teach how to succeed by her example? Is there any such thing as wisdom not applied to life? Is she merely the miller who grinds the finest logic? It is pertinent to ask if Plato got his living in a better way or more successfully than his contemporaries — or did he succumb to the difficulties of life like other men? Did he seem to prevail over some of them merely by indifference, or by assuming grand airs? or find it easier to live, because his aunt remembered him in her will? The ways in which most men get their living, that is, live, are mere makeshifts, and a shirking of the real business of life — chiefly because they do not know, but partly because they do not mean, any better. —"Life Without Principle"

I am grateful for what I am and have. My thanksgiving is perpetual. It is surprising how contented one can be with nothing definite — only a sense of existence. Well, anything for variety. I am ready to try this for the next ten thousand years, and exhaust it. How sweet to think of! my extremities well charred, and my intellectual part too, so that there is no danger of worm or rot for a long while. My breath is sweet to me. O how I laugh when I think of my vague, indefinite riches. No run on my bank can drain it, for my wealth is not possession but enjoyment. —Letter to Harrison Blake, December 6, 1856

On all sides, in swamps and about their edges and in the woods, the bare shrubs are sprinkled with buds, more or less noticeable and pretty, their little *gemmae* or gems, their most vital and attractive parts now, almost all the greenness and color left, greens and salads for the birds and rabbits. Our eyes go searching along the stems for what is most vivacious and characteristic of the concentrated summer gone into winter quarters. For we are hunters pursuing the summer on snow-shoes and skates, all winter long. There is really but one season in our hearts. —Journal, December 6, 1856

We may believe it, but never do we live a quiet, free life, such as Adam's, but are enveloped in an invisible network of speculations. Our progress is only from one such speculation to another, and only at rare intervals do we perceive that it is no progress. Could we for a moment drop this by-play, and simply wonder, without reference or inference! —Journal, December 7, 1838

That grand old poem called Winter is round again without any connivance of mine. As I sit under Lee's Cliff, where the snow is melted, amid sere pennyroyal and frost-bitten catnep, I look over my shoulder upon an arctic scene. I see with surprise the pond a dumb white surface of ice speckled with snow, just as so many winters before, where so lately were lapsing waves or smooth reflecting water. I see the holes which the pickerel-fisher has made, and I see him, too, retreating over the hills, drawing his sled behind him. The water is already skimmed over again there. I hear, too, the familiar belching voice of the pond. It seemed as if winter had come without any interval since midsummer, and I was prepared to see it flit away by the time I again looked over my shoulder. It was as if I had dreamed it. But I see that the farmers have had time to gather their harvests as usual, and the seasons have revolved as slowly as in the first autumn of my life. The winters come now as fast as snowflakes. It is wonderful that old men do not lose their reckoning. It was summer, and now again it is winter. Nature loves this rhyme so well that she never tires of repeating it. So sweet and wholesom is the winter, so simple and moderate, so satisfactory and perfect, that her children will never weary of it. What a poem! an epic in blank verse, enriched with a million tinkling rhymes. It is solid beauty. It has been subjected to the vicissitudes of millions of years of the gods, and not a single superfluous ornament remains. The severest and coldest of the immortal critics have shot their arrows at and pruned it till it cannot be amended. —Journal, December 7, 1856

The remote pastures and hills beyond the woods are now closed to cows and cowherds, aye, and to cowards. I am struck by this sudden solitude and remoteness which these places have acquired. The dear privacy and retirement and solitude which winter makes possible! —Journal, December 8, 1850

Winter has come unnoticed by me, I have been so busy writing. This is the life most lead in respect to Nature. How different from my habitual one! It is hasty, coarse, and trivial, as if you were a spindle in a factory. The other is leisurely, fine, and glorious, like a flower. In the first case you are merely getting your living; in the second you live as you go along. You travel only on roads of the proper grade without jar or running off the track, and sweep round the hills by beautiful curves. —Journal, December 8, 1854

When a noble deed is done, who is likely to appreciate it? They who are noble themselves.... How can a man behold the light who has no answering inward light? —Journal, December 8, 1859

My body is all sentient. As I go here or there, I am tickled by this or that I come in contact with, as if I touched the wires of a battery. I can generally recall — have fresh in my mind — several scratches last received. These I continually recall to mind, reimpress, and harp upon. The age of miracles is each moment thus returned. Now it is wild apples, now river reflections, now a flock of lesser redpolls. In winter, too, resides immortal youth and perennial summer. —Journal, December 11, 1855

Beauty and music are not mere traits and exceptions. They are the rule and character. It is the exception that we see and hear. Then I try to discover what it was in the vision that charmed and translated me. What if we could daguerreotype our thoughts and feelings! for I am surprised and enchanted often by some quality which I cannot detect. I have seen an attribute of another world and condition of things. It is a wonderful fact that I should be affected, and thus deeply and powerfully, more than by aught else in my experience — that this fruit should be borne in me, sprung from a seed finer than the spores of fungi, floated from other atmospheres! finer than the dust caught in the sails of vessels a thousand miles from land! Here the invisible seeds settle, and spring, and bear flowers and fruits of immortal beauty. —Journal, December 11, 1855

How much warmer our woodlands look and *are* for these withered leaves that still hang on! Without them the woods would be dreary, bleak, and wintry indeed. Here is a manifest provision for the necessities of man and the brutes. The leaves remain to keep us warm and to keep the earth warm about their roots. —Journal, December 11, 1858

There is apology enough for all the deficiency and shortcoming in the world in the patient waiting of any bud of character to unfold itself. —Journal, December 12, 1841

I have been surveying for twenty or thirty days, living coarsely, even as respects my diet — for I find that that will always alter to suit my employment — indeed, leading a quite trivial life; and tonight, for the first time, had made a fire in my chamber and endeavored to return to myself. I wished to ally myself to the powers that rule the universe. I wished to dive into some deep stream of thoughtful and

devoted life, which meandered through retired and fertile meadows far from towns. I wished to do again, or for once, things quite congenial to my highest inmost and most sacred nature, to lurk in crystalline thought like the trout under verdurous banks, where stray mankind should only see my bubble come to the surface. I wished to live, ah! as far away as a man can think. I wished for leisure and quiet to let my life flow in its proper channels, with its proper currents; when I might not waste the days, might establish daily prayer and thanksgiving in my family; might do my own work and not the work of Concord and Carlisle, which would yield me better than money. (How much forbearance, aye, sacrifice and loss, goes to every accomplishment! I am thinking by what long discipline and at what cost a man learns to speak simply at last.)
—Journal, December 12, 1851

I cannot say that Swedenborg has been directly and practically valuable to me, for I have not been a reader of him, except to a slight extent; but I have the highest regard for him, and trust that I shall read his works in some world or other. He had a wonderful knowledge of our interior and spiritual life, though his illuminations are occasionally blurred by trivialities. He comes nearer to answering, or attempting to answer, literally, your questions concerning man's origin, purpose, and destiny, than any of the worthies I have referred to. But I think that that is not *altogether* a recommendation; since such an answer to these questions cannot be discovered any more than perpetual motion, for which no reward is now offered. The noblest man it is, methinks, that knows, and by his life suggests, the most about these things. Crack away at these nuts, however, as long as you can — the very exercise will ennoble you, and you may get something better than the answer you expect. —Letter to B.B. Wiley, December 12, 1856

While surveying today, saw much mountain laurel for this neighborhood in Mason's pasture, just over the line in Carlisle. Its bright yellowish-green shoots are agreeable to my eye. We had one hour of almost Indian summer weather in the middle of the day. I felt the influence of the sun. It melted my stoniness a little. The pines looked like old friends again. Cutting a path through a swamp where was much brittle dogwood, etc., etc., I wanted to know the name of every shrub. This varied employment, to which my necessities compel me, serves instead of foreign travel and the lapse of time. If it makes me forget some things which I ought to remember, it no doubt enables me to forget many things which it is well to forget. By stepping aside from my chosen path so often, I see myself better and am enabled to criticise myself. Of this nature is the only true lapse of time. It seems an age since I took walks and wrote in my journal, and when shall I revisit the glimpses of the moon? To be able to see ourselves, not merely as others see us, but as we are, that service a *variety* of absorbing employments does us. —Journal, December 13, 1851

Man lays down his body in the field and thinks from it as a stepping stone to vault at once into heaven, as if he could establish a better claim there when he had left such a witness behind him on the plain. Our true epitaphs are those which the sun and wind write upon the atmosphere around our graves so conclusively that the traveller does not draw near to read the lie on our tombstones. Shall we not be judged rather by what we leave behind us, than what we bring into the world? The guest is known by his leavings. When we have become intolerable to ourselves shall we be tolerable to heaven? —Journal, December 14, 1840

Silence is the communing of a conscious soul with itself. If the soul attend for a moment to its own infinity, then and there is silence. She is audible to all men, at all times, in all places, and if we will we may always hearken to her admonitions. —Journal, December 15, 1838

I seem to see somewhat more of my own kith and kin in the lichens on the rocks than in any books. It does seem as if mine were a peculiarly wild nature, which so yearns toward all wildness. I know of no redeeming qualities in me but a sincere love for some things, and when I am reproved I have to fall back on to this ground. This is my argument in reserve for all cases. My love is invulnerable. Meet me on that ground, and you will find me strong. When I am condemned, and condemn myself utterly, I think straightaway, "But I rely on my love for some things." Therein I am whole and entire. Therein I am God-propped. —Journal, December 15, 1841

One's *life*, the enterprise he is here upon, should certainly be a grand fact to consider, not a mean or insignificant one. A man should not live without a purpose, and that purpose must surely be a grand one. But is this fact of "our life" commonly but a puff of air, a flash in the pan, a smoke, a nothing? It does not afford arena for a tragedy. —Journal, December 15, 1852

Philosophy is a Greek word by good rights, and it stands almost for a Greek thing. Yet some rumor of it has reached the commonest mind. M. Miles, who came to collect his wood-bill today, said, when I objected to the small size of his wood, that it was necessary to split wood fine in order to cure it well, that he had found that that was more than four inches in diameter would not dry, and moreover a good deal depended on the manner in which it was corded up in the woods. He piled his high and tightly. If this were not well done the stakes would spread and the wood lie loosely, and so the rain and snow find their way into it. And he added, "I have handled a good deal of

wood, and I think that I understand the *philosophy* of it."
—Journal, December 15, 1859

Would you be well, see that you are attuned to each mood of nature. —Journal, December 16, 1853

When a man is young and his constitution and body have not acquired firmness, i.e., before he has arrived at middle age, he is not an assured inhabitant of the earth, and his compensation is that he is not quite earthy, there is something peculiarly tender and divine about him. His sentiments and his weakness, nay, his very sickness and the greater uncertainty of his fate, seem to ally him to a noble race of beings, to whom he in part belongs, or with whom he is in communication. The young man is a demigod; the grown man, alas! is commonly a mere mortal. He is but half here, he knows not the men of this world, the powers that be. They know him not. Prompted by the reminiscence of that other sphere from which he so lately arrived, his actions are unintelligible to his seniors. He bathes in light. He is interesting as a stranger from another sphere. He really thinks and talks about a larger sphere of existence than this world. It takes him forty years to accommodate himself to the carapax of this world. This is the age of poetry. Afterward he may be the president of a bank, and go the way of all flesh. But a man of settled views, whose thoughts are few and hardened like his bones, is truly mortal, and his only resource is to say his prayers. —Journal, December 18, 1859

We must heap up a great pile of doing, for a small diameter of being. Is it not imperative on us that we *do* something, if we only work in a treadmill? And, indeed, some sort of revolving is necessary to produce a centre and nucleus of being. What exercise is to the body, employment is to the mind and morals. Consider what an amount of drudgery must be performed — how much humdrum and prosaic labor goes to any work of the least value. There are so many layers of mere white lime in every shell to that thin inner one so beautifully tinted. Let not the shellfish think to build his house of that alone; and pray, what are its tints to him? Is it not his smooth, close-fitting shirt merely, whose tints *are not* to him, being in the dark, but only when he is gone or dead, and his shell is heaved up to light, a wreck upon the beach, do they appear. With him, too, it is a Song of the Shirt, "Work — work — work!" And the work is not merely a police in the gross sense, but in the higher sense a discipline. If it is surely the means to the highest end we know, can any work be humble or disgusting? Will it not rather be elevating as a ladder, the means by which we are translated? —Letter to Harrison Blake, December 19, 1853

I have not yet learned to live, that I can see, and I fear that I shall not very soon. I find, however, that in the long run things correspond to my original idea — that they correspond to nothing else so much; and thus a man may really be a true prophet without any great exertion. The day is never so dark, nor the night even, but that the laws at least of light still prevail, and so may make it light in our minds if they are open to the truth. There is considerable danger that a man will be crazy between dinner and supper; but it will not directly answer any good purpose that I know of, and it is just as easy to be sane. We have got to know what both life and death are, before we can begin to live after our own fashion. —Letter to Harrison Blake, December 19, 1853

Withered leaves! this is our frugal winter diet, instead of the juicy salads of spring and summer. I think I could write a lecture on "Dry Leaves," carrying a specimen of each kind that hangs on in the winter into the lecture-room as the heads of my discourse. They have long hung to some extent in vain, and have not found their poet yet. The pine has been sung, but not, to my knowledge, the shrub oak. Most think it is useless. How glad I am that it serves no vulgar use! It is never seen on the woodman's cart. The citizen who has just bought a sprout-land on which shrub oaks alone come up only curses it. But it serves a higher use than they know. —Journal, December 19, 1856

I am under an awful necessity to be what I am. —Journal, December 21, 1851

One moment of serene and confident life is more glorious than a whole campaign of daring. We should be ready for all issues, not daring to die but daring to live. —Journal, December 1839

In 1845 Walden froze entirely over for the first time on the night of the 22d of December, Flint's and other shallower ponds and the river having been frozen ten days or more; in '46, the 16th; in '49, about the 31st; and in '50, about the 27th of December; in '52, the 5th of January; in '53, the 31st of December. The snow had already covered the ground since the 25th of November, and surrounded me suddenly with the scenery of winter. I withdrew yet farther into my shell, and endeavored to keep a bright fire both within my house and within my breast. —Walden, "House Warming"

It is a record of the mellow and ripe moments that I would keep. I would not preserve the husk of life, but the kernel. —Journal, December 23, 1851

I want to go soon and live away by the pond, where I shall hear only the wind whispering among the reeds. It will be a success if I shall have left myself behind. But my friends ask what I will do when I get there. Will it not be enough to watch the progress of the seasons? —Journal, December 24, 1841

I don't want to feel as if my life were a sojourn any longer. That philosophy cannot be true which so paints it. It is time now that I begin to live. —Journal, December 25, 1841

Do not speak for other men; speak for yourself. They show you as in a vision the kingdoms of the world, and of all the worlds, but you prefer to look in upon a puppet-show. Though you should only speak to one kindred mind in all time, though you should not speak to one, but only utter aloud, that you may the more completely realize and live in the idea which contains the reason of your life, that you may build yourself up to the height of your conceptions, that you may remember your Creator in the days of your youth and justify His ways to man, that the end of life may not be its amusement, speak — though your thought presupposes the non-existence of your hearers — thoughts that transcend life and death.
—Journal, December 25, 1851

The whole duty of life is contained in this question: how to respire and aspire both at once. —Journal, December 26, 1841

To such a pass our civilization and division of labor has come that A, a professional huckleberry-picker, has hired B's field and, we will suppose, is now gathering the crop, perhaps with the aid of a patented medicine; C, a professed cook, is superintending the cooking of a pudding made of some of the berries; while Professor D, for whom the pudding is intended, sits in his library writing a book — a work on the *Vaccinieae*, of course. And now the result of this downward course will be seen in that book, which should be the ultimate fruit of the huckleberry-field and account for the existence of the two professors who come between D and A. It will be worthless. There will be none of the spirit of the huckleberry in it. The reading of it will be a weariness to the flesh. To use a homely illustration, this is to save at the spile but waste at the bung. I believe in a different kind of division of labor, and that Professor D should divide himself between the library and the huckleberry-field. —Journal, December 26, 1860

Talk of fate! How little one can know what is fated to another! — what he can do and what he can not do! I doubt whether one can give or receive any very pertinent advice. In all important crises one can only consult his genius. Though he were the most shiftless and craziest of mortals, if he still recognizes that he has any genius to consult, none may presume to go between him and her. They, methinks, are poor stuff and creatures of a miserable fate who can be advised and persuaded in very important steps. Show me a man who consults his genius, and you have shown me a man who cannot be advised. You may know what a thing costs or is worth to you; you can never know what it costs or is worth to me. All the community may scream because one man is born who will not do as it does, who will not conform because conformity to him is death — he is so constituted. They know nothing about his case; they are fools when they presume to advise him. The man of genius knows what he is aiming at; nobody else knows. And he alone knows when something comes between him and his object. In the course of generations, however, men will excuse you for not doing as they do, if you will bring enough to pass in your own way.
—Journal, December 27, 1858

Both for bodily and mental health, court the present. Embrace health wherever you find her. —Journal, December 28, 1852

It is worth the while to apply what wisdom one has to the conduct of his life, surely. I find myself oftenest wise in little things and foolish in great ones. That I may accomplish some particular petty affair well, I live my whole life coarsely. A broad margin of leisure is as beautiful in a man's life as in a book. Haste makes waste, no less in life than in housekeeping. Keep the time, observe the hours of the universe, not of the cars. What are threescore years and ten hurriedly and coarsely lived to moments of divine leisure in which your life is coincident with the life of the universe? We live too fast and coarsely, just as we eat too fast, and do not know the true savor of our food. We consult our will and understanding and the expectation of men, not our genius. I can impose upon myself tasks which will crush me for life and prevent all expansion, and this I am but too inclined to do.

One moment of life costs many hours, hours not of business but of preparation and invitation. Yet the man who does not betake himself at once and desperately to sawing is called a loafer, though he may be knocking at the doors of heaven all the while, which shall surely be opened to him. That aim in life is highest which requires the highest and finest discipline. How much, what infinite, leisure it requires, as of a lifetime, to appreciate a single phenomenon! You must camp down beside it as for life, having reached your stand for the whole world to you, symbolical of all things. The least partialness is your own defect of sight and cheapens the experience fatally. Unless the humming of a gnat is as the music of the spheres, and the music of the spheres is as the humming of a gnat, they are naught to me. It is not communications to serve for a history — which are science — but the great story itself, that cheers and satisfies us. —Journal, December 28, 1852

I thrive best on solitude. If I have had a companion only one day in a week, unless it were one or two I could name, I find that the value of the week to me has been seriously affected. —Journal, December 28, 1856

One does not soon learn the trade of life. That one may work out a true life requires more art and delicate skill than any other work. —Journal, December 29, 1841

The thoughts and associations of summer and autumn are now as completely departed from our minds as the leaves are blown from the trees. Some withered deciduous ones are left to rustle, and our cold immortal evergreens. Some lichenous thoughts still adhere to us. —Journal, December 29, 1853

We must go out and re-ally ourselves to Nature every day. We must make root, send out some little fibre at least, even every winter day. I am sensible that I am imbibing health when I open my mouth to the wind. Staying in the house breeds a sort of insanity always. Every house is in this sense a hospital. A night and a forenoon is as much confinement to those wards as I can stand. I am aware that I recover some sanity which I had lost almost the instant that I come abroad. —Journal, December 29, 1856

As the least drop of wine tinges the whole goblet, so the least particle of truth colors our whole life. It is never isolated, or simply added as treasure to our stock. When any real progress is made, we unlearn and learn anew what we thought we knew before....

Men claim for the ideal an actual existence also, but do not often expand the actual into the ideal. —Journal, December 31, 1837

In winter even man is to a slight extent dormant, just as some animals are but partially awake, though not commonly classed with those that hibernate. The summer circulations are to some extent stopped; the range of his afternoon walk is somewhat narrower; he is more or less confined to the highway and wood-path; the weather oftener shuts him up in his burrow; he begins to feel the access of dormancy and to assume the spherical form of the marmot; the nights are longest; he is often satisfied if he only gets out to the post-office in the course of the day. The arctic voyagers are obliged to invent and willfully engage in active amusements to keep themselves awake and alive. Most men do not now extend their walks beyond the village street. Even our experience is something like wintering in the pack. —Journal, December 30, 1853

How glorious the perfect stillness and peace of the winter landscape! —Journal, December 31, 1854

SEASONS OF THOREAU

January

The snow is the great betrayer. It not only shows the tracks of mice, otters, etc., etc., which else we should rarely if ever see, but the tree sparrows are more plainly seen against its white ground, and they in turn are attracted by the dark weeds which it reveals. It also drives the crows and other birds out of the woods to the villages for food. We might expect to find in the snow the footprint of a life superior to our own, of which no zoology takes cognizance. Is there no trace of a nobler life than that of an otter or an escaped convict to be looked for in the snow? Shall we suppose that that is the only life that has been abroad in the night? It is only the savage that can see the track of no higher life than an otter. Why do the vast snow plains give us pleasure, the twilight of the bent and half-buried woods? Is not all there consonant with virtue, justice, purity, courage, magnanimity? And does not all this amount to the track of a higher life than the otter's, a life which has not gone by and left a footprint merely, but is there with its beauty, its music, its perfume, its sweetness, to exhilarate and recreate us? Where there is a perfect government of the world according to the highest laws, is there no trace of intelligence there, whether in the snow or the earth, or in ourselves? No other trail but such as a dog can smell? Is there none which an angel can detect and follow? None to guide a man on his pilgrimage, which water will not conceal? Is there no odor of sanctity to be perceived? Is its trail too old? Have mortals lost the scent? The great game for mighty hunters as soon as the first snow falls is Purity, for, earlier than any rabbit or fox, it is abroad, and its trail may be detected by curs of lowest degree. Did this great snow come to reveal the track merely of some timorous hare, or of the Great Hare, whose track no hunter has seen? Is there no trace nor suggestion of Purity to be detected? If one could detect the meaning of the snow, would he not be on the trail of some higher life that has been abroad in the night? Are there not hunters who seek for something higher than foxes, with judgment more discriminating than the sense of foxhounds, who rally to a nobler music than that of the hunting-horn? As there is contention among the fishermen who shall be the first to reach the pond as soon as the ice will bear, in spite of the cold, as the hunters are forward to take the field as soon as the first snow has fallen, so the observer, or he who would make the most of his life for discipline, must be abroad early and late, in spite of cold and wet, in pursuit of nobler game, whose traces are then most distinct. A life which, pursued, does not earth itself, does not burrow downward but upward, which takes not to the trees but to the heavens as its home, which the hunter pursues with winged thoughts and aspiration — these the dogs that tree it — rallying his pack with the bugle notes of undying faith, and returns with some worthier trophy than a fox's tail, a life which we seek, not to destroy it, but to save our own. Is the great snow of use to the hunter only, and not to the saint, or him who is earnestly building up a life? —Journal, January 1, 1854

What mountain are you camping on nowadays? Though I had a good time at the mountains, I confess that the journey did not bear any fruit that I know of. I did not expect it would. The mode of it was not simple and adventurous enough. You must first have made an infinite demand, and not unreasonably, but after a corresponding outlay, have an all-absorbing purpose, and at the same time that your feet bear you hither and thither, travel much more in imagination.

To let the mountains slide — live at home like a traveller. It should not be in vain that these things are shown us from day to day. Is not each withered leaf that I see in my walks something which I have travelled to find?—

travelled, who can tell how far? What a fool he must be who thinks that his El Dorado is anywhere but where he lives! —Letter to Harrison Blake, January 1, 1859

The wonderful purity of nature at this season is a most pleasing fact. Every decayed stump and moss-grown stone and rail, and the dead leaves of autumn, are concealed by a clean napkin of snow. In the bare fields and tinkling woods, see what virtue survives. In the coldest and bleakest places, the warmest charities still maintain a foothold. A cold and searching wind drives away all contagion, and nothing can withstand it but what has a virtue in it, and accordingly, whatever we meet with in cold and bleak places, as the tops of mountains, we respect for a sort of sturdy innocence, a Puritan toughness. All things beside seem to be called in for shelter, and what stays out must be part of the original frame of the universe, and of such valor as God himself. It is invigorating to breathe the cleansed air. Its greater fineness and purity are visible to the eye, and we would fain stay out long and late, that the gales may sigh through us, too, as through the leafless trees, and fit us for the winter — as if we hoped so to borrow some pure and steadfast virtue, which will stead us in all seasons.

There is a slumbering subterranean fire in nature which never goes out, and which no cold can chill. It finally melts the great snow, and in January or July is only buried under a thicker or thinner covering. In the coldest day it flows somewhere, and the snow melts around every tree. This field of winter rye, which sprouted late in the fall, and now speedily dissolves the snow, is where the fire is very thinly covered. We feel warmed by it. In the winter, warmth stands for all virtue, and we resort in thought to a trickling rill, with its bare stones shining in the sun, and to warm springs in the woods, with as much eagerness as rabbits and robins. The steam which rises from swamps and pools is as dear and domestic as that of our own kettle. What fire could ever equal the sunshine of a winter's day, when the meadow mice come out by the wall-sides, and the chickadee lisps in the defiles of the wood? The warmth comes directly from the sun, and is not radiated from the earth, as in summer; and when we feel his beams on our backs as we are treading some snowy dell, we are grateful as for a special kindness, and bless the sun which has followed us into that by-place.

This subterranean fire has its altar in each man's breast; for in the coldest day, and on the bleakest hill, the traveller cherishes a warmer fire within the folds of his cloak than is kindled on any hearth. A healthy man, indeed, is the complement of the seasons, and in winter, summer is in his heart. There is the south. Thither have all birds and insects migrated, and around the warm springs in his breast are gathered the robin and the lark. —"A Winter's Walk" (1843)

Here reign the simplicity and purity of a primitive age, and a health and hope far remote from towns and cities. Standing quite alone, far in the forest, while the wind is shaking down snow from the trees, and leaving the only human tracks behind us, we find our reflections of a richer variety than the life of cities. The chickadee and nuthatch are more inspiring society than statesmen and philosophers, and we shall return to these last as to more vulgar companions. In this lonely glen, with its brook draining the slopes, its creased ice and crystals of all hues, where the spruces and hemlocks stand up on either side, and the rush and sere wild oats in the rivulet itself, our lives are more serene and worthy to contemplate. —"A Winter's Walk" (1843)

Though winter is represented in the almanac as an old man, facing the wind and sleet, and drawing his cloak about him, we rather think of him as a merry woodchopper, and warm-blooded youth, as blithe as summer. The unexplored grandeur of the storm keeps up the spirits of the traveller. It does not trifle with us, but has a sweet earnestness. In winter we lead a more inward life. Our hearts are warm and cheery, like cottages under drifts, whose windows and doors are half concealed, but from whose chimneys the smoke cheerfully ascends. The imprisoning drifts increase the sense of comfort which the house affords, and in the coldest days we are content to sit over the hearth and see the sky through the chimney-top, enjoying the quiet and serene life that may be had in a warm corner by the chimney-side, or feeling our pulse by listening to the low of cattle in the street, or the sound of the flail in distant barns all the long afternoon. No doubt a skillful physician could determine our health by observing how these simple and natural sounds affected us. We enjoy now, not an Oriental, but a Boreal leisure, around warm stoves and fireplaces, and watch the shadow of motes in the sunbeams. —"A Winter's Walk" (1843)

I love nature partly *because* she is not man, but a retreat from him. None of his institutions control or pervade her. There a different kind of right prevails. In her midst I can be glad with an entire gladness. If this world were all man, I could not stretch myself, I should lose all hope. He is constraint, she is freedom to me. He makes me wish for another world. She makes me content with this. —Journal, January 3, 1853

It is now fairly winter. We have passed the line, have put the autumn behind us, have forgotten what these withered herbs that rise above the snow here and there are, what flowers they ever bore. —Journal, January 3, 1854

The true fruit of Nature can only be plucked with a delicate hand not bribed by any earthly reward, and a fluttering heart. No hired man can help us to gather this crop.

How few ever get beyond feeding, clothing, sheltering, and warming themselves in this world, and begin to treat themselves as human beings — as intellectual and moral beings! —Journal, January 3, 1861

After spending four or five days surveying and drawing a plan incessantly, I especially feel the necessity of putting myself in communication with nature again, to recover my tone, to withdraw out of the wearying and unprofitable world of affairs. The things I have been doing have but a fleeting and accidental importance, however much men are immersed in them, and yield very little valuable fruit. I would fain have been wading through the woods and fields and conversing with the sane snow. Having waded in the very shallowest stream of time, I would now bathe my temples in eternity. I wish again to participate in the serenity of nature, to share the happiness of the river and the woods. I thus from time to time break off my connection with eternal truths and go with the shallow stream of human affairs, grinding at the mill of the Philistines; but when my task is done, with never-failing confidence I devote myself to the infinite again. It would be sweet to deal with men more, I can imagine, but where dwell they? Not in the fields which I traverse. —Journal, January 4, 1857

I find that whatever hindrances may occur I write just about the same amount of truth in my Journal; for the record is more concentrated, and usually it is some very real and earnest life, after all, that interrupts. All flourishes are omitted. If I saw wood from morning to night, though I grieve that I could not observe the train of my thoughts during that time, yet, in the evening, the few scrannel lines which describe my day's occupations will make the creaking of the saw more musical than my freest fancies could have been. I find incessant labor with the hands, which engrosses the attention also, the best method to remove palaver out of one's style. One will not dance at his work who has wood to cut and cord before the night falls in the short days of winter; but every stroke will be husbanded, and ring soberly through the wood; and so will his lines ring and tell on the ear, when at evening he settles the accounts of the day. I have often been astonished at the force and precision of style to which busy laboring men, unpracticed in writing, easily attain when they are required to make the effort. It seems as if their sincerity and plainness were the main thing to be taught in schools — and yet not in the schools, but in the fields, in actual service, I should say....

I want to see a sentence run clear through to the end, as deep and fertile as a well-drawn furrow which shows that the plow was pressed down to the beam. If our scholars would lead more earnest lives, we should not witness those lame conclusions to their ill-sown discourses, but their sentences would pass over the ground like loaded rollers, and not mere hollow and wooden ones, to press in the seed and make it germinate. —Journal, January 5, 1842

Nature is full of genius, full of the divinity; so that not a snowflake escapes its fashioning hand. —Journal, January 5, 1856

As a child looks forward to the coming of the summer, so could we contemplate with quiet joy the circle of the seasons returning without fail eternally. As the spring came round during so many years of the gods, we could go out to admire and adorn anew our Eden, and yet never tire. —Journal, January 6, 1838

Very little evidence of God or man did I see just then, and life not as rich and inviting an enterprise as it should be, when my attention was caught by a snowflake on my coat-sleeve. It was one of those perfect, crystalline, star-shaped ones, six-rayed, like a flat wheel with six spokes, only the spokes were perfect little pine trees in shape, arranged around a central spangle. This little object, which, with so many of its fellows, rested unmelting on my coat, so perfect and beautiful, reminded me that Nature had not lost her pristine vigor yet, and why should man lose heart? —Journal, January 6, 1858

The great God is very calm withal. How superfluous is any excitement in his creatures! He listens equally to the prayers of the believer and the unbeliever. The moods of man should unfold and alternate as gradually and placidly as those of nature. The sun shines for aye! The sudden revolutions of these times and this generation have acquired a very exaggerated importance. They do not interest me much, for they are not in harmony with the longer periods of nature. —Journal, January 7, 1842

This is one of those pleasant winter mornings when you find the river firmly frozen in the night, but still the air is serene and the sun feels gratefully warm an hour after sunrise — though so fair, a healthy whitish vapor fills the lower stratum of the air, concealing the mountains — the smokes go up from the village, you hear the cocks with immortal vigor, and the children shout on their way to school, and the sound made by the railroad men hammering a rail is uncommonly musical. This promises a perfect winter day. In the heavens, except the altitude of the sun, you have, as it were, the conditions of summer. Perfect serenity and clarity and sonorousness in the earth. All nature is but braced by the cold. It gives tension to both body and mind. —Journal, January 7, 1852

The delicious soft, spring-suggesting air — how it fills my veins with life! Life becomes again credible to me. A certain dormant life awakes in me, and I begin to love nature again. Here is my Italy, my heaven, my New England. —Journal, January 7, 1855

There is nothing so sanative, so poetic, as a walk in the woods and fields even now, when I meet none abroad for pleasure. Nothing so inspires me and excites such serene and profitable thought. The objects are elevating. In the street and in society I am almost invariably cheap and dissipated, my life is unspeakably mean. No amount of gold or respectability would in the least redeem it — dining with the governor — or a member of congress!! But alone in distant woods or fields, in unpretending sproutlands or pastures tracked by rabbits, even in a bleak and to most, cheerless day like this, when a villager would be thinking of his inn, I come to myself, I once more feel myself grandly related, and that cold and solitude are friends of mine. I suppose that this value, in my case, is equivalent to what others get by churchgoing and prayer. I come to my solitary woodland walk as the homesick go home. I thus dispose of the superfluous and see things as they are, grand and beautiful. I have told many that I walk every day about half the daylight, but I think they do not believe it. I wish to get the Concord — the Massachusetts — the America, out of my head and be sane a part of every day. If there are missionaries for the heathen, why not send them to me? I wish to know something; I wish to be made better. I wish to forget, a considerable part of every day, all mean, narrow, trivial men (and this requires usually to forego and forget all personal relations so long), and therefore I come out to these solitudes, where the problem of existence is simplified. I get away a mile or two from the town into the stillness and solitude of nature, with rocks, trees, weeds, snow about me. I enter some glade in the woods, perchance, where a few weeds and dry leaves alone lift themselves above the surface of the snow, and it is as if I had come to an open window. I see out and around myself. Our *skylights* are thus far away from the ordinary resorts of men. I am not satisfied with ordinary windows. I must have a true *skylight*. —Journal, January 7, 1857

We love not so well the landscape represented as in broad noon, but in a morning or evening twilight, those seasons when the imagination is most active, the more hopeful or pensive seasons of the day. Our mood may then possess the whole landscape, or be in harmony with it, as the hue of twilight prevails over the whole scene. Are we more than crepuscular in our intellectual and spiritual life? Have we awakened to broad noon? The morning hope is soon lost in what becomes the routine of the day, and we do not recover ourselves again until we land on the pensive shores of evening, shores which skirt the great western continent of the night. At sunset we look into the west. For centuries our thoughts fish those grand banks that lie before the newfoundland, before our spirits take up their abode in that Hesperian Continent to which these lie in the way. —Journal, January 8, 1854

As I climbed the Cliff, I paused in the sun and sat on a dry rock, dreaming. I thought of those summery hours when time is tinged with eternity — runs into it and becomes of one stuff with it. How much — how, perhaps, all — that is best in our experience in middle life may be resolved into the memory of our youth! I remember how I expanded. If the genius visits me now I am not quite taken off my feet, but I remember how this experience is like, but less than, that I had long since.

Pulling up the johnswort on the face of the Cliff, I am surprised to see the signs of unceasing growth about the roots — fresh shoots two inches long, white with red leaflets, and all the radical part quite green. The leaves of the crowfoot, also, are quite green, and carry me forward to spring. I dig one up with a stick, and, pulling it to pieces, I find deep in the centre of the plant, just beneath the ground, surrounded by all the tender leaves that are about to precede it, the blossom-bud, about half as big as the head of a pin, perfectly white. There it patiently sits, or slumbers, how full of faith, informed of a spring which the world has never seen, the promise and prophecy of it shaped somewhat like some Eastern temples, in which a bud-shaped dome o'ertops the whole. It affected me, this tender dome-like bud, within the bosom of the earth, like a temple upon the earth, resounding with the worship of votaries. Methought I saw the flamens in yellow robes within it. The crowfoot buds — and how many beside! — lie unexpanded just beneath the surface. May I lead my life the following year as innocently as they! May it be as fair and smell as sweet! I anticipate nature. —Journal, January 9, 1853

To know nature and ourselves well, we must have acquired a certain hardness and habitual equanimity. —Journal, January 10, 1841

We sometimes find ourselves living fast — unprofitably and coarsely even — as we catch ourselves eating our meals in unaccountable haste. But in one sense we cannot live too leisurely. Let me not live as if time was short. Catch the pace of the seasons; have leisure to attend to every phenomenon of nature, and to entertain every thought that comes to you. Let your life be a leisurely progress through the realms of nature. —Journal, January 11, 1852

What of architectural beauty I now see, I know has gradually grown from within outward, out of the character and necessities of the indweller and builder, without even a thought for mere ornament, but an unconscious nobleness and truthfulness of character and life; and whatever additional beauty of this kind is destined to be produced will be preceded and accompanied, aye, created, by a like unconscious beauty of life. One of the most beautiful buildings in this country is a logger's hut in the woods, and equally beautiful will be the citizen's suburban box, when the life of the indweller shall be as simple and agreeable to the imagination, and there is as little straining after effect in the style of his dwelling. —Journal, January 11, 1852

The question is not where did the traveller go? what places did he see? — it would be difficult to choose between places — but who was the traveller? how did he travel? how genuine an experience did he get? For travelling is, in the main, like as if you stayed at home, and then the question is how do you live and conduct yourself at home? What I mean is that it might be hard to decide whether I would travel to Lake Superior, or Labrador, or Florida. Perhaps none would be worth the while, if I went by the usual mode. But if I travel in a simple, primitive, original manner, standing in a truer relation to men and nature, travel away from the old and commonplace, get some honest experience of life, if only out of my feet and homesickness, then it becomes less important whither I go or how far. I so see the world from a new and more commanding point of view. —Journal, January 11, 1852

I sometimes think that I may go forth and walk hard and earnestly, and live a more substantial life and get a glorious experience; be much abroad in heat and cold, day and night; live more, expend more atmospheres, be weary often, etc., etc. But then swiftly the thought comes to me, Go not so far out of your way for a truer life; keep strictly onward in that path alone which your genius points out. Do the things which lie nearest you, but which are difficult to do. Live a purer, a more thoughtful and laborious life, more true to your friends and neighbors, more noble and magnanimous and that will be better than a wild walk. To live in relations of truth and sincerity with men is to dwell in a frontier country. What a wild and unfrequented wilderness that would be! What Saguenays of magnanimity that might be explored! —Journal, January 12, 1852

Perhaps what most moves us in winter is some reminiscence of far-off summer. How we leap by the side of the open brooks! What beauty in the running brooks! What life! What society! The cold is merely superficial; it is summer still at the core, far, far within. It is in the cawing of the crow, the crowing of the cock, the warmth of the sun on our backs. I hear faintly the cawing of a crow far, far away, echoing from some unseen wood-side, as if deadened by the springlike vapor which the sun is drawing from the ground. It mingles with the slight murmur of the village, the sound of children at play, as one stream empties gently into another, and the wild and tame are one. —Journal, January 12, 1855

We should offer up our perfect thoughts to the gods daily. Our writing should be hymns and psalms. Who keeps a journal is purveyor to the gods. There are two sides to every sentence. The one is contiguous to me, but the other faces the gods, and no man ever fronted it. When I utter a thought, I launch a vessel which never sails in my harbor more, but goes sheer off into the deep. Consequently it demands a godlike insight, a fronting view, to read what was greatly written. —Journal, January 13, 1841

We forget to strive and aspire, to do better even than is expected of us. I cannot stay to be congratulated. I would leave the world behind me. We must withdraw from our flatterers, even from our friends. They drag us down. It is rare that we use our thinking faculty as resolutely as an Irishman his spade. To please our friends and relatives we turn out our silver ore in cartloads, while we neglect to

work our mines of gold known only to ourselves far up in the Sierras, where we pulled up a bush in our mountain walk, and saw the glittering treasure. Let us return thither. Let it be the price of our freedom to make that known.
—Journal, January 13, 1852

In our workshops we pride ourselves on discovering a use for what had previously been regarded as waste, but how partial and accidental our economy compared with Nature's. In Nature nothing is wasted. Every decayed leaf and twig and fibre is only the better fitted to serve in some other department, and all at last are gathered in her compost-heap. —Journal, January 13, 1856

I hear one thrumming a guitar below stairs. It reminds me of moments that I have lived. What a comment upon our life is the least strain of music! It lifts me above the mire and dust of the universe. I soar or hover with clean skirts over a field of my life. It is ever life within life, in concentric spheres. The field wherein I toil or rust at any time is at the same time the field for such different kinds of life! The farmer's boy or hired man has an instinct which tells him as much indistinctly, and hence his dreams and his restlessness; hence, even, it is that he wants money to realize his dreams with. The identical field where I am leading my humdrum life, let but a strain of music be heard there, is seen to be the field of some unrecorded crusade or tournament the thought of which excites in us an ecstasy of joy. The way in which I am affected by this faint thrumming advertises me that there is still some health and immortality in the springs of me. What an elixir is sound! I, who but lately came and went and lived under a dish cover, live now under the heavens. It releases me; it bursts my bonds. Almost all, perhaps all, our life is, speaking comparatively, a stereotyped despair; i.e., we never at any time realize the full grandeur of our destiny.

We forever and ever and habitually underrate our fate.
—Journal, January 13, 1857

Pliny says, "*In minimis Natura praestat*" (Nature excels in the least things). The *Wellingtonia gigantea*, the famous California tree, is a great thing; the seed from which it sprang, a little thing; and so are all seeds or origins of things. —Journal, January 14, 1861

In the deepest snows, the path which I used from the highway to my house, about half a mile long, might have been represented by a meandering dotted line, with wide intervals between the dots. For a week of even weather I took exactly the same number of steps, and of the same length, coming and going, stepping deliberately and with the precision of a pair of dividers in my own deep tracks — to such routine the winter reduces us — yet often they were filled with heaven's own blue. —Walden, "Former Inhabitants and Winter Visitors"

In proportion as I have celestial thoughts, it is the necessity for me to be out and behold the western sky before sunset these winter days. That is the symbol of the unclouded mind that knows neither winter nor summer. What is your thought like? That is the hue, that the purity, and transparency, and distance from earthly taint of my inmost mind, for whatever we see without is a symbol of something within, and that which is farthest off is the symbol of what is deepest within. The lover of contemplation, accordingly, will gaze much into the sky. Fair thoughts and a serene mind make fair days. The rainbow is the symbol of the triumph which succeeds to a grief that has tried us to our advantage, so that at last we can smile through our tears. It is the aspect with which we come out of the house of mourning. We have found our relief in tears. As the skies appear to a man, so is his mind. Some see only clouds there; some, prodigies and portents;

some rarely look up at all; their heads, like the brutes', are directed toward earth. Some behold there serenity, purity, beauty ineffable. —Journal, January 17, 1852

When we are so poor that the howling of the wind shall have a music in it, and not declare war against our property — the proprietors may well envy us. We have been seeking riches not by a true industry or building within, but by mere accumulation, putting together was was without, till it rose a heap beside us. We should rather acquire them by the utter renunciation of them. If I hold a house and land as property, am I not disinherited of sun, wind, rain, and all good beside? The richest are only some degrees poorer than nature. —Journal, January 18, 1841

The temperature of the air and the clearness or serenity of the sky are indispensable to a knowledge of a day, so entirely do we sympathize with the moods of nature. It is important to know of a day that is past whether it was warm or cold, clear or cloudy, calm or windy, etc.

They are very different seasons in the winter when the ice of the river and meadows and ponds is bare — blue or green, a vast glittering crystal — and when it is all covered with snow or slosh; and our moods correspond. The former may be called a crystalline winter. —Journal, January 18, 1860

In my experience, I have found nothing so truly impoverishing as what is called wealth, i.e. the command of greater means than you had before possessed, though comparatively few and slight still, for you thus inevitably acquire a more expensive habit of living, and even the very same necessaries and comforts cost you more than they once did. Instead of gaining, you have lost some independence, and if your income should be suddenly lessened, you would find yourself poor, though possessed of the same means which once made you rich. Within the last five years I have had the command of a little more money than in the previous five years, for I have sold some books and some lectures; yet I have not been a whit better fed or clothed or warmed or sheltered, not a whit richer, except that I have been less concerned about my living, but perhaps my life has been the less serious for it, and, to balance it, I feel now that there is a possibility of failure. —Journal, January 20, 1856

Man is the artificer of his own happiness. Let him beware how he complains of the disposition of circumstances, for it is his own disposition he blames. —Journal, January 21, 1838

The pleasures of the intellect are permanent, the pleasures of the heart are transitory....

Associate reverently and as much as you can with your loftiest thoughts. Each thought that is welcomed and recorded is a nest egg, by the side of which more will be laid. Thoughts accidentally thrown together become a frame in which more may be developed and exhibited. Perhaps this is the main value of a habit of writing, of keeping a journal — that so we may remember our best hours and stimulate ourselves. My thoughts are my company. They have a certain individuality and separate existence, aye, personality. —Journal, January 22, 1852

The increased length of days is very observable of late. What is a winter unless you have risen and gone abroad frequently before sunrise and by starlight? Varro speaks of what he calls, I believe, before-light (*antelucana*) occupations in winter, on the farm. Such are especially milking, in this neighborhood.

Speaking of the rustic villa, you must see that the kitchen is convenient, "because some things are done there in the winter before daylight (*antelucana temporibus*); food is prepared and taken." In the study are not some things to be done before daylight, and a certain food to be prepared there? —Journal, January 23, 1854

I do not think much of that chemistry that can extract corn and potatoes out of a barren soil, but rather of that chemistry that can extract thoughts and sentiments out of the life of a man on any soil. It is in vain to write on the seasons unless you have the seasons in you. —Journal, January 23, 1858

Be resolutely and faithfully what you are; be humbly what you aspire to be. Be sure you give men the best of your wares, though they be poor enough, and the gods will help you to lay up a better store for the future. —Journal, January 24, 1841

Improve each occasion when thy soul is reached. Drain the cup of inspiration to its last dregs. Fear no intemperance in that, for the years will come when otherwise thou wilt regret opportunities unimproved. The spring will not last forever. These fertile and expanding seasons of thy life, when the rain reaches thy root, when thy vigor shoots, when thy flower is budding, shall be fewer and farther between. Again I say, Remember thy Creator in the days of thy youth. —Journal, January 24, 1852

A journal is a record of experiences and growth, not a preserve of things well done or said. I am occasionally reminded of a statement which I have made in conversation and immediately forgotten, which would read much better than what I put in my journal. It is a ripe, dry fruit of long-past experience which falls from me easily, without giving pain or pleasure. The charm of the journal must consist in a certain greenness, though freshness, and not in maturity. Here I cannot afford to be remembering what I said or did, my scurf cast off, but what I am and aspire to become. —Journal, January 24, 1856

I would live henceforth with some gentle soul such a life as may be conceived, double for variety, single for harmony — two, only that we might admire at our oneness — one, because indivisible. Such community to be a pledge of holy living. How could aught unworthy be admitted into our society? To listen with one ear to each summer sound, to behold with one eye each summer scene, our visual rays so to meet and mingle with the object as to be one bent and doubled; with two tongues to be wearied, and thought to spring ceaselessly from a double fountain. —Journal, January 26, 1840

If we can listen, we shall hear. By reverently listening to the inner voice, we may reinstate ourselves on the pinnacle of humanity. —Journal, January 26, 1841

I came into this world, not chiefly to make this a good place to live in, but to live in it, be it good or bad. A man has not everything to do, but something; and because he cannot do *everything*, it is not necessary that he should be doing *something* wrong. —"Civil Disobedience" (based on a lecture first delivered January 26, 1848)

Obey the spur of the moment. These accumulated it is that makes the impulse and the impetus of the life of genius. These are the spongioles or rootlets by which its trunk is fed. If you neglect the moments, if you cut off your fibrous roots, what but a languishing life is to be expected. Let the spurs of countless moments goad us incessantly into life. I feel the spur of the moment thrust deep into my side. The present is an inexorable rider. —Journal, January 26, 1852

There are from time to time mornings, both in summer and winter, when especially the world seems to begin anew, beyond which memory need not go, for not behind them is yesterday and our past life; when, as in the morning of a hoar frost, there are visible the effects of a certain creative energy, the world has visibly been recreated in the night. Mornings of creation, I call them. In the midst of these marks of a creative energy recently active, while the sun is rising with more than usual splendor, I look back — I look back for the era of this creation, not into the night, but to a dawn for which no man ever rose early enough. A morning which carries us back beyond the Mosaic creation, where crystallizations are fresh and unmelted. It is the poet's hour. Mornings when men are new-born, men who have the seeds of life in them. It should be a part of my religion to be abroad then. —Journal, January 26, 1853

We begin to die, not in our senses or extremities, but in our divine faculties. Our members may be sound, our sight and hearing perfect, but our genius and imagination betray signs of decay. You tell me that you are growing old and are troubled to see without glasses, but this is unimportant if the divine faculty of the seer shows no signs of decay. —Journal, January 27, 1854

The snow falls on no two trees alike, but the forms it assumes are as various as those of the twigs and leaves which receive it. They are, as it were, predetermined by the genius of the tree. So one divine spirit descends alike on all, but bears a peculiar fruit in each. The divinity subsides on all men, as the snowflakes settle on the fields and ledges and takes the form of the various clefts and surfaces on which it lodges. —Journal, January 30, 1841

But the winter was not given to us for no purpose. We must thaw its cold with our genialness. We are tasked to find out and appropriate all the nutriment it yields. If it is a cold and hard season, its fruit, no doubt, is the more concentrated and nutty. It took the cold and bleakness of November to ripen the walnut, but the human brain is the kernel which the winter itself matures. Not till then does its shell come off. The seasons were not made in vain. Because the fruits of the earth are already ripe, we are not to suppose that there is no fruit left for winter to ripen. It is for man the seasons and all their fruits exist. The winter was made to concentrate and harden and mature the kernel of his brain, to give tone and firmness and consistency to his thought. Then is the great harvest of the year, the harvest of thought. —Journal, January 30, 1854

We too have our thaws. They come of our January moods, when our ice cracks, and our sluices break loose. Thought that was frozen up under stern experience gushes forth in feeling and expression. There is a freshet which carries away dams of accumulated ice. Our thoughts hide unexpressed, like the buds under their downy or resinous scales; they would hardly keep a partridge from starving.
—Journal, January 31, 1854

February

While we preach obedience to human laws and to that portion of the divine laws set forth in the New Testament, the natural laws of genius, of love and friendship, we do not preach nor insist upon....

How much fidelity to law of a kind not commonly recognized, how much magnanimity even, may be thrown away on mankind! is like pearls cast before swine! The hero obeys his own law, the Christian his, the lover and friend theirs; they are to some extent different codes. What incessant tragedy between men when one silently obeys the code of friendship, the other the code of philanthropy, in their dealings with one another. As our constitutions, our geniuses, are different, so are our standards, and we are amenable to different codes. My neighbor asks me in vain to be good as he is good. I must be good as I am made to be good, whether I am heathen or Christian. Every man's laws are hard enough to obey. —Journal, February 1, 1852

We are constantly invited to be what we are; as to something worthy and noble. —Journal, February 3, 1841

I would meet the morning and evening on very sincere ground. When the sun introduces me to a new day, I silently say to myself, "Let us be faithful all round; we will do justice and receive it." Something like this is the secret charm of Nature's demeanor toward us, strict conscientiousness and disregard of us when we have ceased to have regard for ourselves. —Journal, February 3, 1841

The poet will maintain serenity in spite of all disappointments. He is expected to preserve an

unconcerned and healthy outlook over the world, while he lives. *Philosophia practica est eruditionis meta*— Philosophy practiced is the goal of learning; and for that other, *Oratoris est celare artem*, we might read, *Herois est celare pugnam*— the hero will conceal his struggles. Poetry is the only life got, the only work done, the only pure product and free labor of man, performed only when he has put all the world under his feet, and conquered the last of his foes.
—"Thomas Carlyle and His Works" (based on a lecture first delivered February 4, 1846)

Philosophy, certainly, is some account of truths the fragments and very insignificant parts of which man will practice in this workshop; truths infinite and in harmony with infinity, in respect to which the very objects and ends of the so-called practical philosopher will be mere propositions, like the rest. It would be no reproach to a philosopher, that he knew the future better than the past, or even than the present. It is better worth knowing. He will prophesy, tell what is to be, or, in other words, what alone is, under appearances, laying little stress on the boiling of the pot, or, the condition-of-England question. He has no more to do with the condition of England than with her national debt, which a vigorous generation would not inherit. The philosopher's conception of things will, above all, be truer than other men's, and his philosophy will subordinate all the circumstances of life. To live like a philosopher is to live, not foolishly, like other men, but wisely and according to universal laws. —"Thomas Carlyle and His Works"

When I select one here and another there, and strive to join sundered thoughts, I make but a partial heap after all. Nature strews her nuts and flowers broadcast, and never collects them into heaps. A man does not tell us all he has thought upon truth or beauty at a sitting, but, from his last thought on the subject, wanders through a varied scenery of upland, meadow, and woodland to his next. Sometimes a single and casual thought rises naturally and inevitably with a queenly majesty and escort, like the stars in the east. Fate has surely enshrined it in this hour and circumstances for some purpose. What she has joined together, let not man put asunder. Shall I transplant the primrose by the river's brim, to set it beside its sister on the mountain? *This* was the soil it grew in, *this* the hour it bloomed in. If sun, wind, and rain came *here* to cherish and expand it, shall not we come here to pluck it? Shall we require it to grow in a conservatory for our convenience? —Journal, February 6, 1841

I am thankful that this pond was made deep and pure for a symbol. While men believe in the infinite some ponds will be thought to be bottomless. —Walden, "The Pond in Winter"

What I have observed of the pond is no less true in ethics. It is the law of average. Such a rule of the two diameters not only guides us toward the sun in the system and the heart in man, but draws lines through the length and breadth of the aggregate of a man's particular daily behaviors and waves of life into his coves and inlets, and where they intersect will be the height or depth of his character. —Walden, "The Pond in Winter"

Greatness is in the ascent. —Journal, February 7, 1841

I expect that the lichenist will have the keenest relish for Nature in her every-day mood and dress. He will have the appetite of the worm that never dies, of the grub. To study lichens is to get a taste of earth and health, to go gnawing the rails and rocks. This product of the bark is the essence of all times. The lichenist extracts nutriment from the very crust of the earth. A taste for this study is an evidence of titanic health, a sane earthiness. It makes not so much blood as soil of life. It fits a man to deal with the barrenest and rockiest experience. —Journal, February 7, 1859

My journal is that of me which would else spill over and run to waste, gleanings from the field which in action I reap. I must not live for it, but in it for the gods. They are my correspondent, to whom I send off the sheet postpaid. I am clerk in their counting-room, and at evening transfer the account from day-book to ledger. It is as a leaf which hangs over my head in the path. I bend the twig and write my prayers on it; then letting it go, the bough springs up and shows the scrawl to heaven. As if it were not kept shut in my desk, but were as public a leaf as any in nature. It is papyrus by the riverside; it is vellum in the pastures; it is parchment on the hills. I find it everywhere as free as the leaves which troop along the lanes in autumn. The crow, the goose, the eagle carry my quill, and the wind blows the leaves as far as I go. Or, if my imagination does not soar, but gropes in slime and mud, then I write with a reed."
—Journal, February 8, 1841

We may grow old with the vigor of youth. Are we not always in youth so long as we face heaven? We may always live the morning of our days. To him who seeks early, the sun never gets over the edge of the hill, but his rays fall slanting forever. —Journal, February 8, 1841

The times may change, but the laws of integrity and magnanimity are immutable. —"Sir Walter Raleigh" (based on a lecture first delivered February 8, 1843)

Such a life is useful for us to contemplate as suggesting that a man is not to be measured by the virtue of his described actions, or the wisdom of his expressed thoughts merely, but by that free character he is, and is felt to be, under all circumstances. Even talent is respectable only when it indicates a depth of character unfathomed. Surely it is better that our wisdom appear in the constant success of our spirits than in our business, or the maxims which fall from our lips merely. We want not only a revelation, but a nature behind to sustain it. —"Sir Walter Raleigh"

To march sturdily through life, patiently and resolutely looking grim defiance at one's foes, that is one way; but we cannot help being more attracted by that kind of heroism which relaxes its brows in the presence of danger, and does not need to maintain itself strictly, but, by a kind of sympathy with the universe, generously adorns the scene and the occasion, and loves valor so well that itself would be the defeated party only to behold it. —"Sir Walter Raleigh"

A great cheerfulness indeed have all great wits and heroes possessed, almost a profane levity to such as understood them not, but their religion had the broader basis of health and permanence. For the hero, too, has his religion, though it is the very opposite to that of the ascetic. It demands not a narrower cell but a wider world. He is perhaps the very best man of the world; the poet active, the saint willful; not the most godlike, but the most manlike. —"Sir Walter Raleigh"

I would rather be the barrenest pasture lying fallow than cursed with the compliments of kings, than be the sulphurous and accursed desert where Babylon once stood. But when I have only a rustling oak leaf, or the faint metallic chirp of a tree sparrow, for variety in my winter walk, my life becomes continent and sweet as the kernel of a nut. I would rather hear a single shrub oak leaf at the end of a wintry glade rustle of its own accord at my approach, than receive a shipload of stars and garters from the strange kings and peoples of the earth.

By poverty, i.e., simplicity of life and fewness of incidents, I am solidified and crystallized, as a vapor or liquid by cold. It is a singular concentration of strength and energy and flavor. Chastity is perpetual acquaintance with the All. My diffuse and vaporous life becomes as the frost leaves and spiculae radiant as gems on the weeds and stubble in a winter evening. You think that I am impoverishing myself by withdrawing from men, but in my solitude I have woven for myself a silken web or *chrysalis*, and, nymph-like, shall ere long burst forth a more perfect creature, fitted for a higher society. —Journal, February 8, 1857

Is not January alone pure winter? December belongs to the fall; is a wintry November: February to the spring; it is a snowy March. —Journal, February 9, 1854

I go across Walden. My shadow is very blue. It is especially blue when there is a bright sunlight on pure white snow. It suggests that there may be something divine, something celestial, in me. —Journal, February 10, 1855

I should consider it a greater success to interest one wise and earnest soul, than a million unwise and frivolous. —Letter to Calvin H. Greene, February 10, 1856

We go about mending the times, when we should be building the eternity. —Journal, February 11, 1841

The richest gifts we can bestow are the least marketable. We hate the kindness which we understand. A noble person confers no such gift as his whole confidence: none so exalts the giver and the receiver; it produces the truest gratitude. Perhaps it is only essential to friendship that some vital trust should have been reposed by the one in the other. I feel addressed and probed even to the remote parts of my being when one nobly shows, even in trivial things, an implicit faith in me. When such divine commodities are so near and cheap, how strange that it should have to be each day's discovery! A threat or a curse may be forgotten, but this mild trust translates me. I am no more of this earth; it acts dynamically; it changes my very substance. I cannot do what before I did. I cannot be what before I was. Other chains may be broken, but in the darkest night, in the remotest place, I trail this thread. Then things cannot *happen*. What if God were to confide in us for a moment! Should we not then be gods? —Letter to Ralph Waldo Emerson, February 12, 1843

The winter is coming when I shall walk the sky. The ice is a solid sky on which we walk. It is the inverted year. There is an annual light in the darkness of the winter night. The shadows are blue, as the sky is forever blue. In winter we are purified and translated. —Journal, February 12, 1860

Sometimes in our prosaic moods, life appears to us but a certain number more of days like those which we have lived, to be cheered not by more friends and friendship but probably fewer and less. As, perchance, we anticipate the end of this day before it is done, close the shutters, and with a cheerless resignation commence the barren evening whose fruitless end we clearly see, we despondingly think that all of life that is left is only this experience repeated a certain number of times. And so it would be, if it were not for the faculty of imagination. —Journal, February 13, 1859

May I ever be in as good spirits as a willow! How tenacious of life! How withy! How soon it gets over its hurts! They never despair. Is there no moisture longer in nature which they can transmute into sap? They are emblems of youth, joy, and everlasting life. —Journal, February 14, 1856

Why should we not still continue to live with the intensity and rapidity of infants? Is not the world, are not the heavens, as unfathomed as ever? Have we exhausted any joy, any sentiment? —Journal, February 15, 1851

It is because I am allied to the elements that the sound of the rain is thus soothing to me. The sound soaks into my spirit, as the water into the earth, reminding me of the season when snow and ice will be no more, when the earth will be thawed and drink up the rain as fast as it falls. —Journal, February 15, 1855

The unsympathizing man regards the wildness of some animals, their strangeness to him, as a sin; as if all their virtue consisted in their tamableness. He has always a charge in his gun ready for their extermination. What we call wildness is a civilization other than our own. The henhawk shuns the farmer, but it seeks the friendly shelter and support of the pine. It will not consent to walk in the barnyard, but it loves to soar above the clouds. It has its own way and is beautiful, when we would fain subject it to our will. So any surpassing work of art is strange and wild to the mass of men, as is genius itself. —Journal, February 16, 1859

Our work should be fitted to and lead on the time, as bud, flower, and fruit lead the circle of the seasons. —Journal, February 17, 1841

Now for the first time decidedly there is something spring-suggesting in the air and light. Though not particularly warm, the light of the sun (now travelling so much higher) on the russet fields — the ground being nearly all bare — and on the sand and the pines, is suddenly yellower. It is the earliest day-breaking of the year. We now begin to look decidedly forward and put the winter behind us. We begin to form definite plans for the approaching spring and summer. —Journal, February 17, 1855

There is little or nothing to be remembered written on the subject of getting an honest living. Neither the New Testament nor Poor Richard speaks to our condition. I cannot think of a single page which entertains, much less answers, the questions which I put to myself on the subject. How to make the getting our living poetic! for if it is not poetic, it is not life but death that we get. Is it that men are too disgusted with their experience to speak of it? or that commonly they do not question the common modes? The most practically important of all questions, it seems to me, is how shall I get my living, and yet I find little or nothing said to the purpose in any book. Those who are living on the interest of money inherited, or dishonestly, i.e., by false methods, acquired, are of course incompetent to answer it. I consider that society with all its arts, has done nothing for us in this respect. One would think, from looking at literature, that this question had never disturbed a solitary individual's musings. Cold and hunger seem more friendly to my nature than those methods which men have adopted and advise to ward them off. If it were not that I desire to do something here — accomplish some work — I should certainly prefer to suffer and die rather than be at the pains to get a living by the modes men propose. —Journal, February 18, 1851

I think that the most important requisite in describing an animal, is to be sure and give its character and spirit, for in that you have, without error, the sum and effect of all its parts, known and unknown. You must tell what it is to man. Surely the most important part of an animal is its *anima*, its vital spirit, on which is based its character and all the peculiarities by which it most concerns us. Yet most scientific books which treat of animals leave this out altogether, and what they describe are as it were phenomena of dead matter. What is most interesting in a dog, for example, is his attachment to his master, his intelligence, courage, and the like, not his anatomical

structure or even many habits which affect us less.
—Journal, February 18, 1860

Everywhere snow, gathered into sloping drifts about the walls and fences, and, beneath the snow, the frozen ground, and men are compelled to deposit the summer's provision in burrows in the earth like the ground squirrel. Many creatures, daunted by the prospect, migrated in the fall, but man remains and walks over the frozen snow-crust and over the stiffened rivers and ponds, and draws now upon his summer stores. Life is reduced to its lowest terms. There is no home for you now, in this freezing wind, but in that shelter which you prepared in the summer. You steer straight across the fields to that in season. I can with difficulty tell when I am over the river. There is a similar crust over my heart. —Journal, February 19, 1852

When I am going out for an evening I arrange the fire in my stove so that I do not fail to find a good one when I return, though it would have engaged my frequent attention present. So that, when I know I am to be at home, I sometimes make believe that I may go out, to save the trouble. And this is the art of living, too — to leave our life in a condition to go alone, and not to require a constant supervision. We will then sit down serenely to live, as by the side of a stove. —Journal, February 20, 1841

Every gardener practices budding and grafting, but only Van Mons and his equals cultivate seedlings and produce new and valuable varieties. The genius is a seedling, often precocious or made to bear fruit early, as Van Mons treated his pears. The common man is the Baldwin, propagated by mere offshoots or repetitions of the parent stock. —Journal, February 20, 1852

What is hope, what is expectation, but a seed-time whose harvest cannot fail, an irresistible expedition of the mind, at length to be victorious? —Journal, February 20, 1857

My path hitherto has been like a road through a diversified country, now climbing high mountains, then descending to the lowest vales. From the summits I saw the heavens; from the vales I looked up to the heights again.

In prosperity I remember God; in adversity I remember my own elevations, and only hope to see God again.
—Journal, February 21, 1858

A warmth begins to be reflected from the partially dried ground here and there in the sun in sheltered places, very cheering to invalids who have weak lungs, who think they may weather it till summer now. Nature is more genial to them. When the leaves on the forest floor are dried, and begin to rustle under such a sun and wind as these, the news is told to how many myriads of grubs that underlie them! When I perceive this dryness under my feet, I feel as if I had got a new sense, or rather I realize what was incredible to me before, that there is a new life in Nature beginning to awake, that her halls are being swept and prepared for a new occupant. It is whispered through all the aisles of the forest that another spring is approaching.
—Journal, February 21, 1855

Not that ornamental beauty is to be neglected, but, at least, let it first be inward-looking and essential, like the lining of a shell, of which the inhabitant is unconscious, and not mere outside garnishing. —Journal, February 23, 1854

We have lived, not in proportion to the number of years that we have spent on the earth, but in proportion as we have enjoyed. —Journal, February 23, 1860

Measure your health by your sympathy with morning and spring. If there is no response in you to the awakening of nature — if the prospect of an early morning walk does not banish sleep, if the warble of the first bluebird does not thrill you — know that the morning and spring of your life are past. Thus may you feel your pulse. —Journal, February 25, 1859

In the morning I bathe my intellect in the stupendous and cosmogonal philosophy of the Bhagvat-Geeta, since whose composition years of the gods have elapsed, and in comparison with which our modern world and its literature seem puny and trivial; and I doubt if that philosophy is not to be referred to a previous state of existence, so remote is its sublimity from our conceptions. I lay down the book and go to my well for water, and lo! there I meet the servant of the Bramin, priest of Brahma and Vishnu and Indra, who still sits in his temple on the Ganges reading the Vedas, or dwells at the root of a tree with his crust and water jug. I meet his servant come to draw water for his master, and our buckets as it were grate together in the same well. The pure Walden water is mingled with the sacred water of the Ganges. With favoring winds it is wafted past the site of the fabulous islands of Atlantis and the Hesperides, makes the periplus of Hanno, and, floating by Ternate and Tidore and the mouth of the Persian Gulf, melts in the tropic gales of the Indian seas, and is landed in ports of which Alexander only heard the names. —Walden, "The Pond in Winter"

If rivers come out of their icy prison thus bright and immortal, shall not I too resume my spring life with joy and hope? Have I no hopes to sparkle on the surface of life's current? —Journal, February 27, 1852

I desire to speak somewhere without bounds; like a man in a waking moment, to men in their waking moments; for I am convinced that I cannot exaggerate enough even to lay the foundation of a true expression. Who that has heard a strain of music feared then lest he should speak extravagantly any more forever? In view of the future or possible, we should live quite laxly and undefined in front, our outlines dim and misty on that side; as our shadows reveal an insensible perspiration toward the sun. The volatile truth of our words should continually betray the inadequacy of the residual statement. Their truth is instantly translated; its literal monument alone remains. The words which express our faith and piety are not definite; yet they are significant and fragrant like frankincense to superior natures. —Walden, "Conclusion"

The problem of life becomes, one cannot say by how many degrees, more complicated as our material wealth is increased — whether that needle they tell of was a gateway or not — since the problem is not merely nor mainly to get life for our bodies, but by this or a similar discipline to get life for our souls; by cultivating the lowland farm on right principles, that is, with this view, to turn it into an upland farm. You have so many more talents to account for. If I accomplish as much more in spiritual work as I am richer in worldly goods, then I am just as worthy, or worth just as much, as I was before, and no more. I see that, in my own case, money *might* be of great service to me, but probably it would not be; for the difficulty now is, that I do not improve my opportunities, and therefore I am not prepared to have my opportunities increased. Now, I warn you, if it be as you say, you have got to put on the pack of an upland farmer in good earnest the coming spring, the lowland farm being cared for; ay, you must be selecting your seeds forthwith, and doing what winter work you can; and, while others are raising potatoes and Baldwin apples for you, you must be raising apples of the Hesperides for them. (Only hear how he preaches!) No man can suspect that he is the proprietor of an upland farm — upland in the sense that it will produce nobler crops, and better repay cultivation in the long run — but he will be perfectly sure that he ought to cultivate it.

How prompt we are to satisfy the hunger and thirst of our bodies; how slow to satisfy the hunger and thirst of our *souls*! Indeed, we would-be practical folks cannot use this word without blushing because of our infidelity, having starved this substance almost to a shadow. We feel it to be as absurd as if a man were to break forth into a eulogy on *his dog*, who has n't any. An ordinary man will work every day for a year at shoveling dirt to support his body, or a family of bodies; but he is an extraordinary man who will work a whole day in a year for the support of his soul. Even the priests, the men of God, so called, for the most part confess that they work for the support of the body. But he alone is the truly enterprising and practical man who succeeds in *maintaining* his soul here. Have not we our everlasting life to get? and is not that the only excuse at last for eating, drinking, sleeping, or even carrying an umbrella when it rains? A man might as well devote himself to raising pork as to fattening the bodies, or temporal part merely, of the whole human family. If we made the true distinction we should almost all of us be seen to be in the almshouse for souls. —Letter to Harrison Blake, February 27, 1853

On the death of a friend, we should consider that the fates through confidence have devolved on us the task of a double living, that we have henceforth to fulfill the promise of our friend's life also, in our own, to the world. —Journal, February 28, 1840

There was an artist in the city of Kouroo who was disposed to strive after perfection. One day it came into his mind to make a staff. Having considered that in an imperfect work time is an ingredient, but into a perfect work time does not enter, he said to himself, It shall be perfect in all respects, though I should do nothing else in my life. He proceeded instantly to the forest for wood, being resolved that it should not be made of unsuitable material; and as he searched for and rejected stick after stick, his friends gradually deserted him, for they grew old in their works and died, but he grew not older by a moment. His singleness of purpose and resolution, and his elevated piety, endowed him, without his knowledge, with perennial youth. As he made no compromise with Time, Time kept out of his way, and only sighed at a distance because he could not overcome him. Before he had found a stock in all respects suitable the city of Kouroo was a hoary ruin, and he sat on one of its mounds to peel the stick. Before he had given it the proper shape the dynasty of the Candahars was at an end, and with the point of the stick he wrote the name of the last of that race in the sand, and then resumed his work. By the time he had smoothed and polished the staff Kalpa was no longer the pole-star; and ere he had put on the ferule and the head adorned with precious stones, Brahma had awoke and slumbered many times. But why do I stay to mention these things? When the finishing stroke was put to his work, it suddenly expanded before the eyes of the astonished artist into the fairest of all the creations of Brahma. He had made a new system in making a staff, a world with full and fair proportions; in which, though the old cities and dynasties had passed away, fairer and more glorious ones had taken their places. And now he saw by the heap of shavings still fresh at his feet, that, for him and his work, the former lapse of time had been an illusion, and that no more time had elapsed than is required for a single scintillation from the brain of Brahma to fall on and inflame the tinder of a mortal brain. The material was pure, and his art was pure; how could the result be other than wonderful? —Walden, "Conclusion"

I do not say that John or Jonathan will realize all this; but such is the character of that morrow which mere lapse of time can never make to dawn. The light which puts out our eyes is darkness to us. Only that day dawns to which we are awake. There is more day to dawn. The sun is but a morning star. —Walden, "Conclusion"

For Further Exploration

Thoreau wrote on the order of three million words; this book contains around three percent of them. Naturally, his own writings are the primary and best source for his ideas: especially *Walden*, his essays, and his monumental *Journal*.

The selections provided here comprise background material for a companion volume by Peter Saint-Andre entitled *The Upland Farm*.

Among secondary materials on Thoreau and his philosophy, the following are highly recommended:

Philip Cafaro, *Thoreau's Living Ethics: Walden and the Pursuit of Virtue*

Paul Friedrich, *The Gita within Walden*

Robert D. Richardson, *Henry Thoreau: A Life of the Mind*

Ethel Seybold, *Thoreau: The Quest and the Classics*

A Note on the Text

All of the selections excerpted in this book are in the public domain and thus can be freely quoted and reused; although relevant observations can also be found in Thoreau's recently discovered manuscripts (see especially *Wild Fruits*, reconstructed by Bradley P. Dean), they are not included here because doing so would have complicated the copyright status of the book.

www.ingramcontent.com/pod-product-compliance
Lightning Source LLC
LaVergne TN
LVHW051039080426
835508LV00019B/1599